Communications
in Computer and Information Science   2044

Rationale

The CCIS series is devoted to the publication of proceedings of computer science conferences. Its aim is to efficiently disseminate original research results in informatics in printed and electronic form. While the focus is on publication of peer-reviewed full papers presenting mature work, inclusion of reviewed short papers reporting on work in progress is welcome, too. Besides globally relevant meetings with internationally representative program committees guaranteeing a strict peer-reviewing and paper selection process, conferences run by societies or of high regional or national relevance are also considered for publication.

Topics

The topical scope of CCIS spans the entire spectrum of informatics ranging from foundational topics in the theory of computing to information and communications science and technology and a broad variety of interdisciplinary application fields.

Information for Volume Editors and Authors

Publication in CCIS is free of charge. No royalties are paid, however, we offer registered conference participants temporary free access to the online version of the conference proceedings on SpringerLink (http://link.springer.com) by means of an http referrer from the conference website and/or a number of complimentary printed copies, as specified in the official acceptance email of the event.

CCIS proceedings can be published in time for distribution at conferences or as post-proceedings, and delivered in the form of printed books and/or electronically as USBs and/or e-content licenses for accessing proceedings at SpringerLink. Furthermore, CCIS proceedings are included in the CCIS electronic book series hosted in the SpringerLink digital library at http://link.springer.com/bookseries/7899. Conferences publishing in CCIS are allowed to use Online Conference Service (OCS) for managing the whole proceedings lifecycle (from submission and reviewing to preparing for publication) free of charge.

Publication process

The language of publication is exclusively English. Authors publishing in CCIS have to sign the Springer CCIS copyright transfer form, however, they are free to use their material published in CCIS for substantially changed, more elaborate subsequent publications elsewhere. For the preparation of the camera-ready papers/files, authors have to strictly adhere to the Springer CCIS Authors' Instructions and are strongly encouraged to use the CCIS LaTeX style files or templates.

Abstracting/Indexing

CCIS is abstracted/indexed in DBLP, Google Scholar, EI-Compendex, Mathematical Reviews, SCImago, Scopus. CCIS volumes are also submitted for the inclusion in ISI Proceedings.

How to start

To start the evaluation of your proposal for inclusion in the CCIS series, please send an e-mail to ccis@springer.com.

V. N. Manjunath Aradhya · Mufti Mahmud ·
S. Srinath · B. S. Mahanand · R. K. Bharathi
Editors

Cognitive Computing and Information Processing

5th International Conference, CCIP 2023
Mysuru, India, December 15–16, 2023
Proceedings

Springer

Editors
V. N. Manjunath Aradhya
J.S.S. Science and Technology University
Mysuru, India

S. Srinath
JSS Science and Technology University
Mysuru, Karnataka, India

R. K. Bharathi
JSS Science and Technology University
Mysuru, Karnataka, India

Mufti Mahmud
Nottingham Trent University
Nottingham, UK

B. S. Mahanand
JSS Science and Technology University
Mysuru, Karnataka, India

ISSN 1865-0929   ISSN 1865-0937 (electronic)
Communications in Computer and Information Science
ISBN 978-3-031-60724-0   ISBN 978-3-031-60725-7 (eBook)
https://doi.org/10.1007/978-3-031-60725-7

This Springer imprint is published by the registered company Springer Nature Switzerland AG
The registered company address is: Gewerbestrasse 11, 6330 Cham, Switzerland

If disposing of this product, please recycle the paper.

Preface

These proceedings contain a collection of peer-reviewed research papers presented at the 5th International Conference on Cognitive Computing and Information Processing (CCIP 2023), held at the JSS Science and Technology University, Mysuru, India, during December 15–16, 2023. The conference, jointly organized by the Departments of Computer Science & Engineering, Information Science & Engineering and Computer Applications, was the fifth in the series on understanding the recent advancements in cognitive systems that emulate the capability of the human mind. The conference provided a forum for researchers and practitioners to present and discuss new research results and practical applications, and also promoted collaborative research activities in cognitive computing and information processing and related fields.

CCIP 2023 received 127 submissions from fields related to Cognitive Computing and Information Processing and their prospective applications. The submissions underwent a rigorous peer review process from the technical program committee members of the conference. Each submission was checked for originality and was reviewed by a minimum of three reviewers. After the review process, to ensure the highest quality standard, only 14 (including short papers) of the submitted papers were selected for presentation.

The conference featured many distinguished keynote addresses by eminent speakers including Sellappan P., Malaysia University of Science and Technology, Malaysia, Suresh Sundaram, Indian Institute of Science, India, and K. Chidananda Gowda, Kuvempu University, India. We would like to gratefully acknowledge the support received from J.S.S. Mahavidyapeetha in organizing this conference. We are grateful to all the researchers, reviewers, speakers, and the organizing team for helping us attain the objectives of the conference. We are sure that this conference has continued to uphold a platform for researchers to share their ideas catering for continuous improvement of the field. We hope that the conference proceedings will inspire readers to pursue further research in the area of cognitive computing and information processing.

April 2024

V. N. Manjunath Aradhya
Mufti Mahmud
S. Srinath
B. S. Mahanand
R. K. Bharathi

Organization

Chief Patron

His Holiness Jagadguru Sri Shivarathri Deshikendra Mahaswamigalavaru
President, Veerasimhasana Math, Sutturu Srikshethra, India

Patrons

C. G. Betsurmath	JSS Mahavidyapeetha, India
S. P. Manjunath	JSS Mahavidyapeetha, India
M. H. Dhananjaya	JSS Mahavidyapeetha, India
B. Suresh	JSS Mahavidyapeetha, India
A. N. Santosh Kumar	JSS STU, India
S. A. Dhanaraj	JSS STU, India
C. Nataraju	JSS STU, India

Programme Chairs

Srinath S.	JSS STU, India
B. S. Mahanand	JSS STU, India
V. N. Manjunath Aradhya	JSS STU, India

Organising Chairs

Bharathi R. K.	JSS STU, India
K. M. Anilkumar	JSS STU, India
S. P. Shiva Prakash	JSS STU, India

Technical Programme Committee Chairs

Manimala S.	JSS STU, India
Prathibha R. J.	JSS STU, India
Chennamma H. R.	JSS STU, India

International Advisory Board

Sheraz Khan	Harvard University, USA
Alexandre Savio	Technical University of Munich, Germany
Vignesh S.	A*STAR, Singapore
K. Subramanian	Aon, Singapore
Haijun Rong	Xi'an Jiaotong University, China
R. V. Babu	IISc, Bangalore, India
G. Sateesh Babu	AIDA Technologies, Singapore
R. Savitha	A*STAR, Singapore

Special Session Chairs

Pushpalatha M. P.	JSS STU, India
Niranjan S. K.	JSS STU, India

Publication Chairs

Umesh K. K.	JSS STU, India
Trisiladevi C. Nagavi	JSS STU, India
Shashikala B. M.	JSS STU, India

Organising Committee

Harish B. S.	JSS STU, India
Maheshan M. S.	JSS STU, India
Anusuya M. A.	JSS STU, India
Guru R.	JSS STU, India
Manju N.	JSS STU, India
Sheela N.	JSS STU, India

Finance Chairs

Siddesha S.	JSS STU, India
Nandeesh H. D.	JSS STU, India

Publicity Chairs

Prasanna B. T.	JSS STU, India
Vanishri Arun	JSS STU, India
Vani Ashok	JSS STU, India
Shyla Raj	JSS STU, India
Santhosh C. S.	JSS STU, India
Harshitha C. J.	JSS STU, India

Contents

Cognitive Computing and its Applications

Image Analysis

Communications

Evaluating a Deep Learning Model for Cyberattack Detection Based on Network Traffic

Muon Ha[1,2(✉)] [iD] and Duc–Manh Tran[2]

[1] Telecommunications University, Nha Trang, Vietnam
muon.ha@mail.ru
[2] St. Petersburg State Electrotechnical University, St. Petersburg, Russia

Abstract. In the current digital era, Distributed Denial of Service (DDoS) attacks can be recognized as a prevalent and perilous network threat, posing substantial risks to both organizations and individuals. Consequently, the timely identification and notification of DDoS attacks play a vital role in their mitigation and reduction of ensuing harm. Long Short-Term Memory (LSTM) networks, a prevalent form of deep neural network, find extensive application in tasks like natural language processing and forecasting time series data. This study suggests the use of LSTM networks to train and categorize network data features, determining their association with cyberattacks. The effectiveness of our approach in detecting and signaling cyberattacks, especially DDoS attacks, is confirmed through experiments on real-world datasets.

Keywords: Denial of Service Attacks · Artificial Intelligence · LTSM · supervised deep learning · cyberattack

1 Introduction

DDoS attack is a prevalent type of network attack aiming to render services unavailable by overwhelming network traffic on one or multiple target devices. DDoS attacks are often executed by cybercriminal groups or malicious network entities with intentions ranging from extortion to system compromise or espionage activities. According to statistics from [1], as of the second quarter of 2023, there were over 10 million DDoS attack packets carried out across 300 cities in 100 countries worldwide (Fig. 1).

To thwart DDoS attacks, automated attack detection solutions have been researched and developed. Among these, conventional methods often employ statistical analysis to identify attacks by discerning differences between normal network traffic and attack traffic. However, these approaches have been not achieving optimal results when the organizational structure of DDoS attacks becomes increasingly intricate and harder to detect. Therefore, introducing a progressive solution for DDoS attack detection and alerting is really important.

These days, Artificial Intelligence has found widespread application across various domains, notably in cybersecurity, specifically in the realm of network attack detection

V. N. M. Aradhya et al. (Eds.): CCIP 2023, CCIS 2044, pp. 3–13, 2024.
https://doi.org/10.1007/978-3-031-60725-7_1

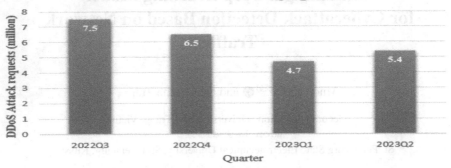

Fig. 1. DDoS attack requests by quarter [1]

and prevention. Artificial intelligence algorithms can be employed to scrutinize network traffic and detect anomalous attacker behavior. Combined with data mining and information analysis techniques, Artificial Intelligence can give a more potent attack detection capability and limit false alarms. This empowers network security experts to swiftly respond and mitigate attacks, thus fortifying network systems.

Our study focuses on evaluating the effectiveness of the LSTM deep learning model in performing the task of detecting and alerting DDoS attacks. This evaluation is based on features extracted from network traffic packets.

This paper is structured as follows: Sect. 2 presents an assessment of relevant studies in the field of cyberattack identification. Section 3 outlines the process of constructing the model and delineates the components of the solution. This encompasses details about the sample dataset and the architecture of the deep learning network employed for detecting anomalies within network traffic. Section 4 encompasses the results and discussion, outlining the model's parameters, training outcomes, and performance evaluation. Finally, the research concludes with a concluding section.

2   Related Works

In recent years, numerous methods for defending DDoS attacks have been developed. Pawel Szynkiewicz [2] introduced a Signature-based technique. This approach is based on a characteristic of modern DDoS attacks, which involves utilizing Packet Generation Algorithms during the attack process. The drawback of Signature-based methods is their inability to detect zero-day attacks. To address this, Y. Afek and colleagues [3] proposed a tool capable of extracting signatures for zero-day attacks, enabling detection and prevention of previously unidentified attacks within a few minutes of their initiation. Several DDoS attack detection models based on entropy [4], destination and legitimate source IP address databases [5], and Mean Availability Parameter for DDoS Mitigation (MAPDDM) [6] have also emerged recently.

However, the most prominent trend in recent years for DDoS attack detection is rooted in Artificial Intelligence. Researchers in [7] performed DDoS attacks using the ping of death technique and employed the Random Forest algorithm to classify attack and legitimate patterns. The NSL-KDD dataset was employed, resulting in a classification accuracy of 99.76%. Meanwhile, [8] employed three datasets, applying Algorithm 1 to capture all packets within a time frame, extracting 11 features from each packet and creating a 2D array—a matrix used as input for CNN. With the ISCX 2012 dataset, their accuracy was 98.88%, with CIC2017 it reached 99.67%, and with CSECIC2018 it reached 99.87%.

Some studies also compared the classification results of various machine learning algorithms to find the best-performing one [9–13]. In [9], researchers compared the accuracy of K-Nearest Neighbor (KNN) and Decision Tree (DT) algorithms for classifying attack and legitimate patterns using the CICIDS2017 dataset with 25 features. They achieved 98.94% accuracy with KNN and 99.91% with DT. [10] applied an Artificial Neural Network (ANN) to detect DDoS attacks, demonstrating that this method is relied on algorithm training through provided datasets. Their suggested methodology was pitted against comparable techniques, such as Backpropagation, Chi-square, Support Vector Machine, and Snort, yielding a detection accuracy of 98%. Authors in [11] evaluated DDoS attack detection in cloud environments and Software Defined Networking (SDN) by employing various models with features applied to both training and testing datasets, highlighting the necessity of performance updates. Among three proposed DDoS attack detection models within SDNs, Mglobal exhibited the highest accuracy at 89.30%. Using the KDDCUp 99 dataset, [12] developed four distinct models, where the Random Forest-based model achieved the highest accuracy of 99.95%. Meanwhile, [13] compared the training results of six different algorithms, with Decision Tree having the highest accuracy.

Not only comparing machine learning algorithms, but researchers also combined algorithms to improve effectiveness [14–16]. In [14], two methods were utilized for DDoS attack detection, specifically K-means clustering and Naive Bayes. They initially grouped similar data based on their behavior and labeled all data according to K clusters. They then labeled data groups through the Naive Bayes algorithm. [15] combined LSTM and Bayes, creating the LSTM-BA model. Initial data were processed to form input for the LSTM module to identify DDoS attacks. Data predictions deemed unreliable (values greater than 0.2 and less than 0.8) were input to the Bayes module for further predictions. Another model named Deep Defense was proposed by [16]. The Deep Defense model consisted of CNN and RNN layers, fully interconnected. They compared the performance of various RNN models, with LSTM having the highest accuracy for the Data14 dataset, and 3LSTM for Data15.

In [17], computer vision techniques were employed, focusing on the detection of DDoS attacks. In this context, traffic flow records were treated as images. Detecting attacks was considered a computer vision problem, and a multivariate joint analysis method was introduced to accurately detect traffic records and transform them into images. This method was named "Earth Mover's Distance - EMD" and computed based on the distance between two measurable distributions.

In [18], authors applied different features to determine whether an attack had occurred. As there are various crucial parameters for evaluating DDoS attacks, determining how these parameters are set is essential. The destination Internet Protocol (IP) address is considered a parameter for attack detection and can be identified using entropy information. The detection method was evaluated using this model and many other parameters.

In conclusion, research on DDoS attack detection has explored various methods to identify attack models. Notably, AI-based methods have been employed to detect DDoS attacks, effectively offloading controllers and switches. Researchers have also concentrated on improving the accuracy and efficiency of attack detection models, along with applying data mining and statistical methods. These methodologies showcase the efficacy of utilizing artificial intelligence for the purpose of detecting DDoS attacks and reinforcing network security.

3   Methology

Currently, cyberattack methods have become increasingly diverse, employing various tactics to avoid detection through traditional approaches such as pattern-based methods, signature recognition, or anomaly detection. Employing intelligent approaches to improve the precision of network intrusion detection systems continues to stand out as one of the most effective strategies available. The holistic model of this approach is illustrated in Fig. 2.

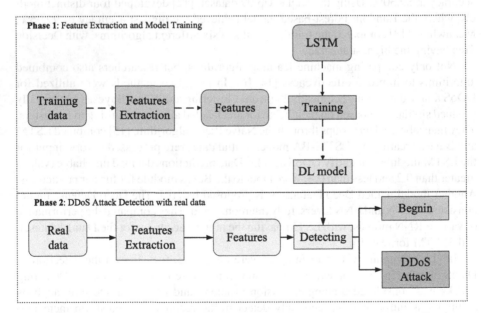

Fig. 2. Deep learning model for DDoS attack detection based on network traffic

The solution that utilizes deep learning model for DDoS attack detection based on network traffic is divided into two distinct phases:

Phase 1: Feature Extraction and Model Training. The aim of this phase is for the model to learn how to capture the essence of features from the data. Once trained, the model can directly apply its knowledge to new data to identify features. Preprocessing of data is also performed in this phase to standardize inputs and modify data formats if necessary.

RNN is a variant of artificial neural network suited for managing sequential data, wherein input information is transmitted from preceding steps in the sequence. LSTM constitutes a specialized form of RNN engineered to effectively handle extensive sequences of data. LSTM addresses the problem of losing critical information during data propagation through time steps of the network. This is achieved by employing additional units like forget gates, input gates, and output gates to regulate the flow of information through hidden state units. LSTM also uses hidden state units like RNNs but supplements them with information control mechanisms to create an improved recurrent neural network model with better learning and prediction capabilities.

In this study, a continuous chain of network packets is utilized and can effectively learn subtle differences between attack and legitimate traffic. Historical information is fed into the LSTM model to identify DDoS attacks. This helps uncover repetitive patterns that represent DDoS attacks and locate them within a long-term traffic sequence.

Phase 2: DDoS Attack Detection Initially, the input data undergoes preprocessing. Then, the model trained in the previous phase is applied to analyze the data's features. Finally, the extracted features are given into a classifier to categorize DDoS attacks based on predefined labels.

3.1 Dataset

The training dataset plays an important role in constructing and evaluating models, such as LSTM, and significantly influences their performance. The quality of training data strongly affects the model's effectiveness. Insufficient diversity or noise within the training dataset can prevent the model's ability from generalizing and making accurate predictions on new data.

In this study, we employed a sample dataset extracted and synthesized from reputable and public sources of network attack data, including CSE-CIC-IDS2018-AWS [19], CICIDS2017 [20]. This dataset encompasses network packets collected within a real-world environment, labeled with distinct attack types. These packets were transformed into network features, encompassing IP addresses, destination ports, protocols, packet sizes, and inter-packet time intervals.

During the training process of the LSTM model for DDoS attack detection, we utilized 84 features. These characteristics include data about the source and destination IP addresses, source and destination ports, as well as communication protocols. This information is accompanied by packet counts, total packet sizes, average inter-packet time intervals, standard deviations of inter-packet time intervals, and the packet size-to-average size ratio.

Prior to training, the data undergoes preprocessing involving the following steps:

Step 1. Data from original datasets is provided in PCAP files, containing details about network packets transmitted and received over a specified timeframe. To enable model training, these PCAP files are converted into CSV format for ease of processing.

Step 2. Within the sample dataset, numerous attributes lack relevance or value in the DDoS attack identification process, such as destination IP addresses and collection dates. These attributes can be removed to reduce data dimensions and expedite processing.

Step 3. Datasets commonly contain missing or null values. During data processing, we identify these missing values and make decisions on their treatment. A common approach is replacing missing values with the mean of the corresponding column.

Step 4. Data normalization improves the model's convergence rate and reduces the influence of outliers. This process is carried out to ensure that attributes within the sample dataset, which might have different value ranges, are adjusted to a uniform range.

Step 5. Subsequent to preprocessing, the data is partitioned into distinct components, namely the training set and the testing set. The primary function of the training set is to facilitate the model training process, while the testing set serves the purpose of evaluating the model's efficacy in handling novel data instances. In the context of this investigation, a partition ratio of 70–30 was employed, apportioning 70% of the dataset to the training set and the residual 30% to the testing set.

3.2 LSTM Network Architecture

In the field of deep learning models, the phenomenon of vanishing gradients has become a common aspect, arising when the derivative gradually decreases, leading to insufficient information to adjust the network's weights. This occurrence leads to the gradual reduction of the gradient, causing it to approach a significantly small value (near 0). As a result, the learning process slows down or can even come to a temporary pause. When this condition occurs, the ability to learn complex relationships between features in the data and the predicted outcomes is limited.

To address this issue, methods like Long Short-Term Memory (LSTM) have been developed to tackle the vanishing gradient problem by employing specialized gates to retain information during the learning process. In our model, we utilize two one-directional LSTM layers, each with 32 units, to cope with this challenge. In the first layer, we apply the tanh(x) activation function, which transforms the input value into a new value within the range of -1 to 1 and exhibits nonlinearity.

In the proposed model, in order to mitigate overfitting, we employ the Dropout layer, randomly discarding a number of input units. Additionally, we apply the Batch-Normalization layer to normalize the input and output values of each layer in the network.

4 Results and Discussion

Once the model structure is established, the subsequent task involves selecting suitable hyperparameters for the model to align with the specific demands of the problem. The model's hyperparameters include:

Number of Layers: This refers to the number of neural network layers used in the model.

Learning Rate of the Adam Optimizer: The Adam optimizer is a popular optimization method, and its learning rate is a crucial parameter that affects the speed of weight updates in the network.

Dropout Rate: Dropout is a regularization technique where a fraction of units in a layer are randomly dropped during each training iteration. This helps reduce the inter-dependence between units, preventing overfitting in neural network training. Overfitting occurs when a model becomes too focused on the details or noise in the training dataset, resulting in poor performance on new or unseen data.

Number of Epochs: The number of epochs is an essential hyperparameter in model training. It determines how many times the entire training dataset is iterated through during training. More epochs allow the model to learn more about the data patterns and potentially improve prediction performance. However, too many epochs can lead to overfitting.

Through the testing process, we have selected the configuration that provides the best performance, as shown in Table 1.

Table 1. Selecting parameters for the model

Hyperparameters	Configuration
Number of Layers	4
Learning Rate of the Adam Optimizer	0.001
Dropout Rate	0.20
Number of Epochs	1000

The training and testing data utilize a sample dataset consisting of 1,048,575 packets, labeled as "normal" and "attack." This dataset contains information about network traffic within a simulated LAN, encompassing various protocols such as TCP, UDP, ICMP, and DNS. Figure 3 illustrates the data distribution of the sample dataset.

Distribution of data in the dataset

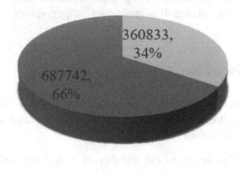

360833, 34%

687742, 66%

▨ Normal ▪ Attack

Fig. 3. Distribution of data in the sample dataset

The testing scenario employs the cross-validation method with 5 iterations. This approach involves evaluating the model by partitioning the data into multiple segments, each of which is sequentially used as the testing set while the remaining segments serve as the training set (Fig. 4).

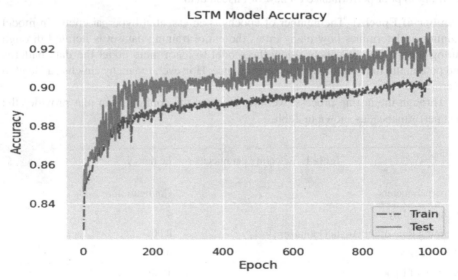

Fig. 4. Model accuracy graph on training and test sets

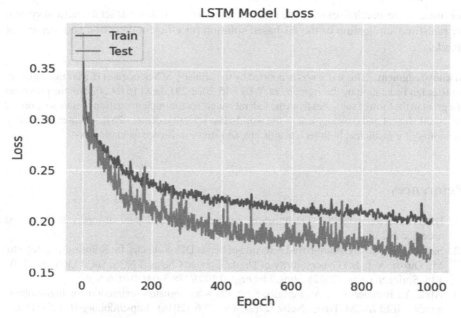

Fig. 5. The loss function graph of the model on the training set and the test set

The assessment outcomes reveal that the model attains an accuracy rate of approximately 91.38% on the testing dataset, with an F1-score of 91.73% for both classes encompassing normal traffic and attacks. Figure 5 illustrates the graphical representation of the model's loss function across both the training and testing datasets. It is evident from the loss function graph that there is a gradual and stable reduction in loss on both the training and testing datasets, indicating the model's effective learning and the absence of pronounced concerns related to overfitting or gradient vanishing.

In summary, the findings demonstrate that the trained model exhibits competence in proficiently predicting both normal network traffic and attack patterns, boasting a high level of accuracy and a favorable F1-score. Nevertheless, it is prudent to note that the model may still encounter challenges in accurately predicting rare instances or novel attack types that have not been previously encountered in the training data corpus.

5   Conclusion

In conclusion, our proposal in this paper involves utilizing LSTM networks for the detection and alerting of DDoS attacks. The evaluation results indicate an accuracy of approximately 91.38%, underscoring the potential of artificial intelligence in detecting and mitigating network attacks, particularly DDoS attacks. This presents a novel direction for network security solutions.

However, during the evaluation process, we also observed certain limitations in our proposed approach. Specifically, the application of this model in real-world environments with large and diverse datasets could impact the accuracy of the solution. We intend to continue our research to expand the range of attack types and construct a practical system for real-time application of the AI-based solution for efficient detection and alerting of attacks.

Acknowledgment. This work was supported by the Ministry of Science and Higher Education of the Russian Federation by the Agreement № 075-15-2022-291 dated 15.04.2022 on the provision of a grant in the form of subsidies from the federal budget for the implementation of state support for the establishment and development of the world-class scientific center «Pavlov center Integrative physiology for medicine, high-tech healthcare, and stress-resilience technologies».

References

1. DDoS threat report for 2023 Q2. https://blog.cloudflare.com/ddos-threat-report-2023-q2/, last accessed 2023/8/19
2. Szynkiewicz, P.: Signature-based detection of botnet DDoS attacks. In: Kołodziej, J., Repetto, M., Duzha, A. (eds.) Cybersecurity of Digital Service Chains. LNCS, vol. 13300, pp., 120–135. Springer, Cham (2022). https://doi.org/10.1007/978-3-031-04036-8_6
3. Afek, Y., Bremler-Barr, A., Feibish, S.L.: Zero-day signature extraction for high-volume attacks. IEEE/ACM Trans. Netw. **27**(2), 691–706 (2016). https://doi.org/10.1109/TNET.2019.2899124
4. Wang, R., Jia, Z., Ju, L.: An entropy-based distributed DDoS detection mechanism in software-defined networking. In: 2015 IEEE Trustcom/BigDataSE/ISPA, pp. 310–317, IEEE, Helsinki, Finland (2015). https://doi.org/10.1109/Trustcom.2015.389
5. Wang, X., Chen, M., Xing, C., Zhang, T.: Defending DDoS attacks in software-defined networking based on legitimate source and destination IP address database. IEICE Trans. Inf. Syst. **99**(4), 850–859 (2016). https://doi.org/10.1587/transinf.2015ICP0016
6. Amuthan, A., Harikrishna, P.: Mean availability parameter-based DDoS detection mechanism for cloud computing environments. In: Zungeru, A., Subashini, S., Vetrivelan, P. (eds.) Wireless Communication Networks and Internet of Things. LNEE, vol. 493, pp. 115–122. Springer, Singapore (2019). https://doi.org/10.1007/978-981-10-8663-2_12
7. Pande, S., Khamparia, A., Gupta, D., Thanh, D.N.: DDOS detection using machine learning technique. In: Khanna, A., Singh, A.K., Swaroop, A. (eds.) Recent Studies on Computational Intelligence. Studies in Computational Intelligence (DoSCI 2020), vol. 921, pp. 59–68. Springer, Singapore (2021). https://doi.org/10.1007/978-981-15-8469-5_5
8. Doriguzzi-Corin, R., Millar, S., Scott-Hayward, S., Martinez-del-Rincon, J., Siracusa, D.: LUCID: a practical, lightweight deep learning solution for DDoS attack detection. IEEE Trans. Netw. Serv. Manag. **17**(2), 876–889 (2020). https://doi.org/10.1109/TNSM.2020.2971776
9. Ramadhan, I., Sukarno, P., Nugroho, M.A.: Comparative analysis of K-nearest neighbor and decision tree in detecting distributed denial of service. In: 2020 8th International Conference on Information and Communication Technology (ICoICT), pp. 1–4, IEEE, Indonesia (2020). https://doi.org/10.1109/ICoICT49345.2020.9166380
10. Saied, A., Overill, R.E., Radzik, T.: Detection of known and unknown DDoS attacks using artificial neural networks. Neurocomputing **172**, 385–393 (2016). https://doi.org/10.1016/j.neucom.2015.04.101
11. Wang, B., Zheng, Y., Lou, W., Hou, Y.T.: DDoS attack protection in the era of cloud computing and software-defined networking. Comput. Netw. **81**, 308–319 (2015). https://doi.org/10.1016/j.comnet.2015.02.026

12. Jyoti, N., Behal, S.: A meta-evaluation of machine learning techniques for detection of DDoS attacks. In: 2021 8th International Conference on Computing for Sustainable Global Development (INDIACom), pp. 522–526. IEEE, India (2021)
13. Gohil, M., Kumar, S.: Evaluation of classification algorithms for distributed denial of service attack detection. In: 2020 IEEE Third International Conference on Artificial Intelligence and Knowledge Engineering (AIKE), pp. 138–141. IEEE, USA (2020). https://doi.org/10.1109/AIKE48582.2020.00028
14. Yassin, W., Udzir, N.I., Muda, Z., Sulaiman, M.N.: Anomaly-based intrusion detection through k-means clustering and Naives Bayes classification. In: Proceedings of the 4th International Conference on Computing and Informatics (ICOCI), pp. 298–303, Malaysia (2013)
15. Li, Y., Lu, Y.: LSTM-BA: ddos detection approach combining LSTM and Bayes. In: 2019 Seventh International Conference on Advanced Cloud and Big Data (CBD), pp. 180–185. IEEE, China (2019). https://doi.org/10.1109/CBD.2019.00041
16. Yuan, X., Li, C., Li, X.: DeepDefense: identifying DDoS attack via deep learning. In: 2017 IEEE International Conference on Smart Computing (SMARTCOMP), pp. 1–8. IEEE, China (2017). https://doi.org/10.1109/SMARTCOMP.2017.7946998
17. Tan, Z., Jamdagni, A., He, X., Nanda, P., Liu, R.P., Hu, J.: Detection of denial-of-service attacks based on computer vision techniques. IEEE Trans. Comput. **64**(9), 2519–2533 (2014). https://doi.org/10.1109/TC.2014.2375218
18. Yan, Q., Gong, Q., Deng, F.A.: Detection of DDoS attacks against wireless SDN controllers based on the fuzzy synthetic evaluation decision-making model. Adhoc Sens. Wirel. Netw. **33**, 275–299 (2016)
19. CSE-CIC-IDS2018 on AWS. https://www.unb.ca/cic/datasets/ids-2018.html. Accessed 19 Aug 2023
20. Intrusion Detection Evaluation Dataset (CIC-IDS2017). https://www.unb.ca/cic/datasets/ids-2017.html. Accessed 19 Aug 2023

Exploring Antarctic Lake Expansion with UAV Data Processing for Mapping Changes and Implications of Climate Research

S. Dhanush, K. R. Raghavendra, B. Mahesh, C. Rakshita, and M. Geetha Priya[✉]

CIIRC, Jyothy Institute of Technology, Bengaluru, India
geetha.sri82@gmail.com

Abstract. In recent years, there has been some concern about the potential impact of climate change and the Antarctic ice sheet, as the presence of meltwater on the surface of the ice sheet can accelerate melting and contribute to ice loss and a rise in sea levels. Increased melting can lead to the formation of melt ponds and glacial lakes. These melt ponds and glacial lakes can vary in size & depth and depend on various factors such as the amount of meltwater and the local climate, which transpire during the Austral summer months. The present study is to investigate the expansion of Adi Shankara Lake (ASL) which is a proglacial lake (70°46′22.13″ S , 11°45′11.62″ E) in central Dronning Maud land (cDML), East Antarctica using real-time kinematics enabled Unmanned Aerial Vehicle (UAV) data over a short duration of 4 days during 20/12/2022–24/12/2022 (austral summer). Research findings show that the area of the proglacial lake expanded more than 2X during the short period. The results obtained are validated using the ground data collected during the field visit Nov 2022–Feb 2023 at Schrimacher oasis, cDML, East Antarctica. This type of lake expansion on the ice sheet over a short period is alarming as an indication of rapid melting of the ice. So, monitoring melt ponds and glacial lakes of Antarctica is an important aspect of understanding and predicting the effects of climate change on the continent's ice sheet.

Keywords: Lake expansion · proglacial Lake · Climate change · UAV data

1 Introduction

Antarctica has seen a significant expansion of its lakes during the austral summer months, and this expansion is believed to be linked to several factors, including increasing temperatures, enhanced melting of glaciers and ice sheets, and changes in precipitation patterns [1, 2]. As meltwater pools on the ice surface, melt ponds and glacial lakes emerge in Antarctica [3, 4]. Studies have shown that the total area of Antarctica lakes had increased by almost 50% between 2003 and 2018, with some lakes growing at a much faster rate than others [5]. This increase in the size and number of lakes has important implications for the understanding of the Antarctica environment and its potential impact on global sea level rise. Satellites offer broad coverage but limited detail, while UAV data can provide more detailed data for smaller areas [6]. The UAV equipped with advanced cameras has emerged as a promising tool for studying the expansion of lakes in Antarctica [7]. UAVs can collect high-resolution data, which facilitates and accelerates monitoring of these lakes [8, 9]. These systems can also enhance atmospheric studies by complementing existing techniques and procedures [10]. One of the main difficulties of collecting UAV data in Antarctica is the extreme weather conditions, low temperatures, and wind velocity which affects the flight stability and battery life of the UAV [11]. Additionally, the limited infrastructure and logistic facility in Antarctica can make it challenging to transit and operate the UAV effectively [10]. The use of UAVs with high spatial resolution in RGB and multispectral bands has made it possible to capture remote-sensing images for efficient monitoring [12].

2 Study Area

Antarctica is a vast continent, predominantly covered by snow and ice, with only a few areas of exposed land. Researchers study a wide range of topics in Antarctica, from climate change to glaciology, geology, and biology. Antarctica can be broadly classified into three main regions, namely, West Antarctica, East Antarctica, and the Antarctic Peninsula. Schirmacher Oasis is a region situated on the Princess Astrid coast of Dronning Maud Land, East Antarctica, which is characterized by a lack of ice cover, and it is 100 m above mean sea level. It has an area of 34 sq. km with more than 100 freshwater lakes, which include landlocked, proglacial, and epi-shelf lakes [13]. The proposed study was conducted on a proglacial lake (70°46′22.13″ S, 11°45′11.62″ E) situated at ~1 km from the Indian Research Station, Maitri (Fig. 1). The lake undergoes ice cover for approximately 8 to 10 months annually, and melts during the Austral summer months (Nov, Dec, Jan & Feb). This proglacial lake has been named as Adi Shankara Lake (ASL) as the CIIRC members are the first team to carry out UAV survey and research activities over the lake in east Antarctica during the Austral summer field season 2022–2023.

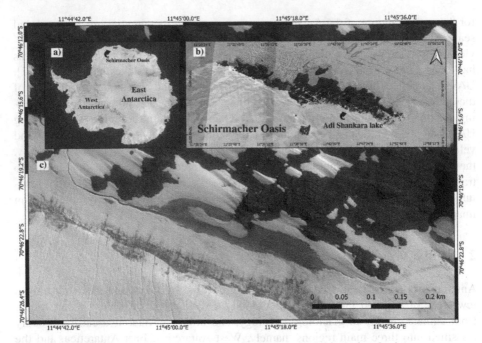

Fig. 1. Location of selected Proglacial Lake in Schirmacher Oasis

3   Materials and Methods

3.1   UAV Surveys and Mission Planning

In recent years, the use of UAVs for remote sensing has increased due to their ability to carry out autonomous or pre-programmed missions, as well as the availability of specialized sensors that can acquire high-resolution imagery. These sensors can capture multispectral, or thermal data with a spectral resolution as fine as 5 cm. The present study utilizes an RTK-enabled UAV with a multispectral imaging sensor. The imaging system comprises of six $1/2.9''$ CMOS sensors, consisting of one RGB sensor intended for capturing visible light images and five monochrome sensors utilized for multispectral imaging with all at 2 megapixels (Fig. 2). Two UAV surveys were conducted on 20/12/2022 and 24/12/2022 (4 days interval) have been considered for the present study out of multiple surveys that were conducted during the field season Nov 2022- Feb 2023.

Fig. 2. Multispectral sensor-based UAV used during the Aerial survey in East Antarctica

In order to cover the study area extent during the UAV survey, multiple autonomous flight missions were planned. The UAV was flown at an altitude of 95 m, with a ground resolution of 5 cm per pixel, at a view angle of 90 degrees. The speed of the UAV was set at 5 m per second to enable hover and capture options to achieve the required overlaps. The survey was planned to achieve a frontal overlap of 75% and a side overlap of 60% which is required for UAV data processing. Figure 3 shows the positioning of cameras and overlapping image fields during the study period [6].

(a)   (b)

Fig. 3. Camera locations and image overlap for (a) 20th December, 2022 and (b) 24th December, 2022

3.2   UAV Data Processing

The images captured by a UAV during the survey are processed using Agisoft Metashape Professional Edition 2.0.1. to create a 3D point cloud of the surveyed area. As these images are unordered and often overlap due to their airborne nature, they require pre-processing to create a georeferenced representation of the surface. Since it is a real-time kinetics (RTK)-enabled UAV, the products are automatically georeferenced, and using a ground control point (GCP) survey the georeferencing is verified and adjusted. Figure 4 Shows the locations of the GCP survey where the location accuracy information was collected using a Global navigation satellite system (GNSS).

Fig. 4. GNSS-based GCP survey for aerial mapping

   The workflow process for UAV data is shown in Fig. 5. The first steps in this process involve camera calibration and image triangulation, which provides a digital elevation model (DEM). Using the DEM and the original imagery, an orthomosaic can be created by projecting the 2D images onto the 3D DEM, resulting in a high-resolution, georeferenced RGB image [14]. This orthomosaic provides a detailed and accurate representation of the surveyed area. In this specific case, the boundary of a lake was manually digitized using the obtained orthomosaicked product, which is utilized to calculate the area and perimeter of the lake using an attribute table. The software known as Quantum Geographic Information System (QGIS) which is freely available as an open-source program is used for digitization and for measuring the length of the lake.

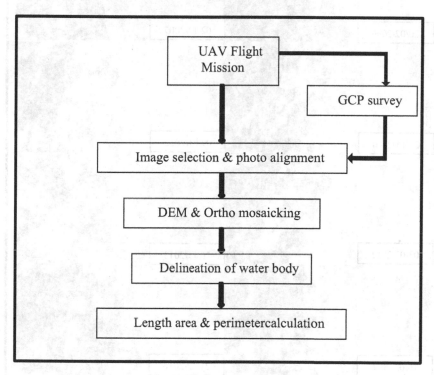

Fig. 5. Workflow process for UAV data

4   Results and Discussions

There are various ways that lakes could form in Antarctica; When meltwater accumulates on the surface of an ice sheet or glacier, it may form ponds or lakes. The evolution of Adi Shankara Lake (ASL) from 2006 to 2016 is shown in Fig. 6. According to observations, the glacial lake did not exist until 2007. The ice sheet deformation over the lake was observed in 2010. Due to the increase in temperature, meltwater ponding was seen in late February 2012. In November 2013, the lake was buried under snow due to the precipitation or no melt conditions. The lake was completely exposed in December 2016.

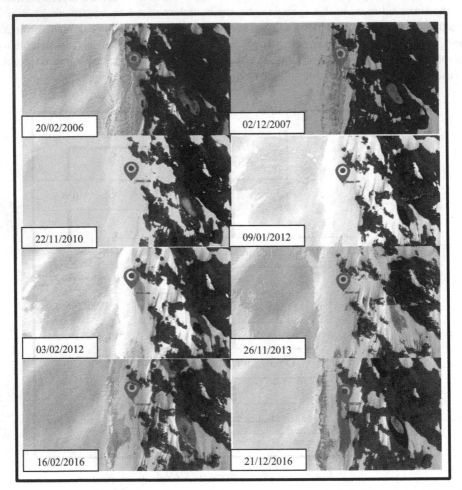

Fig. 6. Evolution of Adi Shankara Lake (ASL) during 2006–2016 (Landmark symbol)

The present study focuses on studying the expansion of Adi Shankara Lake during a short duration of 4 days using UAV datasets during the month of December 2022. The processed UAV image of Adi Shankara Lake on 20th Dec 2022 and 24th Dec 2022 is shown in Fig. 7.

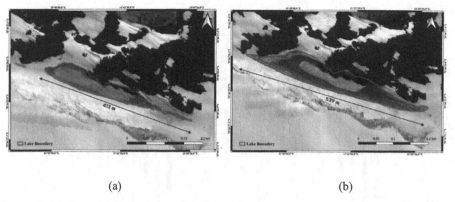

(a)   (b)

Fig. 7. Aerial view of Adi Shankara Lake from UAV on (a) 20th Dec 2022 and (b) 24th Dec 2022

From the aerial survey, it was found that the lake expanded from 413 m to 539 m in length, 957 m to 1184 m in perimeter, and 11,941 sq.m to 24,727 sq.m in terms of area. From Fig. 7, it is evident that the lake area has increased more than 2X times with an increase of 126 m in length. Water bodies in general have a lower albedo than the surrounding ice and hence absorb more solar radiation and melt more. As a result, they can locally increase surface melting, leading to more meltwater formation and further growth of the lake [15, 16]. The lake expansion has been related to the average temperature recorded during December 2022 which ranged from −4.40 °C to 1.80 °C as shown in Fig. 8. The average temperature recorded was −3.20 °C and −0.50 °C, on 20th December 2022 and 24th December 2022 respectively. Despite the average temperatures being below freezing point, it was noted that during the daytime, there existed a positive temperature for a certain duration of time. This rise in temperature in conjunction with albedo effects has resulted in increased melting leading expansion of the lake in a short duration. Glacial lakes can trigger ice shelf collapse by increasing the flow of meltwater to the ice-shelf base, which can cause melting and weaken the ice shelf's structural integrity [17]. This process highlights the complex feedback mechanisms between the ice sheet and climate that can lead to significant impacts on global sea-level rise.

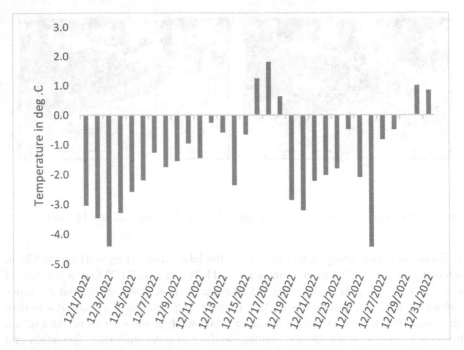

Fig. 8. Average temperature for December 2022 recorded using AWS installed at Maitri Station, East Antarctica (70°46′00″ S and 11°43′55″ E) at an elevation of 117 m above mean sea level (AMSL) by India Meteorological Department (IMD)

5 Conclusion

The proposed work provides new insights to study the dynamics of lakes in Antarctica and the ways in which they can change over time. Specifically, the study focuses on a proglacial lake, which is located near the Schrimacher oasis of East Antarctica. The findings suggest that the proglacial lake has undergone a significant expansion in length and area during a short period. The potential effects of climate change and albedo effect on lake expansion and ice melting highlight the importance of monitoring melt ponds and glacial lakes for undertaking research in this area. UAVs can be used for a variety of specialized research projects as a state-of-art technology since they provide high-resolution imagery. This paper discusses how to effectively use UAV data for studying lake dynamics in Antarctica over a short period.

Acknowledgment. The authors acknowledge the logistical support given by the National Centre for Polar and Ocean Research, Ministry of Earth Sciences, Govt. of India under the Indian Scientific Expedition to Antarctica (ISEA) to undertake this research. The authors gratefully acknowledge the support rendered by Prazim Trading and Investment Company Private Limited (PTICL), MM Forgings, TATA STEEL, Jyothy Industries, Rational Technologies, and Dr. Krishna Venkatesh, Director, CIIRC - Jyothy Institute of Technology, Bengaluru.

References

1. Luis, A.J.: Past, present and future climate of antarctica. Int. J. Geosci. **04**, 959–977 (2013). https://doi.org/10.4236/ijg.2013.46089
2. Rakshita, C., Sowjanya, A., Swathi, P., Geetha Priya, M.: Velocity estimation of east antarctic glacier with SAR offset tracking—an application of image processing. In: Smys, S., Tavares, J.M.R.S., Shi, F. (eds.) Computational Vision and Bio-Inspired Computing. AISC, vol. 1439, pp. 323–331. Springer, Singapore (2023). https://doi.org/10.1007/978-981-19-9819-5_24
3. Phartiyal, B.: Holocene paleoclimatic variation in the schirmacher oasis, East Antarctica: a mineral magnetic approach. Polar Sci. **8**(4), 357–369 (2014). ISSN 1873-9652. https://doi.org/10.1016/j.polar.2014.06.001
4. Geetha Priya, M., Deva Jefflin, A.R., Luis, A.J., Bahuguna, I.M.: Estimation of surface melt induced melt pond depths over amery ice shelf, east antarctica using multispectral and ICESat-2 data. Disaster Adv. **15**, 1–8 (2022). https://doi.org/10.25303/1508da01008
5. Stewart, C.L., Christoffersen, P., Nicholls, K.W., Williams, M.J.M., Dowdeswell, J.A.: Basal melting of ross ice shelf from solar heat absorption in an ice-front polynya. Nat. Geosci. **12**, 435–440 (2019). https://doi.org/10.1038/s41561-019-0356-0
6. Cermakova, I., Komarkova, J.: Modelling a process of UAV data collection and processing. In: International Conference on Information Society (i-Society), pp. 161–164 (2016).https://doi.org/10.1109/i-Society.2016.7854203
7. Geetha Priya, M., Venkatesh, K., Shivanna, L., Devaraj, S.: Detecting short-term surface melt over vestre broggerbreen, arctic glacier using indigenously developed unmanned air vehicles. Geocarto Int. **37**, 3167–3178 (2022). https://doi.org/10.1080/10106049.2020.1849416
8. Fair, Z., Flanner, M., Brunt, K.M., Amanda Fricker, H., Gardner, A.: Using ICESat-2 and operation icebridge altimetry for supraglacial lake depth retrievals. Cryosphere **14**, 4253–4263 (2020). https://doi.org/10.5194/tc-14-4253-2020
9. Moussavi, M., Pope, A., Halberstadt, A.R.W., Trusel, L.D., Cioffi, L., Abdalat, W.: Antarctic supraglacial lake detection using landsat 8 and sentinel-2 imagery: towards continental generation of lake volumes. Remote Sens. **12** (2020). https://doi.org/10.3390/RS12010134
10. Pina, P., Vieira, G.: UAVs for science in antarctica. Remote Sens. **14**, 1–39 (2022). https://doi.org/10.3390/rs14071610
11. Bello, A.B., Navarro, F., Raposo, J., Miranda, M., Zazo, A., Álvarez, M.: Fixed-wing UAV flight operation under harsh weather conditions: a case study in livingston Island Glaciers, Antarctica. Drones **6** (2022). https://doi.org/10.3390/drones6120384
12. Feng, H., Tao, H., Li, Z., Yang, G., Zhao, C.: Comparison of UAV RGB imagery and hyperspectral remote-sensing data for monitoring winter wheat growth. Remote Sens. **14** (2022). https://doi.org/10.3390/rs14153811
13. Phartiyal, B.: Holocene paleoclimatic variation in the schirmacher oasis, east antarctica: a mineral magnetic approach. Polar Sci. **8**, 357–369 (2014). https://doi.org/10.1016/j.polar.2014.06.001
14. Ismail, M.A.M., Kumar, N.S., Abidin, M.H.Z., Madun, A.: Systemic approach to elevation data acquisition for geophysical survey alignments in hilly terrains using UAVs. J. Phys. Conf. Ser. **995** (2018). https://doi.org/10.1088/1742-6596/995/1/012104
15. Kakareka, S.V., et al.: Spatial features of the chemical composition of Thala Hills surface snow, East Antarctica. Arct. Antarct. Res. **67**, 28–43 (2021). https://doi.org/10.30758/0555-2648-2021-67-1-28-43

16. Priya, M.G., Varshini, N., Chandhana, G., Deeksha, G., Supriya, K., Krishnaveni, D.: Study on snowmelt and algal growth in the Antarctic Peninsula using spatial approach. Curr. Sci. **120**, 932–936 (2021). https://doi.org/10.18520/cs/v120/i5/932-936
17. Banwell, A.F., MacAyeal, D.R., Sergienko, O.V.: Breakup of the Larsen B Ice Shelf triggered by chain reaction drainage of supraglacial lakes. Geophys. Res. Lett.. Res. Lett. **40**, 5872–5876 (2013). https://doi.org/10.1002/2013GL057694

MVR Delay: Cooperative Light Weight Detection and Prevention of False Emergency Message Dissemination in VANET

Mahabaleshwar Kabbur[(⊠)] and M. Vinayaka Murthy

School of Computer Science and Applications, REVA University, Bengaluru-64, Bengaluru, India

mskabbur.reva@gmail.com, vinayaka.murthy@reva.edu.in

Abstract. The fake emergency message propagation is one of the major problems in VANET networks where attackers propagate false emergency messages for their selfish needs and disrupt the reliability of VANETs. Emergency messages are intended to be delivered fast and the network should be optimized for faster delivery of emergency messages. A complex authentication procedure disturbs the utilities of emergency messaging in VANET. Towards this end, the emergency message propagation must pass through light weight verification without affecting the speed of propagation of genuine messages. Since the attack behavior changes over a period of time, the detection system must consider temporal correlation between attack characteristics over a period of time. This work proposes a secure path for emergency message dissemination in VANET networks wherein the authenticity of message is verified using Long short-term memory (LSTM) classifier using the temporal correlation between the events. The emergency message along the path is verified and fake messages are dropped by the Road side units (RSU). Simulation of proposed scheme shows more than 96% accuracy in filtering fake emergency messages and at the same time it does not introduces any significant delay in message delivery.

Keywords: VANET · emergency message · fake message · secure

1 Introduction

Emergency message dissemination over VANET networks can ensure the travel safety and reduce fatalities. Since its inception various mechanisms have been proposed for emergency message dissemination [1]. Though message dissemination can provide a significant value add to driving experience, it also exposes the network and makes it vulnerable to various malicious intentions by attackers. Attacker can create fake messages and propagate them in the network. Since the VANET network message propagation protocols given higher priority to emergency message forwarding, attacker exploit this to accelerate the propagation of fake messages [2]. Frequent propagation of fake emergency messages creates a trust deficit factor in VANETs and the vehicles cannot ascertain the creditability of the messages. Some of the existing works proposed for preventing

V. N. M. Aradhya et al. (Eds.): CCIP 2023, CCIS 2044, pp. 25–38, 2024.
https://doi.org/10.1007/978-3-031-60725-7_3

fake message propagation are based trust [3]. But these approaches fail in presence of sparseness in the networks. Also, the complexity in verification of message introduces higher latency in emergency delivery disturbing the utility of emergency message dissemination. Thus, it becomes necessary to prevent the fake emergency propagation in VANET in a light weight manner without introducing a significant delay in genuine message propagation.

In this work, a secure emergency message propagation mechanism is proposed to prevent the propagation of fake emergency messages in a light weight manner without introducing significant delay for genuine messages. The proposed approach constructs a backbone channel for emergency message propagation. The nodes in the path learn and built up the knowledge for fake message propagation in a cooperative manner. The knowledge learnt is encoded into a Long Short-term memory (LSTM) model and model is distributed among the Road side units (RSU). Emergency messages detected as fake are marked as fake by the RSU and other vehicles never forward them. By this way the propagation of fake messages is prevented in the network.

2 Related Work

Trust score based scheme for false message injection was proposed by Ullah et al. [4]. Trust for vehicle nodes is calculated based on social utility and kept at RSU. RSU authenticates the messages from the vehicle before disseminating in the network. But this scheme fails in presence of sparseness and has higher false positives. Routing the emergency messages on reliable link instead of broadcast is adopted by Due et al. [5]. The reliability of links is calculated based on game theory involving speed and trajectory. But the method has higher computational complexity. Liu et al. [6] proposed a false message detection scheme in VANET based on traffic flow theory and machine learning. The authenticity of message is validated in relation to the traffic scenario resulting from it. A Bayesian model is trained to predict the likelihood of the event. Park et al. [7] proposed a two directional data verification scheme to prevent false message propa-gation in VANET. This approach receives messages from vehicles travelling in both directions of a two-way road and verifies the integrity of data. The approach is based on assumption that it is difficult for an adversary to have two collaborative vehicles on both driving directions in the same region. Though the method is simple to implement without any need for a public key infrastructure, it is applicable to only highway scenarios. Arshad et al. [8] presented a false message detection scheme based on witness data and machine learning. Vehicles located at scene are used as witness and information collected from them is passed to a Bayesian model to predict the likelihood of the emergency event. But reliability of the witness vehicles was not considered before processing the data from them. Mohamed et al. [9] proposed a message authentication scheme based on cryptography. Symmetric key was generated and exchanged using Diffe-Hellman protocol. Since every message is authenticated for source, there are least changes of valid entity spreading fake messages. Even it spreads, it can be blocked, as the source is known. But the complexity of approach is high and affects the utility of emergency messaging. Chen et al. [10] proposed a trust-based message evaluation framework. Peers evaluate the messages in a cooperative manner and authenticate it before propagating it in the network.

But the scheme introduces a significant latency in authentication spoiling the utilities of emergency messaging. Zhang et al. [11] used SVM classifier to detect fake messages and authenticated the source using Dempster-Shafer theory. But decision was at local end and there was no uniformity in decision logic globally. Asian et al. [12] proposed a genetic programming-based trust computation model to authenticate messages. Data from attack scenarios are used to extract features and genetic programming model-based attack classification model is built. Using this model, fake messages are classified. But the approach has zero-day problem. Muhammad et al. [13] used physical features like radio signal strength to detect the authenticity of contents in the message. From the radio signal strength, distance estimate is made and this is checked for consistency in the message to detect authenticity of the message. The message works well to detect Sybil based attacks but the scheme fails for relayed messages. Rassam et al. [14] proposed a context aware detection approach to classify fake messages. Features extracted from vehicular context are used to train a unsupervised clustering algorithm to classify the messages to two classes of genuine and fake. Contexts considered were snapshot based without any temporal correlation. Ghaleb et al. [15] proposed a Hybrid and Multifaceted Context-aware Misbehavior Detection model for filtering fake messages. Data and behavior features are used to build a vehicular context. Consistency against this model is checked and if any deviation, the messages are filtered as fake messages. The computational complexity is higher in this model for emergency messages. Sharshembiev et al. [16] used selective flow sampling and entropy change to detect misbehaving nodes in the network. Once the misbehaving nodes are detected, messages from it are blocked. The method proposed here was based on observing the statistical difference in flow between flooding and multi hop routing. The work does not analyze contents of message. Guo et al. [17] proposed a reinforcement learning based trust management scheme to filter fake messages. The evaluation strategy to filter fake messages is continuously updated using reinforcement learning. Though the model is adaptive to different driving condition, it does not con-sider temporal correlation between the events. Sedjelmaci et al. [18] presented a rule-based message filtering scheme for VANETs. The rules to spot malicious vehicles are framed and based on rules, vehicles and their message are filtered. The scheme is not adaptive and requires frequent rule update. Zaidi et al. [19] used statistical techniques to detect false information attacks. Data collected in various attack scenarios are analyzed for statistical correlation and rules are built based on it to detect false information messages. The analysis is based only on behavior data and contents are not considered. Liang et al. [20] proposed a message filtering system for VANET based on hidden generalized mixture transition distribution model. Multi objective optimization combined with expectation maximization is used to predict the future state of neighboring vehicles. Message filtering is done based on forecasted future state of the vehicle. The analysis did not consider the temporal correlation between the message contexts of attackers. Bujari et al. (2019) [21] proposed a fast multi-hop broadcast protocol to propagate emergency messages. The solution is distributed. Each vehicle dynamically estimates the transmission range and speeds up multi hop propagation through broadcast according to the estimate. But the solution fails in high way scenarios. Gonzalez et al. (2019) [22] proposed a present delay broadcast protocol for a fast and reliable dissemination. The solution is a subset of existing schemes of like count-based, geographical, distance-based, and opportunistic emergency message dissemination. But the solution has higher retransmission and works only for dense scenarios.

Most of the approaches discussed in this section can be categorized to two types: trust based and behavior based. They are not computationally efficient and can create higher latency. This distorts the purpose of emergency messages. Thus, it becomes necessary to validate the emergency message in a light weight manner at same time without compromising on accuracy of fake detection.

3 Cooperative Light Weight Detection and Prevention

The proposed cooperative light weight detection and prevention of false message propagation is designed for infrastructure based VANET involving RSU placed at certain locations along the road. The proposed mechanism architecture is given in Fig. 1. In this RSU registers to trusted authority and vehicles register to RSU. Vehicles sends an emergency event to RSU, which is validated and only genuine events are propagated on the emergency path. A graph G is constructed with RSU as vertices and distance between them are considered as weights. A Steiner minimal tree is constructed with G as input. Steiner minimal tree is the minimal latency path connecting all the RSU's. Emergency message verification is carried out by the RSU entities, which are near to the location of reported event. The structure of fake message detection is shown in Fig. 1.

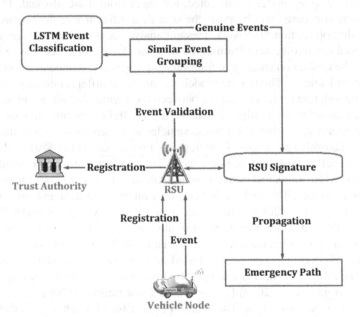

Fig. 1. VANET fake message detection architecture

An event agreement model involving RSU's and the vehicles is designed to measure the confidence of the event. Along with this, reputation of the reporting source and environmental conditions are used to ascertain the occurrence of the further event. As the confidence increases, emergency message is propagated along the Steiner path. The proposed solution has following important stages (i) Registration (ii) Steiner path computation (iii) Event validation and forwarding. Each of these stages are detailed in below subsections.

3.1 Registration

In this proposed mechanism RSU must register to a trusted authority. RSU selects its identifier as RID_a, , creates public key $(PURID_a)$ and private key $(PRRID_a)$ for further operations. RSU sends $(PRRID_a, PURID_a)$ to the Trusted authority (TA) and public key of RSU stores in public key information table. TA provides a key K which is used for sharing any information among the RSU. The vehicle node of the VANET must register themselves to RSU before generating or forwarding any emergency messages. Vehicle initiates registration with the RSU by calculating two numbers called S_1 and S_2.

$$S_1 = a.(P_{pub} + h_1(G).P)$$
$$S_2 = h_1([e(P, P)]^a, G) \oplus (ID, b) \tag{1}$$

where, ID is the unique ID assigned by the system randomly to the vehicle and a, b are two random numbers generating in the range of m_{min} and n_{max} values specified dynamically. Later stage e, G, S_1 and S_2 are sent to RSU and RSU finds the ID of the vehicle node as given below.

$$k = e\left(\frac{1}{S_1 + h_1(G)}.P, S_1\right)$$
$$v = h_1(k, G)$$
$$(ID, b) = S_2 \oplus v \tag{2}$$

At the RSU, it computes two number called R_1 and R_2 as follows,

$$SK = b.S_1$$
$$R_1 = b.(h_1(G).P + P_{pub})$$
$$R_2 = b.(h_1(h_1(ID), h_1(G), b, ID, G, SK)) \tag{3}$$

The updated values of R_1 and R_2 are sent back to vehicle. On receiving it, sensing node computes $\overline{R}_2$ as follows,

$$SK = H_1(a.R_1)$$
$$\overline{R}_2 = H_1(h_1(h_1(ID), h_1(G), b, ID, G, SK)) \tag{4}$$

If the computed $\bar{R}_2$ is equal to R_2, then vehicle gets authenticated. Next, vehicle node computes S_3 as given below and send it back to the RSU.

$$S_3 = (b + H_1(ID, SK, R_2, S_1)) \times \left(\frac{P}{S_1 + h_1(ID)} \right) \tag{5}$$

On receiving S_3, RSU verifies the validity of S_3 by checking following relation.

$$e\left(S_3.\left(P_{pub} + h_1(ID).P\right)\right) = k.g^{h_1(ID,SK,R_2,S_1)} \tag{6}$$

If the relation is true, then vehicle is registered at the sink. The random number b is generated by the vehicle is available at vehicle and RSU both. The session key for communication is created as,

$$sk = h_1(ID) \oplus h_1(G) \oplus h_1(EG) \oplus h_1(b) \tag{7}$$

Every vehicle entering into the RSU area, must register itself before posting any event. This ensures a mutual authentication between Vehicle and RSU and creates a secret session key for communication between vehicle and RSU.

3.2 Steiner path Computation

Given set of N RSU's, Steiner minimal tree is constructed with S Steiner points in a way that, minimum spanning tree (MST) cost over $NRSU$ is minimized. The solution to the Steiner minimal tree problem is found using Graph Iterated 1-Steiner (GI1S) algorithm with KMP heuristics [23]. In GI1S, a weighted graph G is created with N RSU's. The edge weight between any two RSU A and B is given as the delay cost [24]. Delay is modeled as probability mass function of delay distribution as,

$$Delay = \begin{cases} \sum\limits_{i=0}^{\infty} f_i(a).f_i(b), \ x = 0 \\ \sum\limits_{i=0}^{\infty} f_i(a)f_i(a).f_{2x+i}(b) + \sum\limits_{i=0}^{\infty} f_i(b).f_{2x+i}(a), \ x > 0 \end{cases} \tag{8}$$

where a, b are forward and backward directions from transmitter to receiver. f(z) is the probability mass function of delay of direction z. GI1S finds a set S of potential Steiner points such that,

$$\Delta KMB(N, S) = cost(KMB(N)) - cost(KMB(N \cup S)) \tag{9}$$

where N is the subset of V RSU's.

The output of GI1S algorithm is the Steiner points connecting all the V RSU's with minimal path length. This minimal delay path is used for emergency message propagation.

3.3 Event Validation and Forwarding

A vehicle which detects any emergency event must forward it first to its registered RSU. RSU after accepting the emergency event from the registered vehicle must validate the event using a cooperative agreement scheme. In this scheme, the event is held at RSU for a tolerable time t, and its agreement to other event received in time t is measured.

The agreement is measured between the emergency event E_m and other similar events reported by vehicles over time t. The similarity is measured by calculating distance between the features of the event and thresholding them. The features of the event are reported location, reported time, Term frequency – inverted document frequency (TF-IDF) of event contents etc. The similar events are sorted by time. A Long short-term memory (LSTM) classifier is trained to learn the temporal correlation between the events and to classify them as fake or genuine events.

LSTM is an extension of RNN (Recurrent Neural Networks). It has gated mechanism with cell activation state, in addition to the existing hidden state [25]. It will be learned when to forget long-term information and when to incorporate new information. Separating the hidden state with the cell activation state also allows for the network to learn controlling how much of the cell activation it outputs. The structure of LSTM is given in Fig. 2 as follows.

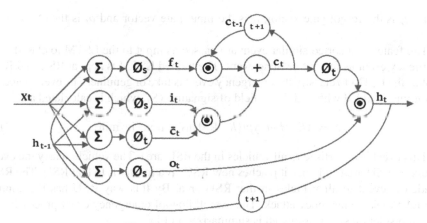

Fig. 2. Structure of LSTM classifier

A combination of an input vector x and the previous hidden state is taken as input by the LSTM node. A new candidate cell activation ~c is calculated by LSTM as the weighted sum of the inputs and bias b. Later the result is passed to a hyperbolic tangent activation function to calculate (c_t) as given below.

$$c_t = \emptyset_t(W_c x_t + U_c h_{t-1} + b_c) \tag{10}$$

where, c_t is the candidate cell activation, x_t is the input vector, W and U are the weight matrices, h_{t-1} is the hidden state vector at the previous time step and b_c is the bias.

The gates control how much of activation must be retained and how much must be forgot. Input gate control how much activation to retain and forget gate decided how much cell activation must be forgot. The final gate is incorporated to calculate the hidden state.

$$f_t = \emptyset_s\left(W_f x_t + U_f h_{t-1} + b_f\right) \tag{11}$$

$$i_t = \emptyset_s(W_i x_t + U_i h_{t-1} + b_i) \tag{12}$$

$$o_t = \emptyset_s(W_o x_t + U_o h_{t-1} + b_o) \tag{13}$$

where, f_t is the forgot gate vector, i_t is the input gate vector and o_t is the output gate vector.

The features of sorted similar event are passed as input to the LSTM to classify the emergency event as fake or genuine event. The trained LSTM is kept at RSU and RSU invokes the LSTM to classify the emergency event is fake or genuine. The event detected as genuine is added with additional field of signature (S), which is calculated as,

$$S = AES\_Encrypt(K, RSU_{ID} + time\ in\ min) \tag{14}$$

This event is advertised to all vehicles in the RSU area. The vehicles carry the event to outside RSU area and once it reaches new RSU area forwards to that RSU. The RSU broadcasts event to all vehicles in that RSU area. By this way RSU has the control over fake replay emergency attack. The overall flow of emergency event processing in proposed solution so far discussed is summarized in Fig. 3.

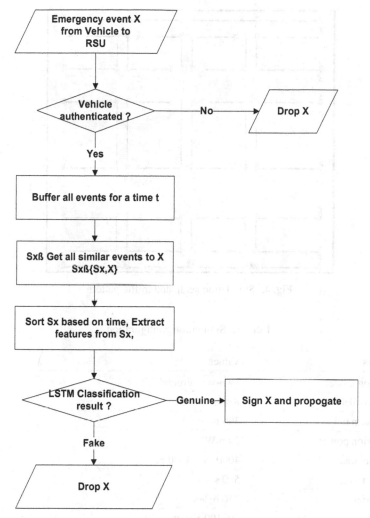

Fig. 3. Proposed emergency event processing diagram

4 Results

The proposed solution is simulated in NS2.34 simulator for vehicle mobile pattern generation. The simulation for proposed solution has been conducted with the traffic pattern given in Fig. 4 using the parameters given in Table 1.

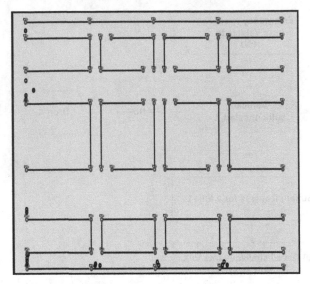

Fig. 4. Simulation setup and traffic pattern

Table 1. Simulation configuration

Parameters	Values
Propagation model	Two-way ground
Mobility model	Krauss
Transmission range	300 m
Transmission power	20 mW
Simulation area	4000 m * 4000 m
Simulation time	500 s
Message size	256 bytes
Speed	20–100 Kmph
Density	25–150 km
Performance rate	5 times/second with 5–20 different patterns

The performance is measured in terms of (i) Fake Detection accuracy, (ii) False positive (iii) Fake detection rate and (iv) latency. The performance is compared against traffic flow model approach proposed by Liu et al. [6], context aware approach proposed by Rassam et al. [14] and multifaceted context approach proposed by Ghaleb et al. [15].

4.1 Fake Message Detection Accuracy

The fake message detection accuracy is measured by varying the attacker's proportion and the result is given in Fig. 5.

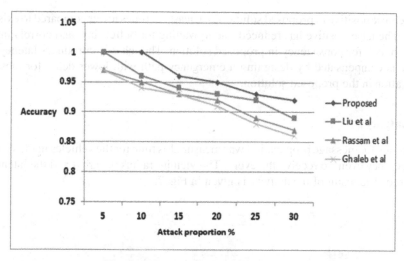

Fig. 5. Fake message detection accuracy

The fake detection accuracy in proposed solution is 2% more than Liu et al., 4% more than Rassam et al. and 5% more than Ghaleb et al. The fake detection accuracy is higher in proposed solution due to use of temporal correlation between events using LSTM classifier.

4.2 False Positive

The false positive is measured varying the attack's proportion and the result is given in Fig. 6.

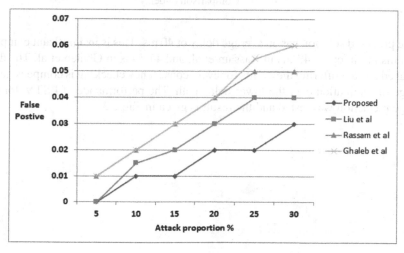

Fig. 6. False positive

The false positive in proposed solution is at least 1.6 times lower compared to existing works. The false positive has reduced due to waiting for buffer time and correlating all events to look for consistency in proposed solution. Though this introduces latency, the latency is compensated by designing a emergency path with lower delay for message propagation in the proposed solution.

4.3 Latency

The latency for message propagation was measured as time for the vehicles in the vicinity of emergency event to receive the event. The vicinity radius is varied and the latency is measured. The result of the activity is given in Fig. 7.

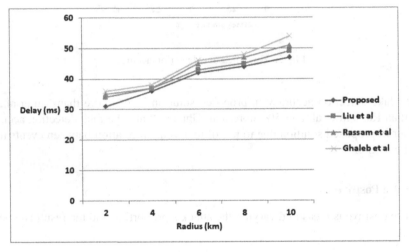

Fig. 7. Comparison of delay

The proposed solution has an average delay of 40 ms. This is insignificant compared to 41.6 ms in Liu et al., 43 ms in Rassam et al. and 44.4 ms in Ghaleb et al. The delay introduced due to buffering the events for event consistency checking is compensated by message dissemination over the lower delay path. The performance of LSTM for fake message prediction was tested and the result is given in Table 2.

Table 2. LSTM classifier results

Properties	Result
Sensitivity/Recall	0.909
Specificity	0.918
Precision	0.903
F1-Score	0.920
AUC	0.911

As per the results generated through the proposed solution, the LSTM classifier is able to achieve about 91% accuracy in detection of fake emergency events.

5 Conclusion

This proposed mechanism is the complete solution to detect fake emergency message and prevention solution based on LSTM classifier. In this, the emergency events are verified for temporal consistency with similar events reported in a buffer time. Based on the temporal consistency, the emergency event is classified as fake or genuine. Only authenticate vehicles can generate emergency events and are forwarded on low latency path for propagation after proving its truthness. The proposed solution is able to detect fake messages with average accuracy of 96% without any significant latency.

References

1. Latif, S., Mahfooz, S., Jan, B., Ahmad, N., Cao, Y., Asif, M.: A comparative study of scenario-driven multi-hop broadcast protocols for VANETs. Veh. Commun. **12**, 88–109 (2018)
2. Wu, J., Lu, H., Xiang, Y., Wang, F., Li, H.: SATMAC: self-Adaptive TDMA-based MAC protocol for VANETs. IEEE Trans. Intell. Transp. Syst. **23**(11), 21712–21728 (2022)
3. Li, W., Song, H.: Art: an attack-resistant trust management scheme for securing vehicular ad hoc networks. IEEE Trans. Intell. Transp. Syst. **17**(4), 960–969 (2016)
4. Ullah, N., Kong, X., Ning, Z., Tolba, A., Alrashoud, M., Xia, F.: Emergency warning messages dissemination in vehicular social networks: a trust-based scheme. Veh. Commun. 100199. https://doi.org/10.1016/j.vehcom.2019.100199
5. Dua, A., Kumar, N., Bawa, S.: ReIDD: reliability-aware intelligent data dissemination protocol for broadcast storm problem in vehicular ad hoc networks. Telecommun. Syst. **64**(3), 439–458 (2017)
6. Liu, J., Yang, W., Zhang, J., Yang, C.: Detecting false messages in vehicular ad hoc networks based on a traffic flow model. Int. J. Distrib. Sens. Netw. **16**(2) (2020)
7. Park, S., Zou, C.C.: Reliable traffic information propagation in vehicular Ad-Hoc networks. In: 2008 IEEE Sarnoff Symposium, Princeton, NJ, USA, pp. 1–6 (2008)
8. Arshad, M., Ullah, Z., Ahmad, N., et al.: A survey of local/cooperative-based malicious information detection techniques in VANETs. J. Wirel. Commun. Netw. **2018**, 62 (2018)
9. Mohamed, T.M., Ahmed, I.Z., Sadek, R.A.: Efficient VANET safety message delivery and authenticity with privacy preservation. PeerJ Comput. Sci. **4**(7), e519 (2021)

10. Chen, C.: A Trust-based Message Evaluation and Propagation Framework in Vehicular Ad-Hoc Networks. UWSpace (2010). http://hdl.handle.net/10012/4929

11. Zhang, C., Chen, K., Zeng, X., Xue, X.: Misbehavior detection based on support vector machine and Dempster-Shafer theory of evidence in VANETs. IEEE Access **6**, 59860–59870 (2018)

12. Aslan, M., Sen, S.: Evolving trust formula to evaluate data trustworthiness in VANETs using genetic programming. In: Kaufmann, P., Castillo, P. (eds.) Applications of Evolutionary Computation. EvoApplications 2019. LNCS, vol. 11454, pp. 413–429. Springer, Cham (2019). https://doi.org/10.1007/978-3-030-16692-2_28

13. Muhammad, M., Kearney, P., Aneiba, A., Arshad, J., Kunz, A.: RMCCS: RSSI-based message consistency checking scheme for V2V communications. In: di Vimercati, S.D.C., Samarati, P. (eds.), Proceedings of the 18th International Conference on Security and Cryptography, SECRYPT 2021, pp. 722–727, SCITEPRESS, July 6–8 2021

14. Ghaleb, F.A., Zainal, A., Maroof, M.A., Rassam, M.A., Saeed, F.: Detecting Bogus Information Attack in Vehicular Ad Hoc Network, A Context-Aware Approach (2019)

15. Ghaleb, F.A., Maarof, M.A., Zainal, A., Al-Rimy, B.A.S., Saeed, F., Al-Hadhrami, T.: Hybrid and multifaceted context-aware misbehavior detection model for vehicular Ad Hoc network. IEEE Access **7**, 159119–159140 (2019)

16. Sharshembiev, K., Yoo, S.M., Elmahdi, E., Kim, Y.K., Jeong, G.H.: Fail-safe mechanism using entropy based misbehavior classification and detection in vehicular Ad Hoc networks. In: Proceedings of the 2019 International Conference on Internet of Things (iThings) and IEEE Green Computing and Communications (GreenCom) and IEEE Cyber, Physical and Social Computing (CPSCom) and IEEE Smart Data (SmartData), Atlanta, GA, USA, pp. 123–128, 14–17 July 2019

17. Guo, J., et al.: TROVE: a context-awareness trust model for VANETs using reinforcement learning. IEEE Internet Things J. **7**, 6647–6662 (2020)

18. Sedjelmaci, H., Senouci, S.M., Abu-Rgheff, M.A.: An efficient and lightweight intrusion detection mechanism for service-oriented vehicular networks. IEEE Internet Things J. **1**, 570–577 (2014)

19. Zaidi, K., Milojevic, M.B., Rakocevic, V., Nallanathan, A., Rajarajan, M.: Host-based intrusion detection for VANETs: a statistical approach to rogue node detection. IEEE Trans. Veh. Technol. **65**, 6703–6714 (2016)

20. Liang, J., Lin, Q., Chen, J., Zhu, Y.A.: Filter model based on hidden generalized mixture transition distribution model for intrusion detection system in vehicle Ad Hoc networks. IEEE Trans. Intell. Transp. Syst. **10**, 2707–2722 (2019)

21. Bujari, A., Gottardo, J., Palazzi, C.E., Ronzani, D.: Message dissemination in urban IoV. In: Proceedings of the 23rd IEEE/ACM International Symposium on Distributed Simulation and Real Time Applications (DS-RT '19), pp. 211–214. IEEE Press (2019)

22. Gonzalez, S., Ramos, V.: Preset delay broadcast: a protocol for fast information dissemination in vehicular Ad Hoc networks (VANETs). J. Wirel. Commun. Netw. **2016**, 117 (2016)

23. Kou, L., Markowsky, G., Berman, L.A.: Fast algorithm for steiner trees. Acta Informatica **15**, 141–145 (1981)

24. Khan, M.U., Hosseinzadeh, M., Mosavi, A.: An intersection-based routing scheme using Q-learning in vehicular Ad Hoc networks for traffic management in the intelligent transportation system. Mathematics **10**(20), 3731 (2022)

25. Habelalmateen, M.I., Ahmed, A.J., Abbas, A.H., Rashid, S.A.: ACRP: traffic-aware clustering-based routing protocol for vehicular Ad-Hoc networks. Designs **6**(5), 89 (2022)

Antarctic Ice Sheet Surface Mass Balance Using UAV-Based Digital Elevation Model

B. Mahesh, S. Dhanush, C. Rakshita, K. R. Raghavendra, and M. Geetha Priya$^{(\boxtimes)}$

CIIRC, Jyothy Institute of Technology, Bengaluru, India
geetha.sri82@gmail.com

Abstract. A glacier's mass balance is the difference between the quantity of snow that accumulates in the winter and quantity of the ice that melts in the summer. A positive mass balance indicates that the glacier is gaining ice, whereas a negative mass balance indicates that the glacier is losing ice. Ice sheets are continental glaciers whose thickness of ice varies from several kilometers at the center to tens of meters at the edges. The main objective of the study is to quantify the net change in mass over a short period of 7 days during Austral summer (2022–2023) over a portion of the ice sheet margin (70°46′22.13″S, 11°45′11.62″E) located in central Dronning Maud Land, East Antarctica using unmanned aerial vehicle (UAV) based multispectral datasets. Two digital elevation models (DEMs) were generated from UAV (real-time kinematics enabled) data for estimating the change in mass by calculating the elevation change. The findings revealed that the study area experienced a significant elevation change of 1.60 m within a week-long duration (10/12/2022–17/12/2022), which is an exceptional rate of change for 7 days of interval. The outcomes of this research, therefore, provide crucial data for understanding the hydrological processes and climate dynamics that govern the sea level increase.

Keywords: UAV · Mass balance · Antarctica · DEM · Glacier

1 Introduction

The world's largest freshwater body is the Antarctic Ice Sheet (AIS) [1], small variation in the mass balance of the ice sheet plays a significant role in rising the sea level globally and climatic changes so it is vital to study the Antarctic mass balance. Snowfall continuously adds mass to the ice sheets, which is then continuously removed by basal melting, iceberg calving, and surface melting [2]. The AIS has been experiencing a significant reduction in its mass, which is a major cause for concern. Recent research has revealed that this mass loss has accelerated over the past ten years, and it is thought to be one of the major contributors to the rise in the sea level worldwide [3]. The process of mass loss in the AIS is complex, involving a combination of melting and ice flow acceleration, and it is mainly driven by the warming of ocean waters, according to scientific research [3]. The proposed study makes use of unmanned aerial vehicles (UAV) data, which produce high-resolution digital elevation models (DEMs) that can be used to estimate the mass balance over the region of our interest because these models are not well-represented in lower-resolution satellite-derived products [4].

V. N. M. Aradhya et al. (Eds.): CCIP 2023, CCIS 2044, pp. 39–49, 2024.
https://doi.org/10.1007/978-3-031-60725-7_4

To guarantee the exactness of the DEM and Ortho-mosaic, a considerable number of ground control points (GCPs) were employed. In polar environments, the utilization of GCPs is crucial to incorporate additional control into survey results and shall be considered mandatory, especially in RTK UAV surveys.

2 Study Area

Antarctica is the southernmost continent, which serves as a crucial site for scientific exploration, with numerous research stations operated by various countries. The AIS is the world's largest ice sheet which covers 14 million km^2 [5]. Antarctica is experiencing very harsh extreme climatic conditions with temperatures of around −50 °C (−58°F) and around −10 °C (14°F) in the summer at the shelf regions. The temperature distribution across the ice sheet is influenced by several factors such as elevation, atmospheric conditions, and proximity to the sea. Antarctica is known for its strong and persistent katabatic winds [6], which are cold and dry winds that blow from high elevations down to lower elevations, with speeds reaching up to 200 km per hour in general.

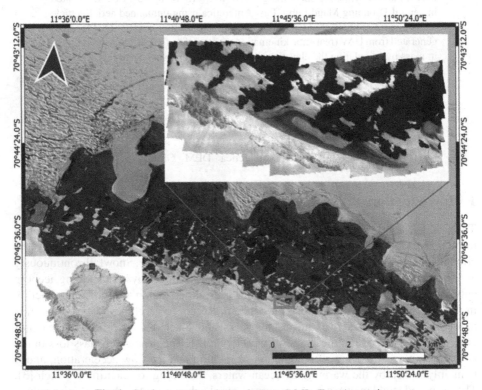

Fig. 1. Study Area (Ice sheet edge) at cDML, East Antarctica

The area considered for this mass balance study is a region at the periphery of the AIS (edges around 70°46′22.13″S, 11°45′11.62″E) in central Dronning Maud land (cDML), East Antarctica, which is located at an aerial distance of 1 km from the Maitri Indian research station at Antarctica on the Schirmacher Oasis which is shown in Fig. 1. The region also consists of a proglacial lake with an area of 9500 m^2. This region is chosen as the study area because the Ice sheets are sensitive to climate change, with rising temperatures causing them to melt and shrink [7]. This process can contribute to sea-level rise, which can have significant impacts on coastal areas around the world.

3 Materials and Methods

3.1 UAV Mission and Data Collection

UAV survey is a technique of conducting aerial surveys using unmanned aerial vehicles equipped with cameras and sensors [8]. These drones can capture high-resolution images and videos. These images are used to produce highly accurate 3D models, maps, and other conceptions of the survey area, which can be utilized for analysis and decision-making. The UAV used for the present study has a feature of Real-Time Kinematics enabled [9] for positional accuracy with a multispectral sensor and of net weight of 1487 g. It was operated with a maximum flight time of 27 min with a field temperature of −12° to 2 °C. The UAV utilized during the study has one RGB camera and a multispectral camera array with 5 cameras in it which cover Red, Blue, Green, Near-infrared(NIR), and Red Edge bands all at 2 megapixels with global shutter, on a 3-axis stabilized gimbal. Two UAV surveys (10/12/2022 & 17/12/2022) were planned for data acquisition with 3 missions to cover the study area extent and to achieve the best possible spatial resolution of 5 cm. Mission parameters are shown in Table 1. A survey utilizing the Global Navigation Satellite System (GNSS) was also conducted for collecting Ground Control Points (GCPs) [10].

Table 1. UAV Mission planning parameters

Setting	values
Flight altitude	95 m
ground resolution	5 cm
view angle	900
Flight speed	5 m/s
Frontal overlap	75%
Side overlap	60%

3.2 UAV Flight Challenges Faced

Operating a UAV in Antarctica requires overcoming significant challenges caused by harsh climate conditions. The negative temperatures and strong katabatic winds pose a significant risk to the UAV's battery performance and flight time. In such cold weather, the battery drains much faster, and wind gusts can easily destabilize the UAV. To overcome these challenges, adjustments in flight altitude were necessary to ensure that the required ground resolution was achieved. However, this led to a trade-off between area covered and resolution, making it challenging to obtain high-quality data. The field photograph is shown in Fig. 2.

Fig. 2. Field photograph captured during Austral summer 2022–2023 over the Ice sheet edge

3.3   Process Flow and DEM Generation

The process flow shown in Fig. 3 was incorporated to carry out to process the UAV data over the study region. A professional edition of Agisoft Metashape 2.0.1 software was used to construct a DEM of the Ice sheet surveyed area [11]. This was done through photogrammetric processing using a triangulation algorithm which produces maps by overlapping aerial images [12]. The UAV survey carried out on 10th December 2022 had 1005 images with a reprojection error of 0.672pixel/survey and the survey on 17th December had 1655 images with a reprojection error of 0.631pixel/survey [13]. The sensor used in the UAV survey has an image resolution of 1600*1300 and a focal length of 5.74 mm. All the images are selected and aligned based on the camera position and these images are used to generate Dense point clouds which is a three-dimensional representation of an object or scene created by capturing a large number of data points. Every point in the dense point cloud represents a specific location in space and contains information about its X, Y, and Z coordinates, where X represents longitude, Y represents latitude and Z represents altitude. The XY error and Z error for the first survey was

0.17 cm and 0.34 cm, for the second survey the XY and Z error was observed to be 0.21 cm and 0.45 cm as given by the software.

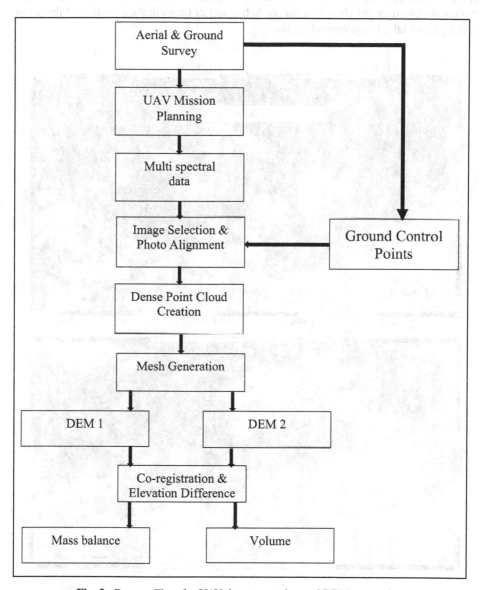

Fig. 3. Process Flow for UAV data processing and DEM generation

The resulting point density achieved during the process was approximately 125 points per sq.m. for the first survey and 112 points per sq.m. for the second survey. A mesh was created connecting all the point clouds. The DEMs obtained from the process provides a spatial resolution of 8.5 cm and are georeferenced with the help of 9 GCP points setup on the surveyed area as given in the Fig. 4. Even with Real-Time Kinematic (RTK) enabled UAVs, conducting a GCP survey of the area under consideration is required to ensure accuracy [14]. The surveyed area encompasses the periphery of the ice sheet in the south direction and shelters a part of Schirmacher Oasis in the direction of the north and a glacial lake in the central region.

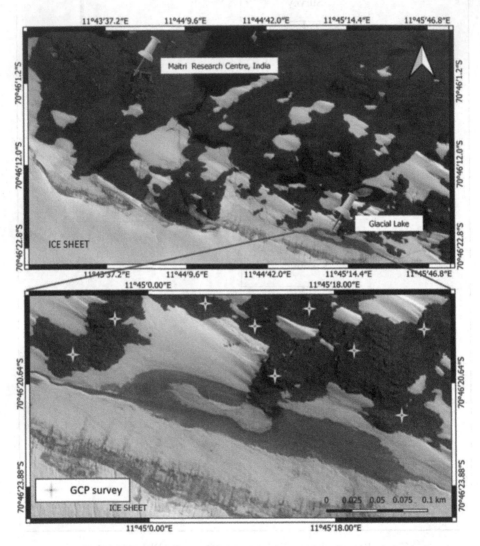

Fig. 4. GCP points established on stable regions

4   Results

The process flow was followed as discussed in the methodology to produce the DEM from UAV raw images. Two DEMs generated on 10th Dec, 2022 and 17th Dec,20222 cover an approximate area of 34.5 acres and 43 acres respectively as given in Fig. 5(a & b). The elevation difference between the two DEMs was computed after the bias correction of the individual DEMs and co-registration. The GCPs obtained in the GNSS survey over stable (non-glaciated) regions are utilized to minimize the elevation-dependent bias for the generated DEMs.

Additionally, the root mean square error (RMSE) was computed by considering the elevations of the stable regions for over 100 points, from the two DEMs using (Eq. 1).

$$RMSE = \sqrt{\sum_{i=1}^{Y} \frac{(x_i - x_i')^2}{Y}} \qquad (1)$$

where Y represents the number of points considered, x_i is the elevation value of the DEM1 and x_i' is the elevation of the DEM2. The elevation changes greater than 2 m and less than -7.5 m were considered outliers and removed from the difference DEM which usually represents the DEM edges as seen in Fig. 5(c & d). Pixels with an absolute elevation difference greater than three standard deviations from the mean were also excluded, in addition to the outlier threshold. Figure 6 represents the minimum, maximum, and average elevations obtained from the DEMs and the differenced DEMs. The study revealed that there was no difference in elevation across the stable region, but there were significant changes observed at the edges of the ice sheet, which were caused by the dynamic movement of the ice sheet.

The computed elevation difference is used to compute the mass balance (Eqs. 2–5) of the ice sheet portion over a short duration of 7-day interval. The area under consideration is approximately 78,200 m^2 after the removal of outliers and non-overlapping regions. The findings showed that the average elevation lost is around 1.6 m with a mass loss of 1.446 mwe.

$$\text{Volume} = \text{Average depth} * \text{total area} \qquad (2)$$

$$\text{Mass} = \text{Density of Ice} * \text{Volume} \qquad (3)$$

$$\text{Mass per unit area} = \text{Mass/Total area} \qquad (4)$$

$$\text{Mass balance} = \text{Mass per unit area/Density of water} \qquad (5)$$

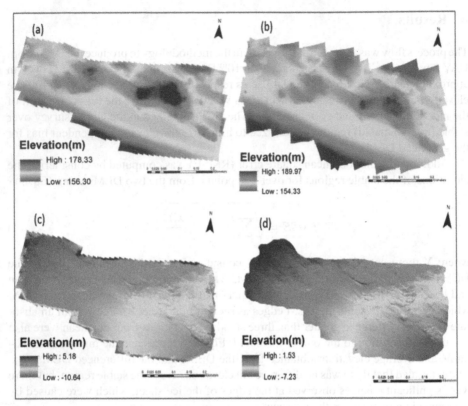

Fig. 5. (a) DEM from 10th Dec 2022 UAV survey, (b)DEM from 17th Dec 2022 UAV survey (c) Elevation difference with outliers, and (d) Elevation difference without outliers with an area of 1,11,037 m^2

The mass balance and mass change rate were calculated by considering two values for the density of ice as shown in Table 2. The study shows a significant amount of mass loss over a small region of an ice sheet during a brief 7-day period, compared to the annual mass balance computed for Himalayan glaciers [15]. The increased mass loss and rate of change shown in Table 2 indicate that the ice sheet frontal edge experiences rapid movement with increased velocity daily which was also manually visualized during the fieldwork (Fig. 7) by the team members [16].

By analyzing the results obtained, it is interpreted that the elevation diminished at a rate of 23 cm/day with a rate of mass change of approximately 15.26 Kt/day in the surveyed area during the study period. These results were estimated only over the surveyed area for a week-long period and may vary with time for the other regions of the Antarctic ice sheet.

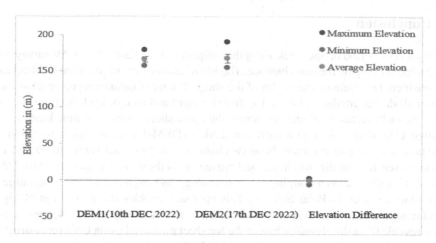

Fig. 6. Elevation Profile

Table 2. Mass balance and mass change rates during the study period

Parameter (10th Dec, 2022-17th Dec, 2022)	Density scenario 1 (850 ± 60 kgm^{-3})	Density scenario 1 (900 ± 60 kgm^{-3})
Mass balance (m.w.e)	-1.37 ± 0.09	-1.47 ± 0.09
Rate of change of mass/day (Kt)	16.16 ± 1.07	15.26 ± 1.07

Fig. 7. Field photograph showing the ice sheet frontal edge as seen from a pro-glacial lake.

5 Conclusion

During a brief period of one week along the periphery of the East AIS, a UAV survey was conducted to compute the mass balance. The Mass balance estimated for the ice sheet can be considered to evaluate the health of the sheet. The mass balance represents the total sum of all the accumulation (snow, ice, freezing rain) and melt or ice loss (from calving icebergs, melting, and sublimation) across the entire sheet. Using real-time kinematics-enabled UAV data, two digital elevation models (DEMs) were produced to calculate elevation changes and compute the mass changes. The proposed study shows that ice sheets are sensitive to climate change and movement of the sheet is evident from the UAV survey. This study aims to employ UAV technology and engineering design techniques to conduct research in Polar Science. This approach enables the acquisition of high-resolution ground data that is not obtainable from satellite datasets. The outcomes of the study revealed that the elevation loss of the Ice sheet measured using UAV reconstructed images is 23 cm per day with a mass loss of 113.13 ktons/week during the study period. The analysis suggests that conducting UAV surveys on an annual basis would aid in comprehending the characteristics and patterns of ice sheet parameters.

Acknowledgment. The authors acknowledge the logistical support given by the National Centre for Polar and Ocean Research, Ministry of Earth Sciences, Govt. of India under the Indian Scientific Expedition to Antarctica (ISEA) to undertake this research. The authors gratefully acknowledge the support rendered by Prazim Trading and Investment Company Private Limited (PTICL), MM Forgings, TATA STEEL, Jyothy Industries, Rational Technologies, and Dr. Krishna Venkatesh, Director, CIIRC - Jyothy Institute of Technology, Bengaluru.

References

1. Mottram, R., et al.: What is the surface mass balance of Antarctica? An intercomparison of regional climate model estimates (2021). https://doi.org/10.5194/tc-15-3751-2021
2. Alley, K.E., Scambos, T.A., Miller, J.Z., Long, D.G., MacFerrin, M.: Quantifying vulnerability of Antarctic ice shelves to hydrofracture using microwave scattering properties. Remote Sens. Environ. **210**, 297–306 (2018). https://doi.org/10.1016/j.rse.2018.03.025
3. Priya, M.G., Varshini, N., Chandhana, G., Deeksha, G., Supriya, K., Krishnaveni, D.: Study on snowmelt and algal growth in the Antarctic Peninsula using spatial approach. Curr. Sci. **120**, 932–936 (2021). https://doi.org/10.18520/cs/v120/i5/932-936
4. Lamsters, K., Ješkins, J., Sobota, I., Karušs, J., Džeriņš, P.: Surface characteristics, elevation change, and velocity of high-arctic valley glacier from repeated high-resolution UAV photogrammetry. Remote Sens. **14** (2022). https://doi.org/10.3390/rs14041029
5. Artemieva, I.M.: Antarctica ice sheet basal melting enhanced by high mantle heat. Earth-Science Rev. **226**, 103954 (2022). https://doi.org/10.1016/j.earscirev.2022.103954
6. Lindbäck, K., et al.: Spatial and temporal variations in basal melting at Nivlisen ice shelf, East Antarctica, derived from phase-sensitive radars. Cryosphere **13**, 2579–2595 (2019). https://doi.org/10.5194/tc-13-2579-2019
7. Geetha Priya, M., Deva Jefflin, A.R., Luis, A.J., Bahuguna, I.M.: Estimation of surface melt induced melt pond depths over Amery Ice Shelf, East Antarctica using Multispectral and ICESat-2 data. Disaster Adv. **15**, 1–8 (2022). https://doi.org/10.25303/1508da01008

8. Geissler, J., Mayer, C., Jubanski, J., Münzer, U., Siegert, F.: Analyzing glacier retreat and mass balances using aerial and UAV photogrammetry in the Ötztal Alps Austria. Cryosphere **15**, 3699–3717 (2021). https://doi.org/10.5194/tc-15-3699-2021
9. Sefercik, U.G., Nazar, M.: Coherence analysis of DSMS generated by multispectral RTK and RGB NON-RTK UAVS' simultaneous data. In: International Geoscience and Remote Sensing Symposium, July 2022, pp. 7733–7736 (2022). https://doi.org/10.1109/IGARSS46834.2022.9884157
10. Belloni, V., Fugazza, D., Di Rita, M.: UAV-based glacier monitoring: gnss kinematic track post-processing and direct georeferencing for accurate reconstructions in challenging environments. Int. Arch. Photogramm. Remote Sens. Spat. Inf. Sci. - ISPRS Arch. **43**, 367–373 (2022). https://doi.org/10.5194/isprs-archives-XLIII-B1-2022-367-2022
11. Darji, K., Patel, D.: Creating the high resolution DEM for flood assessment using UAV techniques. In: ISRS-ISG National Symposium, p. 185 (2020)
12. Groos, A.R., Aeschbacher, R., Fischer, M., Kohler, N., Mayer, C., Senn-Rist, A.: Accuracy of UAV photogrammetry in glacial and periglacial alpine terrain: a comparison with airborne and terrestrial datasets. Front. Remote Sens. **3** (2022). https://doi.org/10.3389/frsen.2022.871994
13. Geetha Priya, M., Venkatesh, K., Shivanna, L., Devaraj, S.: Detecting short-term surface melt over Vestre Broggerbreen, Arctic glacier using indigenously developed unmanned air vehicles. Geocarto Int. **37**, 3167–3178 (2022). https://doi.org/10.1080/10106049.2020.1849416
14. Lin, Y., Liu, Y., Yu, Z., Cheng, X., Shen, Q., Zhao, L.: Uncertainties in mass balance estimation of the Antarctic Ice Sheet using the input-output method. 1–26 (2021)
15. Pratap, B., Dobhal, D.P., Bhambri, R., Mehta, M., Tewari, V.C.: Four decades of glacier mass balance observations in the Indian Himalaya. Reg. Environ. Chang. **16**, 643–658 (2016). https://doi.org/10.1007/s10113-015-0791-4
16. Rakshita, C., Sowjanya, A., Swathi, P., Geetha Priya, M.: Velocity estimation of east antarctic glacier with SAR offset tracking—an application of image processing. In: Smys, S., Tavares, J.M.R.S., Shi, F. (eds.) Computational Vision and Bio-Inspired Computing, pp. 323–331. Springer, Singapore (2023). https://doi.org/10.1007/978-981-19-9819-5_24

Estimation of Glacier Velocity of Ny-Ålesund, Arctic Using Sentinel-1 Remote Sensing Data

C. Rakshita, L. Yashwanth Krishna, B. S. Yeshwanth, and M. Geetha Priya$^{(\boxtimes)}$

CIIRC, Jyothy Institute of Technology, Bengaluru, India
geetha.sri82@gmail.com

Abstract. Glaciers serve as crucial indicators of climate change and global warming through a variety of mechanisms. The objective of the current study is to determine the Line-of-sight (LOS) velocity of Vestre Brøggerbreen (VB), Austre Brøggerbreen (AB), Midtre Lovénbreen (ML), Austre Lovénbreen (AL), Edithbreen (EB), Pedersenbreen (PB), and Botnfjellbreen (BB) glaciers of Ny-Ålesund, Svalbard in the Arctic region, as a means of elucidating the effects of global warming and climatic change. It is important to estimate the glacier velocity to have a precise understanding of glacier dynamics and climatic change. Obtaining in-situ measurements of dynamic glaciological parameters poses significant challenges. The use of Interferometric Synthetic Aperture Radar (InSAR) data, serves as a valuable tool for monitoring and estimating the LOS velocity at sub-millimeter levels. In the proposed study, Sentinel-1 Synthetic Aperture Radar (SAR) data was acquired from 04/06/2019 to 02/10/2019 with a 12-day temporal resolution. The data were processed using the OpenSAR Jupyter Notebook, employing specialized conda environments and tools, including the Hybrid Plugable Processing Pipeline (HyP3) and Miami InSAR Time Series Python (MintPy). The analysis yielded a maximum LOS velocity rate of 10 cm between June 4, 2019, and October 10, 2019.

Keywords: Ny-Ålesund · LOS Velocity · InSAR · HyP3 · MintPy

1 Introduction

Glaciers encompass roughly 10% of the Earth's landmass and exert significant influence on both the global climate and sea level rise [1]. Glaciers are the continuous mass of ice driven by gravitational forces, they play a critical and vulnerable role in the ecosystem. Glaciers exhibit high sensitivity to long-term climatic variations, rendering them valuable tools for tracking climate change, such as temperature, precipitation, and wind speed. Understanding glacier dynamics and climatic changes is of utmost importance, particularly regarding Arctic and Greenland glaciers/ice sheets, as they significantly contribute to global climate regulation [2]. The study focuses on estimating LOS velocity across the seven glaciers (VB, AB, ML, AL, EB, PB, and BB) located in Ny-Ålesund, Svalbard, Arctic [3].

© The Author(s), under exclusive license to Springer Nature Switzerland AG 2024
V. N. M. Aradhya et al. (Eds.): CCIP 2023, CCIS 2044, pp. 50–59, 2024.
https://doi.org/10.1007/978-3-031-60725-7_5

Remote sensing technologies are extensively employed to understand glacier dynamics and the estimation of glacier surface flow velocity. SAR Interferometry has gained widespread usage for high-resolution measurements of ground surface ice velocity. In the present study, InSAR time series analysis is employed, utilizing a set of SAR images to estimate the glacier surface ice velocity. Time series techniques in InSAR represent potent geodetic remote sensing methods for measuring sub-millimetric LOS velocities from a spaceborne perspective. The Sentinel-1 mission, launched under the Copernicus Earth observation program in collaboration between the European Commission and the European Space Agency (ESA), enables a systematic global mapping of the Earth's surface using the Terrain Observation by Progressive Scans (TOPS) technique as its core methodology. Sentinel-1 provides images with both high resolution and short repeat times, improving the viability of SAR images for glacier motion monitoring [4]. This results in a remarkable time series dataset for InSAR. In the proposed study, LOS velocity has been estimated with a cloud-based OpenSAR lab conda environment using Sentinel 1 SAR data with HyP3 products in MintPy of Jupyter Notebook.

2 Study Area

Ny-Ålesund (78.9N, 11.9E) which Encompasses an area of roughly 0.25 square kilometers is a small village located on the Brogger Peninsula within the Arctic region of Svalbard [7]. It is situated on the shores of Kongsfjorden Bay and is surrounded by seven glaciers Vestre Brøggerbreen, Austre Brøggerbreen, Midtre Lovénbreen, Austre Lovénbreen, Edithbreen, Pedersenbreen, and Botnfjellbreen [5] as shown in Fig. 1 and Table 1. The primary island in the Svalbard archipelago is known as Spitzbergen, and it benefits from the climatic influence of the Gulf Stream, enabling the existence of small communities in the region. The main aim of this study is to determine the LOS velocity of the seven glaciers located in Ny-Ålesund. These glaciers hold immense significance in climate change due to their minimal human interference and low pollution levels, providing a pristine environment for investigation, It serves as a research base and is a prominent center for Arctic research activities [6]. The current study holds substantial importance in advancing our understanding of glacier dynamics.

Table 1. List of Glaciers

Sl. no	Glaciers	Area (sq. Km)	Max Slope (Degrees)
1.	Vestre Brøggerbreen (VB)	4.63	56.9
2.	Austre Brøggerbreen (AB)	9.64	54.2
3.	Midtre Lovénbreen (ML)	5.02	57.9
4.	Austre Lovénbreen (AL)	4.83	66.4
5.	Edithbreen (EB)	3.48	66.2
6.	Pedersenbreen (PB)	6.02	60.8
7.	Botnfjellbreen (BB)	5.66	62.1

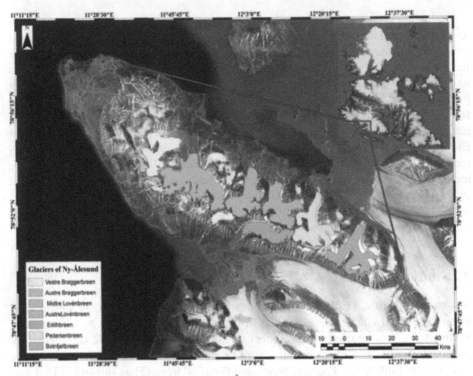

Fig. 1. Glaciers of Ny-Ålesund, Svalbard, Arctic

3 Data Used

The present study utilizes Sentinel-1 microwave Single Look Complex (SLC) data; as a part of the Copernicus Earth observation program launched by ESA. The Sentinel-1 mission consists of a pair of identical satellites, Sentinel-1A and Sentinel-1B, Both launched in the year 2014 and 2016 [7] respectively with a combined revisit of 6 days. It provides a fine spatial resolution of 5X20 meters and a wide swath coverage of 250 km in the Interferometric Wide (IW) mode with dual polarization. Data was obtained from the Alaska Satellite Facility (ASF) Vertex portal, available at (https://search.asf.alaska.edu/). The data sets used in the present study are given in Table 2 which is acquired in descending mode in VV+VH polarization from flight path 154.

The Global Copernicus DEM GLO-30 was employed in the proposed study which provides medium-resolution coverage with a spatial resolution of 30 m [8]. For correcting the propagation delays induced by the Earth's troposphere, ERA5 climate reanalysis data, which is accessible through the European Centre for Medium-Range Weather Forecasts (ECMWF) at the website (https://cds.climate.copernicus.eu/) was utilized. The dataset incorporates various atmospheric parameters, such as humidity, pressure, and temperature derived from a combination of satellite observations, ground-based measurements, and numerical weather prediction models. The dataset used was of descending orbit and was processed with WGS 84/Arctic Polar Stereographic projection.

Table 2. List of Data sets used

Sl. no	Product Identifier	Date of Acquisition
1.	70E5	04/06/ 2019
2.	C822	16/06/ 2019
3.	46B9	28/06/ 2019
4.	E482	10/07/2019
5.	2968	22/07/ 2019
6.	7879	03/08/2019
7.	E309	15/08/2019
8.	02A0	27/08/2019
9.	97B4	08/09/2019
10.	9918	20/09/2019
11.	0E57	02/10/2019

4   Methodology

InSAR time series analysis stands as a reliable geodetic technique employed to calculate ice surface velocity using SAR images [9]. Figure 2 illustrates a typical processing work-flow for the time series analysis of InSAR data was implemented in the present study. The initial step involved the downloading of Sentinel-1 SAR SLC data from 04/06/2019 to 02/10/2019. Interferograms were generated using the ASF HyP3 platform through the On-Demand process. Subsequently, the generated interferograms underwent unwrapping to obtain phase measurements, resulting in the construction of an unwrapped stack [10]. Inversion and correction of the unwrapped interferogram stack were performed using a multithreaded processing approach using dask within a cloud-based laboratory environment. MintPy, a specialized Python software package for InSAR time series analysis, was employed for this purpose [11]. The entire analysis was conducted within the OpenSAR lab Jupyter Notebook, utilizing the specialized conda environment. To mitigate the impact of unwrapping errors on the analysis, the software incorporated a network modification feature. Two key blocks were implemented: Block 1, which addressed unwrapping errors in the raw phase, and Block 2, which mitigated noise from various sources to create a time series for surface ice flow velocity. The temporal interval between the master and slave images used to generate the interferogram was utilized to calculate velocity. The analysis aimed to provide accurate and reliable estimates of the surface ice flow velocity for the glaciers in Ny-Ålesund over a defined time duration.

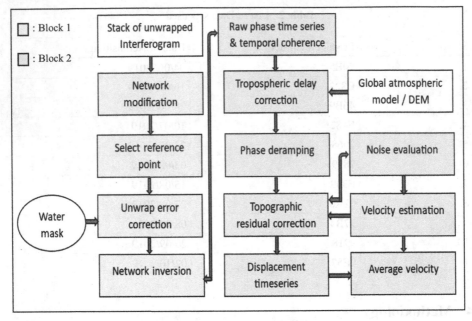

Fig. 2. Workflow of Hyp3 + MintPy Conda environment

5   Results

A time series analysis was conducted using a sequence of images acquired during the ablation period 04/06/2019 to 2/10/2019 over the Svalbard region with HyP3+MintPy Conda environment from ASF. The first image, acquired on 4/06/2019, is typically denoted as the master image, while the subsequent images are commonly termed as slave images. Utilizing the comprehensive analysis technique of InSAR time series data, the ice surface flow velocity of the glaciers in Ny-Ålesund, Svalbard, Arctic was estimated and is given in Fig. 3. Overall 10 cm surface ice flow velocity was observed during the ablation season of the hydrological year 2018–2019. From the time series surface ice flow velocity, the annual LOS velocity has been derived and shown in Fig. 4 [12]. From Fig. 5, considering their maximum and average velocities within the context of glacial dynamics and environmental factors, detailed interpretations and analyses were conducted. Figure 6, shows the field photograph of the VB glacier taken on 16th 2019 during the field visit under the Indian Arctic Expedition Program by the National Centre for Polar and Ocean Research (NCPOR), Government of India.

Starting with Vestre Broggerbreen, it exhibits a notable maximum velocity of 18.32 cm/year, signifying periods of vigorous ice flow. This glacier's faster pace could be influenced by factors such as steep terrain, potential crevasses, and localized variations in temperature and meltwater availability. The high maximum velocity implies intermittent bursts of rapid ice movement that might be associated with ice avalanches or other dynamic processes. Additionally, its average velocity of 4.72 cm/year suggests consistent, though not overly rapid, overall movement. Austre Broggerbreen displays a slightly lower maximum velocity of 12.19 cm/year, indicating less pronounced bursts of rapid ice flow. This glacier's movement might be influenced by similar factors as Vestre Broggerbreen but to a lesser extent. Its average velocity of 3.01 cm/year indicates a relatively steady pace of movement, reflecting a consistent ice flow over time. Midtre Loverbreen has a maximum velocity of 7.61 cm/year, suggesting moderate episodes of accelerated ice movement. This glacier's slower pace might be due to a less steep terrain or different ice dynamics. The average velocity of 1.68 cm/year indicates a consistent but comparatively slow overall movement.

Austre Loverbreen showcases a maximum velocity of 11.48 cm/year, pointing to relatively frequent periods of faster ice flow. This glacier's movement could be influenced by various factors, including its geometry and the presence of meltwater. The higher average velocity of 3.41 cm/year suggests a consistent, moderately paced flow over time. Edithbreen, with a maximum velocity of 5.35 cm/year, exhibits a more moderate pattern of ice movement. This glacier's movement might be influenced by a variety of factors, including its specific topography and local climate conditions. The lower average velocity of 1.55 cm/year implies a slow, but relatively consistent pace of ice flow. Pedersenbreen stands out with a maximum velocity of 12.16 cm/year, indicating intermittent bursts of rapid ice flow. This glacier's dynamics could be influenced by steep gradients and variations in ice thickness. Its average velocity of 2.70 cm/year suggests a moderate, consistent pace of movement. Lastly, Botnjelbreen has a maximum velocity of 10.06 cm/year, reflecting occasional bursts of faster ice movement. This glacier's ice flow might be influenced by factors such as its terrain and localized conditions. The average velocity of 2.74 cm/year mirrors a consistent, moderate movement pattern.

In summary, the variations in maximum and average velocities among these glaciers highlight the complexity of glacial dynamics. Factors such as terrain steepness, ice thickness, meltwater, and local climate conditions can all contribute to these variations, offering valuable insights into the intricate interplay between glaciers and their environments. Monitoring these velocities over time is essential for understanding the response of glaciers to changing climatic conditions and their potential impacts on sea levels and surrounding ecosystems.

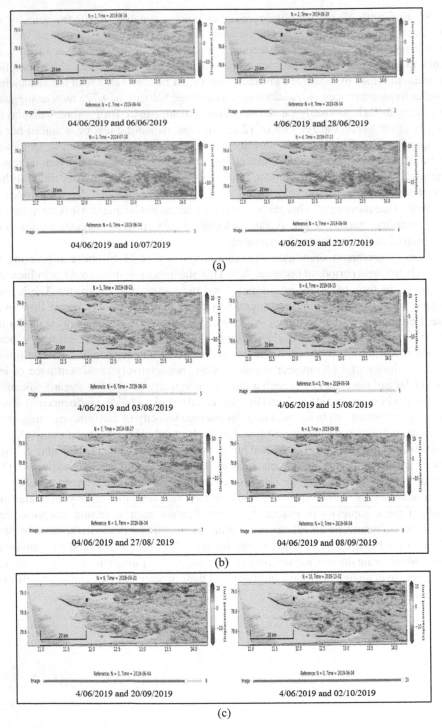

Fig. 3. (a), (b), (c): LOS velocity of the glaciers in Svalbard, Arctic

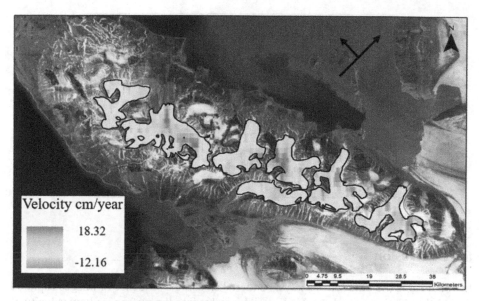

Fig. 4. Annual LOS velocity of the glaciers in Ny-Ålesund, Svalbard, Arctic

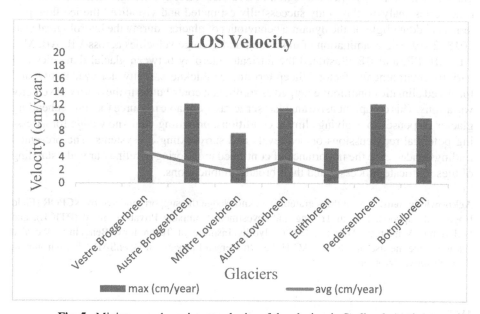

Fig. 5. Minimum and maximum velocity of the glaciers in Svalbard, Arctic

Fig. 6. Field photograph of VB Glacier

6 Conclusion

In conclusion, the time series analysis undertaken using a sequence of images captured during the ablation period provided crucial insights into the surface ice flow velocity of glaciers within the Ny-Ålesund region of Svalbard, Arctic. Through meticulous InSAR time series analysis, this study successfully estimated and visualized the ice flow patterns, shedding light on the dynamic behaviours of glaciers during the hydrological year 2018–2019. The examination of maximum and average velocities across VB, AB, ML, AL, EB, PB, and BB illustrated the intricate interplay between glacial dynamics and various environmental factors. Steep terrain, ice thickness, meltwater availability, and localized climatic conditions emerged as significant contributors to the observed velocity variations. This comprehensive analysis serves as a valuable resource for comprehending glacier responses to evolving climate conditions, providing vital knowledge for assessing potential repercussions on sea levels and surrounding ecosystems. The presented findings underscore the importance of continued monitoring to refine our understanding of these intricate processes and their broader implications.

Acknowledgment. The authors gratefully acknowledge the support rendered by NCPOR (Field Logistical support), Prazim Trading and Investment Company Private Limited (PTICL), and Dr.Krishna Venkatesh, Director, CIIRC, Jyothi Institute of Technology, Bengaluru. We also acknowledge the use of ASF DAAC HyP3 On-Demand process in OpenSAR lab environment through Jupyter Notebook.

References

1. Priya, M.G., Krishnaveni, D.: Greenland glacier velocity estimation using sar offset tracking (2020)
2. Muhuri, A., Bhattacharya, A., Natsuaki, R., Hirose, A.: Glacier surface velocity estimation using stokes vector correlation. In: Proceedings of the 2015 IEEE 5th Asia-Pacific Conference on Synthetic Aperture Radar, APSAR 2015, pp. 606–609 (2015). https://doi.org/10.1109/APSAR.2015.7306281

3. Shashank, B., Geetha Priya, M.: Monitoring of melting glaciers of Ny-Ålesund, Svalbard, Arctic using space-based inputs. In: Subhashini, N., Morris, A.G., Ezra, S.-K. (eds.) VICFCNT 2021, pp. 381–390. Springer, Singapore (2023). https://doi.org/10.1007/978-981-19-8338-2_31

4. Gundersen, R., Norland, R., Denby, C.R.: Monitoring glacier flow in Ny-Ålesund with a high temporal resolution ground-based interferometric-phased array radar. Polar Res. **38**, 1–18 (2019). https://doi.org/10.33265/polar.v38.3382

5. Geetha Priya, M., Venkatesh, K., Shivanna, L., Devaraj, S.: Detecting short-term surface melt over Vestre Broggerbreen, Arctic glacier using indigenously developed unmanned air vehicles. Geocarto Int. **37**, 3167–3178 (2022). https://doi.org/10.1080/10106049.2020.1849416

6. Dhanush, S., Geetha Priya, M.: Supraglacial debris cover for Ny-Ålesund using Sentinel-2 data. In: Subhashini, N., Morris, A.G., Ezra, S.-K. (eds.) VICFCNT 2021, pp. 391–400. Springer, Singapore (2023). https://doi.org/10.1007/978-981-19-8338-2_32

7. Rakshita, C., Sowjanya, A., Swathi, P., Geetha Priya, M.: Velocity estimation of east antarctic glacier with SAR offset tracking—an application of image processing. In: Smys, S., Tavares, J.M.R.S., Shi, F. (eds.) Computational Vision and Bio-Inspired Computing, pp. 323–331. Springer, Singapore (2023). https://doi.org/10.1007/978-981-19-9819-5_24

8. Piter, A., Vassileva, M., Haghshenas Haghighi, M., Motagh, M.: Exploring cloud-based platforms for rapid insar time series analysis. Int. Arch. Photogramm. Remote Sens. Spat. Inf. Sci. - ISPRS Arch. **43**, 171–176 (2021). https://doi.org/10.5194/isprs-archives-XLIII-B3-2021-171-2021

9. Yunjun, Z., Fattahi, H., Amelung, F.: Small baseline InSAR time series analysis: unwrapping error correction and noise reduction. Comput. Geosci. **133**, (2019). https://doi.org/10.1016/j.cageo.2019.104331

10. Choopani, A., Dehghani, M., Nikoo, M.R., Zeinali, S.: Time series analysis of insar data to study land subsidence induced by groundwater level decline in Sirjan Plain. Int. Arch. Photogramm. Remote Sens. Spat. Inf. Sci. - ISPRS Arch. **42**, 51–57 (2017). https://doi.org/10.5194/isprs-archives-XLII-4-W4-51-2017

11. Cigna, F., Del Ventisette, C., Liguori, V., Casagli, N.: Advanced radar-interpretation of InSAR time series for mapping and characterization of geological processes. Nat. Hazards Earth Syst. Sci. **11**, 865–881 (2011). https://doi.org/10.5194/nhess-11-865-2011

12. Sadiq, M., Dutta, S., Kumar, P., Jat, S., Gajbhiye, D.Y., Dharwadkar, A.: Ice dynamics of Vestre Brøggerbreen glaciers, Ny-Ålesund, Svalbard, Arctic. J. Earth Syst. Sci. **131** (2022). https://doi.org/10.1007/s12040-021-01750-8

Implementation of ECPM for High-Speed Area-Efficient Processor on FPGA

U. B. Mahadevaswamy[✉], N. Indhu, and D. M. Mounitha[✉]

SJCE, JSS Science and Technology University, Mysuru, India
mahadevaswamy@sjce.ac.in, indunagaraj92@gmail.com,
mounadm26@gmail.com

Abstract. The Cryptography and network protocols call for the development of high-performance elliptic curve cryptographic (ECC) processors that are fast and low-powered, to address key challenges in Protecting data This study presents an ECC processor that is low-area, high-speed, and immune to side-channel attacks (SCAs) using field-programmable gate arrays (FP-GAs). Twisted wards curve for 256-bit Elliptic Curve Point Multiplication (ECPM) on the Edwards 25519 curve is supported by this processor as part of the high-security Edwards curve digital signature technique (EdDSA). This work presents a new hardware architecture or point-double operations on twisted Edwards curves, wherein point additions and point doublings are processed in a mere 257 and 512 clock cycles, respectively. Using only 14,245 slices on the Xilinx Virtex 7 FPGA platform, the proposed ECC processor performs single point multiplication for a 256-bit key in 1.21 ms, operating at a maximum clock frequency of 107.932 MHz in a cycle count of 130,815 with a throughput of 209.41 kbps, where the points are represented in projective coordinates. Due to the design's fast multiplication rate and low hardware utilization, the implemented design can offer an extremely time- and space-efficient solution without compromising security levels.

Keywords: Elliptic curve cryptography (ECC) · elliptic curve point multiplication (ECPM) · twisted Edwards curve · side-channel attacks (SCAs) · field-programmable gate array (FPGA)

1 Introduction

Wireless communication is proliferating, and the requirement of IoT security is becoming more and more necessary every day. An important concern in the current state of the Internet has emerged with the introduction of Internet of Things (IoT) security. Data is typically stored in the cloud since most of those devices are resource-constrained, so users can download and upload data from anywhere via the net. The information management within the cloud-computing environment is unmanaged, posing security concerns for data owners. We install lightweight cryptographic schemes to satisfy the special requirements of IoT devices regarding security and low-power consumption, while also ensuring that IoT devices have limited resources.

© The Author(s), under exclusive license to Springer Nature Switzerland AG 2024
V. N. M. Aradhya et al. (Eds.): CCIP 2023, CCIS 2044, pp. 60–73, 2024.
https://doi.org/10.1007/978-3-031-60725-7_6

In a wireless network, asymmetric cryptography, also known as public-key cryptography (PKC), is a great way to meet sensor node demand since it provides a key agreement procedure between new nodes and guards against unwanted access to private information. Using public and private keys, asymmetric cryptography—also referred to as public-key cryptography—is a method of data security. Discrete logarithms are the foundation of elliptic curve cryptography (ECC), which has far stronger encryption than earlier methods put forth by Victor Miller [16] and Koblitz [17]. Public-key cryptography is a cryptographic technique based on Elliptic Curve Discrete Logarithm Problems (ECDLPs) of elliptic curves over infinite fields. Two well-known and generally acknowledged PKC algorithms are elliptic curve cryptography (ECC) and rival-Shamir-Adleman (RSA) [18]. It uses integer factorization, the strength of which is dictated by the size of the key you select for encryption. In 1978, Adleman, Shamir, and Rivest proposed RSA. Authentication, encoding, digital signatures, and key exchange are just a few of the security applications that ECC provides. The primary advantage of ECC, besides its smaller key size and better performance at the same security level, is when compared to public key cryptosystems such as RSA. For the same level of security, the ECC key length is shorter than the RSA key length. For instance, the security of a 1024-, 2048-, or 3072-bit RSA key is equal to that of a 160-, 224-, or 256-bit ECC key. ECC is perfect for IoT devices with limited resources and high-speed cryptographic processors because of its tiny size.

2 Proposed Work

This article presents the FPGA implementation of a 256-bit ECC processor over GFp that is area time efficient. Additionally, the goal of point multiplication computation time reduction is to minimize the number of clock cycles. The hardware requirements for the modular multiplication and point operations are to be minimized so that the processor occupies less area in terms of area time product. The important operations of this paper can be outlined as given below:

1. A green layout for the Elliptic curve Point Multiplication on an Edwards 25519 curve is a proposal made to realize quicker ECPM with better protection.
2. The approach used is the Montgomery adder algorithm for the Elliptic curve point Multiplication operation to provide notable protection against probable side Channel Attacks (for ex: timing and power analysis attacks).
3. To avoid computationally expensive modular inversion work, the layout is expressed in projective coordinates rather than relative coordinates.
4. The layout is represented in projective coordinates in place of related ordinates to keep away from modular inversion operation, which is computationally expensive.
5. Edwards25519 hardware of the curve organization function (more details) aims to reduce latency and math performance by modifying the parallelization process.
6. Time – optimized hardware architecture is preferred for radix 4 nested modular multiplication to perform the group operations faster with less area consumption.
7. Additionally, the area-time model of the proposed elliptic curve point multiplication layout maybe very, and therefore the throughput of the layout is very high, which makes higher overall performance of the ECC Processor higher.

A green layout for Elliptic Curve Point Multiplication on an Edwards25519 curve is preferred to comprehend quicker point multiplication with better protection. The Montgomery ladder approach and its set of rules are followed for the Point multiplication layout to provide sizeable safety towards likely Side Channel Attacks(for example: power analysis and timing attacks) and the curves are represented in projective co-ordinates in place of related co-ordinates to keep away from modular inversion operation, as it is computationally expensive.

The modular multiplication of the processor is responsible for all the speed and area occupied by the processor. A higher Radix modular multiplier offers fewer clock cycles but requires more area, and similarly, a Lower Radix modular multiplier requires much less area but consumes a lot of clock cycles for execution. Due to its high latency and the fact that it consumes more clock cycles than Radix-2, Radix-4 is preferred for the modular multiplication operation over Radix-2. To multiply two n bit integers A and B over the GF (p) field, the radix-4 modular multiplier requires $(n/2) + 1$ clock cycles (CCs), whereas radix-2 requires $(n + 1)$.

3   An Overview of Mathematical Backgrounds

The twisted Edwards curve is presented in this segment, as well as the group regulation of this curve. Here are the formulas for add-on and doubling points in projective coordinates for the Edwards25519 curve.

3.1   Twisted Edwards Curve (Edwards25519)

The selection of the desired elliptic curve among various elliptic curves is the objective of this section. We prefer Edwards curves that are twisted, which is the generalization of Edwards curves and their group laws. In terms of prime field Fp, an Edwards curve with twisted parameters is given by,

$$e_{a,d}: ax^2 + y^2 = 1 + dx^2 y^2 \tag{1}$$

a = 1, is for the curve which is untwisted. a = −1 for the twisted elliptic curve.

$$e_d: -x^2 + y^2 = 1 + dx^2 y^2 \tag{2}$$

3.2   Arithmetic on Edwards25519 Curve

Two Arithmetic operations are performed on the elliptic curve are Addition of 2 affine points (Point Addition) and the Doubling of 2 affine points (Point Doubling) on the curve. Along with that, group operations are also performed in Projective coordinates, where affine points are converted to projective points and Point Addition and Point Doubling operations are performed on curves using projective points.

Point Addition: Twice the affine point A (x_1, y_1) and B(x_2, y_2) on the curve $e_{a,d}$ is given by the formula

$$A(x_1, y_1) + B(x_2, y_2) = R(x_3, y_3) \tag{3}$$

where,

$$x_3 = \frac{x_1 y_2 + x_2 y_1}{1 + d x_1 x_2 y_1 y_2} \tag{4}$$

$$y_3 = \frac{y_1 y_2 - a x_1 y_2}{1 - d x_1 x_2 y_1 y_2} \tag{5}$$

Point Doubling: The doubling of the affine point A $(x1, y1)$ on the curve $e_{a,d}$ is given by the formula $2A\ (x1,\ y1) + B(x2, y2) = R(x3,\ y3)$.

3.3 Edwards25519-Group Operation

Each Three-point coordinates, such as (X, Y, Z), are used to represent each point (x, y) on the curve. With respect to the projective point P (X = x, Y = y, Z = 1), the point P(x, y) is related. The point P (x = X/Z, y = Y/Z) with Z $\neq$ 0 is related to the projective point P (X, Y, Z). The following mathematical statement permits the projective representation of the curve:

$$E_{a,d}: \left(aX^2 + Y^2\right)Z^2 = Z^4 + dX^2 Y^2 \tag{6}$$

The origin of the Ed curve is given by the following mathematical expression:

$$E_d: \left(-X^2 + Y^2\right)Z^2 = Z^4 + dX^2 Y^2 \tag{7}$$

Ed An additional point can be made on the as curve.

$$A(X_1, Y_1, Z_1) + B(X_2, Y_2, Z_2) = R(X_3, Y_3, Z_3) \tag{8}$$

where,

$$X_3 = Z_1 Z_2 \left(Z^2 Z^2 - dX_1 X_2 Y_1 Y_2\right)(X_1 Y_2 + Y_1 X_2) \tag{9}$$

$$Y_3 = Z_1 Z_2 \left(Z^2 Z^2 + dX_1 X_2 Y_1 Y_2\right)(X_1 Y_2 + Y_1 X_2) \tag{10}$$

$$Z_3 = \left(Z^2 Z^{2+} dX_1 X_2 Y_1 Y_2\right)\left(Z^2 Z^2 - dX_1 X_2 Y_1 Y_2\right) \tag{11}$$

Point doubling can be done on the E_d curve by $2A\ (X_1, Y_1, Z_1) = R\ (X_2, Y_2, Z_1)E$
Where,

$$X_2 = (2X_1 Y_1)\left(Y^2 - X^2 - 2Z^2\right) \tag{12}$$

$$Y_2 = \left(X^2 - Y^2\right)\left(X^2 + Y^2\right) \tag{13}$$

$$Z_2 = \left(Y^2 - X^2\right)\left(Y^2 - X^2 - 2Z^2\right) \tag{14}$$

4 Proposed Hardware Architecture

This section discusses all hardware architecture ideas for Modular multiplication, point addition, point doubling, and Elliptic curve point multiplication.

4.1 Modular Multiplication

Modular multiplication is the most important function before ECPM. The area in terms of slice and LUTs consumed, and the efficiency of the whole proposed work majorly depend on it. A higher Radix modular multiplier offers fewer clock cycles but requires more area, and similarly, a Lower Radix modular multiplier requires much less area but consumes a lot of clock cycles for execution. So as shown in the Fig. 1 Radix 4 modular multiplier requires (k/2) + 1 clock cycles by falling in with pair k-bit integers A then B above the top discipline *GFp*, where p is a k-bit prime number whereas radix-2 requires (k + 1) clock cycles. Soaadix-4 Interleaved Modular Multiplication is preferred over Radix-2. Modular multiplication is near via work done iterative summation on its meantime half products reducing by modulo p.

Figure 1 shows a shift left "Register R" that was once used to execute left in imitation of proper multiplication in bitwise and it is used for loop operation until the contents of the register are empty. Initially, R [(k + 1) down to 2] is computed before the loop operation in the same way that the multiplicator H is, except R [1: 0] is precomputed as

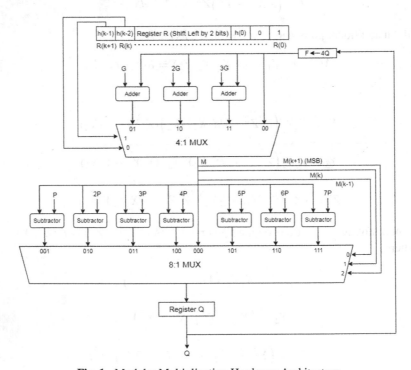

Fig. 1. Modular Multiplication Hardware Architecture

"01". These two bits are added to the Register R's last 2 LSB bit places to determine the suitable end of the loop operation between the laws of $h0 = 0$ and $h1 = 0$. At the start of each cycle, the register Q value is multiplied 4 times, resulting in F. G, 2G, and 3G being introduced independently in imitation of F for bitwise multiplication. Based entirely on the three bits R [(k + 1): k], 4:1 MUX is supposed to select one of the 4 outcomes.

F, F + G, F + 2G, or F + 3G as M. If both R(k + 1) and R(k) are zero, F remains static, and M becomes F. At the end of each cycle, M is decreased modulo p and the R register is shifted left two. The modular function, M mod p, is obtained by subtracting a larger number p from M with respect to (i − 1) p; where M is generally less than ip; (i- 3,4, 5.). (M mod p) is learned by subtracting the number p 6p from M, since M is usually less than 8p. Isolation is done with the help of extraction. 8:1 MUX selects M, M-p, M-2p, M-3p, M-4p, M-5p, M-6p and M-7p as comparators.

≥ 2p, M ≥ 3p, M ≥ 4p, M ≥ 5p, M ≥ 6p and M ≥ 7p. ≥ 2p, M ≥ 3p, M ≥ 4p, M ≥ 5p, M ≥ 6p and M ≥ 7p. These contrasts are present via observing the first 3 MSB bits M [(k + 1) *down to* (k − 1)]. After $k/2$ number of cycles, H namely a s well as R [(k − 1) *down to* 0], is shifted to nil or the contents of Register are empty then the operations are finished. The final value stored in the Reg Q is the output of the MM of G and H.

4.2 Group operation on Elliptic Curve

In ECPM, several arithmetic modules are used: the modular multiplier, adder, subtractor, and squarer in successive data flows. The arithmetic modules also represent arithmetic modules within successive levels. A projective coordinate system is used to design the Point Addition and Point Doubling architectures. According to Fig. 2(a), the PA hardware design is based on the formula (9), which consists of five levels requiring twelve multiplication operations, one squaring operation, three addition operations, and one subtraction operation, which are named (12M + 1S+ 3A + 1S). PD is illustrated in Fig. 2(b). According to (10), there are four consecutive stages with four multiplications, three squares, three additions, and three subtractions. These two metrics are indicated as (4M + 3S + 6A). To reduces the number of arithmetic and hardware components of the Twisted Edwards curve shown in [14] and [15], modification of the point addition and doubling model has been introduced. Effectively balanced architectures and horizontally parallelized arithmetic operations among the levels ensure the shortest data path and the shortest latency.

The diagram in Fig. 2 describes the hardware architecture of point addition and doubling. Addition and subtraction each require one clock cycle to complete; where k is the number of bits to be processed. Multiplication and squaring each take (k + 1) clock cycles. For each level which contains one or more multiplications or squares, (k + 1) clock cycles need to be spent, while for the levels that contain no multiplications or squares, it only takes one clock cycle. The proposed Point Addition and Point Doubling architectures have latencies of (4k + 5) clock cycles and (2k + 4) clock cycles, respectively.

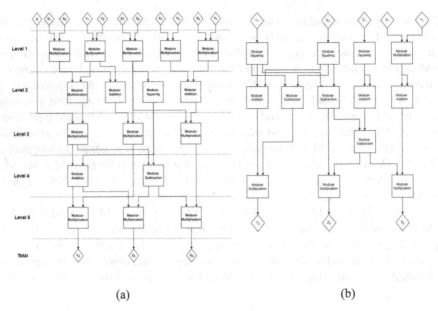

(a)   (b)

Fig. 2. Hardware Architecture (a) Point Addition (b) Point Multiplication

4.3 Elliptic Curve Point Multiplication

Point multiplication, also known as scalar multiplication, is the most important operation in elliptic curve cryptography and accounts for most of the execution time. We've lB = B + B +... + B during this process, where B could be a point on the curve and l could be any positive integer. Because of this, it is simple to compute the purpose multiplication using the self-using PA and PD operations as well as the l times addition of point B. The basic operation of ECPM will be C = lB, where B could be the base point of a curve. Ed, l could represent the secret key as a scalar, and C could represent the public key as a point on the curve. If l is even, then C can be found by either doubling B log2l times or by adding B to itself (l − 1) times. Multiplication is now done using the binary or double and add approach, which is a combination of PA and PD. This method has two temporal and power consumption profiles: one that merely doubles points and another that adds points after doubling. This approach is vulnerable to SCAs because the secret key's binary bit pattern can be easily obtained by tracking power consumption trends using simple power analysis (SPA) [21].

Figure 3 shows how the inputs to the point addition module are precomputed in B and 2D. The preliminary calculation of the Point doubling module depends on the (k − 2)th point of l; where k is the length of l. MUX 1 is used to select the ith bit of l from l0 to lk-1 via the log2k select line. If lk−2 = 0, MUX 2 selects the first entry of the double parameter as B; If lk−2 = 1, choose 2D. The XOR gate is used to decide when to change the comparison point by calculating li ⊕ li−1; where li is the current operation of l and li−1 is the next operation of l in parallel from left to right. If the EX-OR gate's output is low, no state change happens, and the Point Doubling module's output is sent back into its input through a feedback loop. If the EX-OR gate's output is high, the state changes, and the PA module's output is connected to the PD module's input. To choose the input for the Point Doubling module, MUX 3 is used. One of the 2 inputs of the Point Addition module is its own output through a feedback loop in both situations, while the other is the output of the Point Doubling module. The midway outputs of the Point Addition and Point Doubling modules are respectively stored in Register A' and Register D'. After $(k-1)$ iterations, MUX 4 selects the output of the dual point module if $k0 = 0$ or selects the output of the insertion point module such that the result is $k0 = 1$. The PA module determines the number of iterations, and due to the delay of the ECPM and the simultaneous completion of PA and PD, additional module points must have more cycles than the dual point of the module to complete its work.

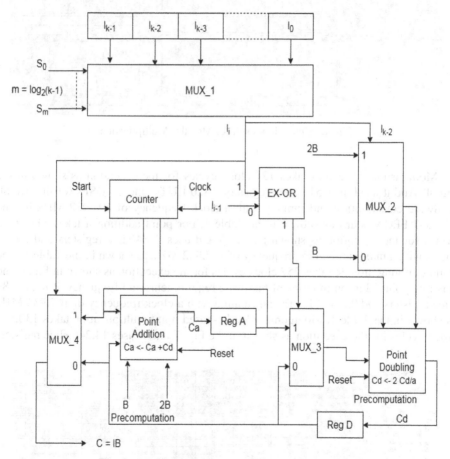

Fig. 3. Proposed Hardware Architecture for ECPM

5 Simulation Results

The Modelsim simulator is used to model the design, which is implemented in the Xilinx ISE 14.5 software. The necessary modules' Python code implementation is used to confirm the simulation findings using the same inputs. Each of the synthesized modules is independently tested for timing and power analysis on the Xilinx Virtex 7 and 6 FPGA platforms. The XC7VX690T is the device used in Virtex 7, while the XC6VHX380T is used in Virtex 6.

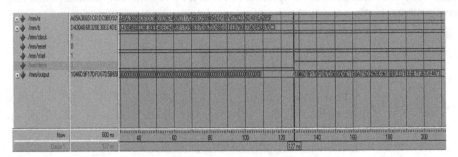

Fig. 4. Simulation result for Modular Multiplication

Modular multiplication takes 127 clock cycles for the execution as shown in the Fig. 4. And it used over 513 slice registers, 1820 LUTs, and 24 DSPs for the overall hardware consumption and running with a clock frequency of 107.932 MHz for the Virtex-7 FPGA board as shown in the Table 1. For point addition it takes 512 clock cycles for the execution as shown in Fig. 5 and uses 7184 slice registers and 29731 LUTs with a maximum clock frequency of 107.932 MHz as shown in the Table 1. The Point doubling module takes 257 clock cycles for the execution as shown in Fig. 6 and it is like point addition in terms of hardware requirements and frequency, it uses 7184 slice registers and 229433 LUTs and running with a clock frequency of 107.932 MHz as shown in the Table 1. Montgomery ladder-based point multiplication takes 130,815 clock cycles for the execution as shown in the Fig. 7 and it uses 14,245 slice registers

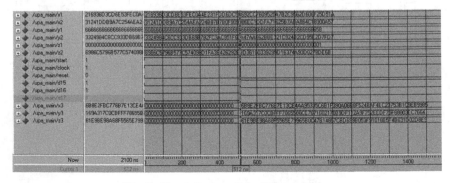

Fig. 5. Simulation result for Point Addition

and 60,166 LUTs for Hardware consumption and running with a clock frequency of 107.932 MHz as shown in the Table 1.

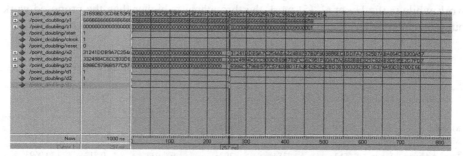

Fig. 6. Simulation result for Point Multiplication

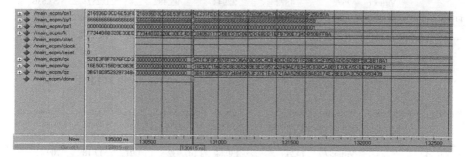

Fig. 7. Simulation result for Point Multiplication

6 Performance Comparison of Proposed Work with Existing Work

The Area - Time product comparison between different works is given in Table 2. The Area - Time product of the analysis of the purpose addition, point doubling, modular multiplication, and Montgomery ladder algorithm ECPM are shown in the Fig. 8 and Fig. 9. The area-time product of the proposed work in Virtex 7 (a) and Virtex 6 (b) are closely similar and less making it more efficient, comparing to other existing works where the area-time product is high and therefore it is less efficient.

The Throughput comparison between different works is given in Table 2, the throughput of the proposed work in Virtex 7 is high as compared to the throughput obtained from Virtex 6 platform. The throughput of some existing works is less than the proposed work while in the Hu et al. [5] work the throughput is higher than the proposed work but it has more Area - Time product as shown in Fig. 8 and Fig. 9 of this design.

Table 1. Outcomes of the Proposed work on 2 Platforms of FPGA

Operation	Platform	Clock cycle	No of slices	No of LUTs	Max Frequency (MHz)	Time (μs)	Throughput (Mbps)
Modular Multiplication	Virtex 7	127	513	1820	107.932	0.127	217.563
	Virtex 6	127	513	1812	95.482	0.127	192.467
Point Addition	Virtex 7	512	7184	29731	107.932	0.512	30.0693
	Virtex 6	512	7184	29731	95.482	0.512	28.359
Point Doubling	Virtex 7	257	4872	22943	107.932	0.257	65.512
	Virtex 6	257	4872	22943	95.482	0.257	57.636
ECPM	Virtex 7	130815	14245	60166	107.932	1.21 ms	209.41 kbps
	Virtex 6	130815	14245	60169	95.485	1.36 ms	186.82 kbps

Table 2. Outcomes of the Proposed work on 2 Platforms of FPG

Work	Publishing year	Platform	Area Consumed (slices)	Clock cycles (k)	Maximum Frequency (MHz)	Time (ms)	Area Time (AT)	Throughput (kbps)
This work (a)	–	Virtex-7	14.2k	130.8k	107.932	1.21	17.18	209.41
This work (a)	–	Virtex-6	14.2k	130.8k	95.485	1.36	19.45	186.82
Islam et al. [1]1	2019	Virtex-7	8.9k	262..7	177.7	1.48	13.17	173.80
Islam et al. [1]1	2019	Virtex-6	9.2k	262.7	161.1	1.63	15.00	157.00
Hu et al. [5]	2019	Virtex-6	27.655k	14.24	38.045	0.37	50.35	683.95
Hu et al. [4]	2018	Virtex-4	9.4k+14DSP	610	20.43	29.80	280.51	8.57
shah et al. [2]	2018	Virtex-6	65.6K	153	327	0.469	30.82	546.41
Javeed et al. [3]	2017	Virtex-4	20.6K	191.5	49	3.9	80.54	65.46

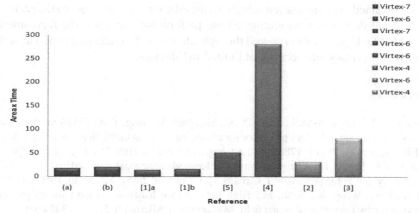

Fig. 8. Contrast of Performance in terms of Area × Time product

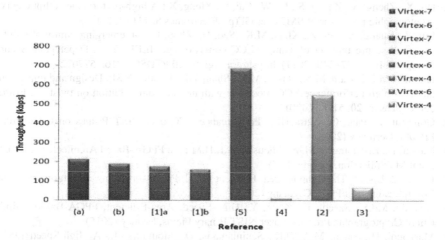

Fig. 9. Contrast of Performance in terms of Throughput

7 Conclusions

This paper uses the twisted Edwards curve represented by the plot to develop a high-speed anti-elliptic curve cryptographic processor with a functional space that is high-performance and resistant to side-channel attacks. Modular multiplication uses nested modular multipliers of radix 4. Because the sum of two k-bit numbers requires (k/2) + 1 cycle. For two additional points and doubling, a new hardware is proposed that requires (4k + 5) clock cycles to complete PA and (2k + 4) clock cycles to PD. Since this algorithm is a fast algorithm with high SCA, it is used as ECPM. Modular and group studies are carried out on 256-bit arithmetic on Xilinx Virtex 7 and Virtex 6 platforms. An elliptical spline point object takes 130, 815 cycles and 0.00121 seconds to complete. The transmission of ECPM is 209.41 kbps. Virtex-7 FPGA uses 14245 slice regions. It is more effective for the product delay area because the product delay area is low and the material obtained after simulation is high, so the efficiency is also high, so the protection level will not decrease. Considering all the performance analysis, the recommended radix 4 MM ECC processor is overall the right choice for fast data encryption as well as protecting the privacy and security of limited IoT devices.

References

1. Islam, M.M., Hossain, M.S., Hasan, M.K., Shahjalal, M., Jang, Y.M.: FPGA implementation of high-speed area-efficient processor for elliptic curve point multiplication over prime field. IEEE Access 7, 178811–178826 (2019). https://doi.org/10.1109/ACCESS.2019.2958491
2. Shah, Y.A., Javeed, K., Azmat, S., Wang, X.: Redundant signed digit based high-speed elliptic curve cryptographic processor. J. Circuits Syst. Comput. 28(5), Article no. 1950081 (2018)
3. Javeed, K., Wang, X., Scott, M.: High performance hardware support for elliptic curve cryptography over general prime field. Microprocess. Microcyst. 51, 331–342 (2017)
4. Hu, X., Zheng, X., Zhang, S., Cai, S., Xiong, X.: A low hardware consumption elliptic curve cryptographic architecture over GF(p) in embedded application. Electronics 7(7), 104 (2018)
5. Hu, X., Zheng, X., Zhang, S., Li, W., Cai, S., Xiong, X.: A high-performance elliptic curve cryptographic processor of SM2 over GF(p). Electronics 8, 431 (2019)
6. Liu, Z., Huang, X., Hu, Z., Khan, M.K., Seo, H., Zhou, L.: On emerging family of elliptic curves to secure Internet of Things: ECC comes of age. IEEE Trans. Dependable Secure Comput. 14(3), 237–248 (2017). https://doi.org/10.1109/TDSC.2016.2577022
7. Islam, M.M., Hossain, M.S., Hasan, M.K., Shahjalal, M., Jang, Y.M.: Design and implementation of high-performance ECC processor with unified point addition on twisted edwards curve. Sensors 20, 5148 (2020)
8. Guneysu, T., Paar, C.: Ultra High Performance ECC over NIST Primes on Commercial FPGAs, Germany (2008)
9. Nassar, D., El-Kharashi, M.W., Shousha, A.E.H.M.: An FPGA-Based Architecture for ECC Point Multiplication, Egypt (2017)
10. Khan, Z.-U.-A.: Throughput/Area Efficient ECC Processor Using Montgomery Point Multiplication on FPGA, Germany (2015)
11. Hossain, Md.S., Saeedi, E., Kong, Y.: High-Speed, Area-Efficient, FPGA-Based Elliptic Curve Cryptographic Processor over NIST Binary Fields, Sydney (2015)
12. Marzouqi, H., Salah, M.A.-Q.K., Schinianakis, D., Stouraitis, T.: A High-Speed FPGA Implementation of an RSD-Based ECC Processor, Egypt (2015)
13. Islam, Md.M., Hossain, Md.S., Hasan, Moh.K., Shahjalal, Md., Jang, Y.M.: Design and Implementation of High-Performance ECC Processor with Unified Point Addition on Twisted Edwards Curve, Korea (2019)
14. Hossain, Md.S., Saeedi, E., Kong, Y.: An Efficient FPGA Implementation of ECC Modular Inversion over F256, Pune (2018)
15. Shylashree, N., Bhat, N., Sridhar, V.: FPGA Implementations of High-Speed Elliptic Curve Cryptography, Germany (2016)
16. Miller, V.S.: Use of elliptic curves in cryptography. In: Williams, H.C. (ed.) CRYPTO 1985. LNCS, vol. 218, pp. 417–426. Springer, Heidelberg (1986)
17. Koblitz, N.: Elliptic curve cryptosystems. Math. Comput. 48(1987), 203–209 (2003)
18. Hankerson, D., Menezes, A., Vanstone, S.: Guide to Elliptic Curve Cryptography, 1st edn. Springer, New York (2003)
19. Kudithi, T., Potdar, M., Sakthivel, R.: Radix-4 interleaved modular multiplication for cryptographic applications. In: 2019 International Conference on Vision Towards Emerging Trends in Communication and Networking (ViTECoN), Vellore, India, pp. 1–5 (2019). https://doi.org/10.1109/ViTECoN.2019.8899461

20. Joye, M., Yen, S.-M.: The Montgomery powering ladder. In: Kaliski, B.S., Koç, çK., Paar, C. (eds.) CHES 2002. LNCS, vol. 2523, pp. 291–302. Springer, Heidelberg (2003). https://doi.org/10.1007/3-540-36400-5_22
21. Joye, M.: Elliptic curves and side-channel analysis. ST J. Syst. Res. 4(1), 1721 (2003)

Comparative Analysis of Machine Learning Approaches to Assess Stability in Micro Grid

M. Neethi[✉] [iD] and B. Sahana [iD]

Department of Electrical and Electronics Engineering, JSS Science and Technology University, Mysuru, India
neethi@jssstuniv.in

Abstract. Traditionally, electricity generation was localized, with a single power plant supplying power to surrounding towns and using only fossil fuels, but as modernization began, increasing electricity demand meant many Blackouts, distribution imbalances, and unavailability of power supply all these issues have resulted in high energy costs also in terms of pollution. The idea of a microgrid is growing in popularity as a means of addressing environmental pollution and raising energy demands. The features of Micro grid differ significantly from those of the traditional grid because distributed energy sources (DERs) are typically interfaced with the utility grid by inverters. In this work algorithms like Deep Learning, and LSTM, are compared with KNN a Machine learning Algorithm and both are used to evaluate for transient, frequency, and small signal stability in an 18-bus test system while comparing.

Keywords: Micro Grid · Stability Analysis · Machine learning · Deep learning · LSTM · KNN

1 Introduction

Transient, frequency, small signal, and voltage stability collectively constitute the robustness of a power grid [1, 2]. Numerous situations, such as day-ahead planning real-time operation, and strategic planning, capitalize on swift evaluations of system stability. Time-domain simulation is the basis of traditional approaches for assessing the stability of systems, however, this approach is highly dependent on the availability of real-time modelling of power systems and requires large computing resources [3–7].

Data-driven methods are another category of stability evaluation techniques in addition to model simulation. Artificial intelligence-based methodologies as well as measurement-based methods make up data-driven stability assessment methods. When compared to simulation-based time-domain models, calculation-based methods use metrics info to construct simple yet good models for stability assessment [10–13]. However creating measurement-based, less complicated models is not an easy job [16]. Contrarily, stability evaluation based on artificial intelligence is based on data and not primarily based on physical principles. These AI models can perform assessments based on system inputs after being trained using simulation or measurement data [17–20].

V. N. M. Aradhya et al. (Eds.): CCIP 2023, CCIS 2044, pp. 74–89, 2024.
https://doi.org/10.1007/978-3-031-60725-7_7

Numerous research have already attempted to examine the stability of power systems using artificial intelligence [21]. A review of previous studies is given in this paper. The majority of currently used ML-based methods can evaluate a single type of stability. Typically, inputs are chosen using a particular machine-learning model through trial and error. In this paper ML and Deep learning methods are simultaneously used to evaluate the frequency, small signal, and transient stability of a power system. On an 18-bus system, the proposed approach's correctness and effectiveness in stability assessment are confirmed [1].

1.1 Artificial Intelligence-Based Stability Assessment

For effective energy-efficient operation, microgrids use a wide range of AI Techniques, which include Deep learning, Machine learning, and Artificial Neural Networks [23]. Various deep-learning methodologies were put forth to forecast electrical loads for a microgrid. The authors concentrate on the usage of various deep-learning technologies in the smart grid for load prediction. Further, they assessed the accuracy results of the generated applications in terms of mean absolute error and root-mean-square error, and the outcomes revealed that the convolutional neural network with the k-means algorithm had a considerable probability of minimizing RMSE [24, 25].

1.2 Machine Learning Applications in Grid Management

Ali Kashif Bashir [8] in the paper titled "Comparative analysis of ML algorithms for predicting grid stability", International Electrical Energy Syst. 2021 employed models such as Least squares support vector machine - multi-input multi-output, Artificial neural networks, QOABC optimization algorithm, and GMI for examining different machine learning tools in the Correlation of irregular patterns in the electrical load and price signals. Without taking into account the previous data for a specific forecast day, this model forecasts the load and power signals, but it might not be more precise [23]. The analysis took into account several problem statements, including the demand prediction for each consumer's household load, STLF inside microgrids, predicting district-level long- and medium-term energy consumption, and early warning systems to anticipate.

Blackout incidents to prevent cascading failure As a result, machine learning algorithms are needed for preserving the stability of the microgrid due to their capacity to anticipate client electricity needs. Mamoun Alazab [24] in the paper titled "Multidirectional LSTM Model-Predicting the Stability of a Grid", published, in 2020, they have used the MLSTM technique to predict the stability of the grid network. The Results were compared to those of other well-liked DL techniques, including Recurrent Neural Networks, standard LSTM, and Gated Recurrent Units. The results of the experiments show that the LSTM strategy works better than the other Machine learning approaches. A greater accuracy of 99.07% than other cutting-edge deep learning models is attained. CPS System is taken into account here. A cyber-physical system (CPS) combines computation, networks, and physical processes. Although numerous research studies have shown that successful prediction models exist, there is still room for accuracy improvements. The examined literature shows that the proposed neural network incorporates hyperparameter adjustment for improved prediction accuracy to address these issues.

Despite the advancements, further study is required to improve AI-based models and guarantee the reliability and effectiveness of smart grids in real-time applications [25, 26].

2 Problem Statement and Objective

The primary challenge is to address those concerns in terms of reliability, continuity, and secure operation, It is important to develop precise and effective prediction models that can handle the complexities of Microgrids such as fluctuating loads, renewable energy sources integration, and other uncertainties. A power grid's robustness is determined by its transient, frequency, and small signal stability characteristics taken as a whole.

To overcome the above said problem the following Objectives are defined in this work,

1) Test and Train the KNN Algorithm for frequency, small signal, and voltage stability in an 18-bus test system using MATLAB.
2) Test and Train the LSTM Algorithm for frequency, small signal, and voltage stability in an 18-bus test system using MATLAB.
3) Comparative Analysis of KNN and LSTM Algorithm.

3 System Modelling

This method uses a prediction model using complete input data that is data collection, analysis, and pre-processing come first and second step comprises the prediction model to forecast stability using the input data, which begins with identifying the input data.

3.1 KNN Algorithm

K-Nearest Neighbours (Fig. 1) is one of the most primitive yet significant categorization techniques in ML. It is often employed in the detection of intrusions, mining data, and identification of patterns and relates to the area of supervised learning [27]. It is widely practical in real-world situations since it is non-parametric and makes no fundamental presumptions about the distribution of the data (unlike other methods, like GMM, which assume a Gaussian distribution of the input data). To be able to build coordinates according to a trait, we offer some prior knowledge, which is referred to as training data [28–30]. The use of datasets labelled to train algorithms that accurately group data or predict events is a major aspect of supervised learning, also known as supervised. This Algorithm fits the data perfectly.

Here the new data is placed in the category that most closely matches the current categories after assessing the new and old data sets. After saving all of the previous data, a new data point is classified using the K-NN algorithm based on resemblance. This indicates that recent information can be reliably and quickly categorized utilizing the K-NN approach. The K-NN method can be employed in regression even though classification problems are where it is most typically applied. As a result of saving the training dataset rather than instantly learning from it, the approach is also known as a lazy learner. However, when sorting data, it makes use of the dataset to take action [34].

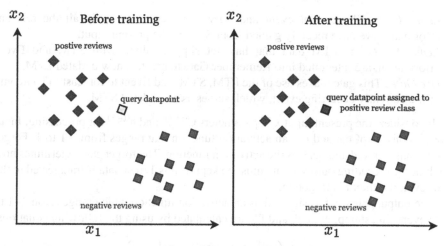

Fig. 1. KNN Methodology

3.2 LSTM Algorithm

To conduct calculations using both long-term and short-term memory, LSTMs use the concept of gates as shown in Fig. 2. First, the dataset for the electrical grid from several power plants is combined. After that, minimum and maximum normalization is employed to normalize the data. These values of the data are retrieved and reinstituted during this process using Eq. (1). Where X stands for an attribute in the fed dataset, min (X) and max (X) represent the attribute's minimum and maximum values. Every element in a dataset has an updated value indicated by 'L'. The 'I' corresponds to the dataset's prior values. new_max (X) and new_min (X) stand for the upper and lower boundaries of the specified range [24, 35–38].

$$L = [I - min(X)/(max(X) - min(X))](new\_min(X) - new\_max(X)) + new\_min(X)$$
$$(1)$$

The values in the dataset cannot be processed by ML algorithms. For this reason, the Label encoding technique is used to transform the categorical data in the dataset into numbers that can be processed by the ML formulas.

The proposed LSTM technique is then used to train the Microgrid dataset [40]. The proposed model's performance is subsequently compared with KNN by using metrics such as accuracy.

LSTM contains several neural network modules and a chain structure. RNN employs a greater number of network layers, making it difficult to understand the parameters from earlier layers [41, 42]. The LSTM network is a widely used strategy to address this difficulty in recent studies.

The LSTM design is made up of an input gate, an exit gate, and a memory gate [24].

1. *Memory gate/Forget Gate.*: When LTM reaches to forget gate, it slips undesirable information.

2. *Learn Gate.*: The current event and STM are merged to apply all the relevant information we have recently gained from STM to the present input.
3. *Remember Gate.*: LTM data that has not slipped, along with STM and Event information, are integrated into Remember Gate to create a new updated LTM.
4. *Use Gate.*: This gate makes use of the LTM, STM, and Event to forecast the outcome of the currently occurring event, which serves as an updated STM.

It considers the present input $x^{(t)}$, parameters $C^{(t-1)}$, and $h^{(t-1)}$ for processing. Input gate $i^{(t)}$ consists of tan and has an activation function that ranges from -1 to 1. Forget gate $f^{(t)}$ has sigmoid and tan h as the activation function. The forget gate determines how much of the preceding output's data must be kept. If it is 1 then data is transferred to the next level, if 0 then it's forgotten.

The output gate $o^{(t)}$ has sigmoid as an activation function which ranges from -1 to 1. At every timestamp, $i^{(t)}$, $o^{(t)}$, and $f^{(t)}$ are calculated by using the following equations.

$$i^{(t)} = \sigma\left(W^i\left[C^{t-1}, h^{(t-1)}, x^{(t)}\right] + b^i\right)$$

$$o^{(t)} = \sigma\left(W^o\left[C^{t-1}, h^{(t-1)}, x^{(t)}\right] + b^i\right)$$

$$f^{(t)} = \sigma\left(W^f\left[C^{t-1}, h^{(t-1)}, x^{(t)}\right] + b^i\right)$$

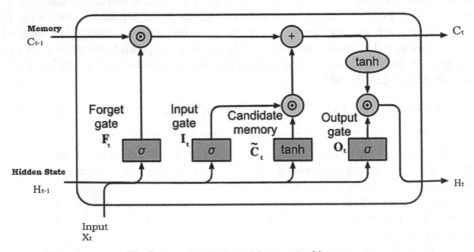

Fig. 2. Long Short-Term Memory Architecture

4   Experimental Dataset and Methodology

The simulation results of 18 bus systems for GA and optical placement in dispersed networks were utilized as the source for the dataset used in the suggested approaches [1]. For load data and line data, two distinct datasets are collected from standard 18-bus IEEE test system. We have employed MATLAB Simulink to construct a testing system, purpose-built for gathering the necessary dataset. Within this system, a workspace is established to store specific signals, which are connected to the output requiring monitoring. These signals are then stored in an array format. The process of dataset classification typically involves the development of models tailored for classification tasks using various methods. In this context, the extracted data from model are classified or separated with individual folders del (del 1 to del 4), freq (F1 to F19) and Inputs (Vabc 1 to Vabc 19). These data are utilised for training and testing purpose, where 80% of data are used for training and 20% for testing.

This work suggests an efficient stability assessment tool to all together evaluate frequency, small signal, and transient stability. The methodological flowchart is shown in Fig. 3. Firstly, dispatch data from the scheduling model is altered to AC power flow. Then, by executing a time-domain simulation, numerous scenarios their stability margins are determined. The artificial intelligence model is then trained using the stability indicators. The trained model can forecast the stability margin for new power flow scenarios. Table 1 contains a list of the inputs, outputs, and two AI models employed in this assessment. Data from the transmission network and generator dispatch levels are among the input features. The stability margin indicators for various stability issues are the outputs. An 18-bus test system is used to conduct the stability assessment.

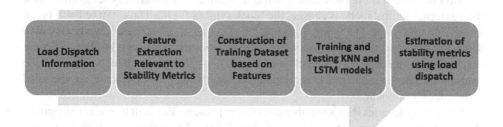

Fig. 3. Methodology

The system has four sources coal, gas, and two Hydro plants each consisting of one conventional generator, There is one more Solar PV power facility towards the east. The suggested system's main goal is to evaluate the bus systems' stability using load angles. A VCPI value is used to define each bus. The bus is stable if it equals 1, and the bus network is weak or unstable if it equals 0. This classification is crucial for evaluating bust stability. With the VCPI index, the stability rises.

Table 1. Input and Output Stability Assessment

Stability	Inputs	Output	Algorithm
Frequency	Transmission Network data and Generator dispatch levels	Frequency after simulation	KNN
Transient		CCT	LSTM
Small Signal		Oscillations	

The Three-Phase V-I Measurement unit is employed for evaluating the instantaneous three-phase voltages and currents in a system. It returns the three phase-to-ground or phase-to-phase maximum voltages and currents when connected in series with three-phase elements. The block has an output range of volts, amperes, and per unit (pu) values for both voltages and currents. A three-phase circuit breaker's opening and shutting times can be controlled by either an in-house timer utilizing multiple modes or an external Simulink® signal by using the single-phase to the ground or three-phase fault blocks, respectively. Phase-to-phase faults, phase-to-ground faults, or a combination of phase-to-phase and ground faults can be controlled using the Three-Phase Fault block, which makes use of three Breaker blocks that can be sequentially turned on and off. The Three-Phase Fault block's arc extinction mechanism is the same as the Breaker block's. If the ground fault option is not preset, the ground resistance is automatically set to 106 ohms. If an external control mode is chosen, the block symbol for the Three-Phase Fault block shows a control input. The fourth Simulink input's control signal must either be 0 (which opens the breakers) or any positive value (which closes the breakers). The breakers tend to stay closed for readability using the one-digit signal. In the event that the Three-Phase Fault block is set up in internal control mode, the switching times and status are specified in the block's dialogue box.

In the model, series Rs-Cs snubber circuits are present. The fault breakers can optionally be attached to them. They can be employed if the Three-Phase Fault block is connected in series to an inductive circuit, an open circuit, or a current source. The Simulink® input signal is transformed into an equivalent voltage source via the Controlled Voltage Source block. The block's input signal drives the generated voltage.

5 Results

5.1 KNN Method Training and Testing

Training KNN Model To begin with training KNN Model—using the inputs acquired from running the Simulink model. The training for the KNN gives accuracy around 55%.

Testing KNN Model
Later Testing is carried out and command windows display every bus system's status as shown below. In the command window, the bus number and voltage will be displayed if the bus is malfunctioning meaning faulty bus; if there is no malfunction or fault, it will indicate NO. Table 2 displays the voltage readings and fault bus status for each of the 18 buses.

Table 2. Faulty Bus and non-faulty Bus data from KNN Testing

Bus No.	Fault Status	Voltage Value
1	Yes	0.9572
2	Yes	0.9565
3	Yes	0.9574
4	Yes	0.9567
5	No	0.9736
6	No	0.9636
7	No	0.9732
8	No	0.9746
9	No	0.9673
10	No	0.9769
11	No	0.9736
12	No	0.9636
13	No	0.9735
14	No	0.9746
15	No	0.9736
16	No	0.9636
17	No	0.9735
18	No	0.9746

Based on results obtained busses are classified as faulty and non-faulty busses for further predictions. In the later phase after testing is done Load angle, Bus voltage, and Frequency of the system are graphically displayed as shown in Figs. 4, 5 and 6 respectively representing the actual state of the system.

A fault is created between 2 and 3 s (x-axis) as a result fluctuations will be present in the system, but at the end of the third second even though oscillations exist in the system, it recovers and comes back to stability.

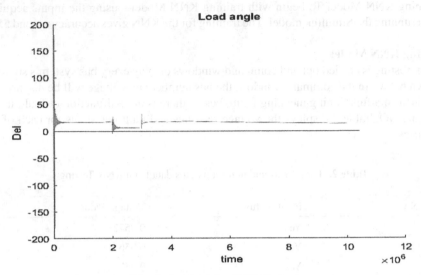

Fig. 4. Load Angle- KNN Testing

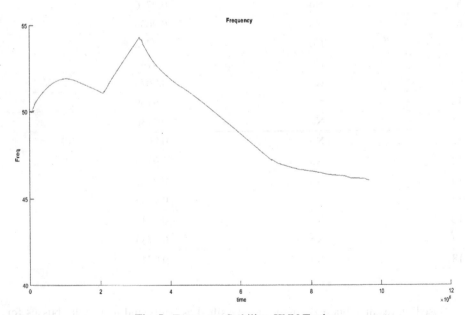

Fig. 5. Frequency Stability- KNN Testing

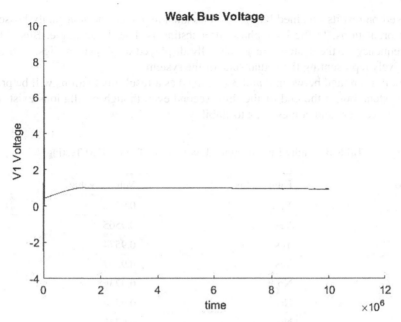

Fig. 6. Weak bus voltage- KNN Testing

In the case of voltage, we are providing the values after the fault is recovered to find a weak bus hence the graphical depiction remains unchanged prior to, during and after fault.

5.2 LSTM Method Training and Testing

Training and Testing LSTM Model

Testing of LSTM Model: To begin with training LSTM Model—using the inputs acquired from running the Simulink model. The training for the LSTM gives accuracy around 99.995%. Later Testing is carried out and command windows display every bus system's status as shown below. In the command window, the bus number and voltage will be displayed if the bus is malfunctioning meaning faulty bus; if there is no malfunction or fault, it will indicate NO. Table 3 displays the voltage readings and fault bus status for each of the 18 buses.

Based on results obtained busses are classified as faulty and non-faulty busses for further predictions. In the later phase after testing is done Load angle, Bus voltage, and Frequency of the system are graphically displayed as shown in Figs. 7, 8 and 9 respectively representing the actual state of the system.

A fault is created between 2 and 3 s (x-axis) as a result fluctuations will be present in the system, but at the end of the third second even though oscillations exist in the system, it recovers and comes back to stability.

Table 3. Faulty Bus and non-faulty Bus data from LSTM Testing

Bus No.	Fault Status	Voltage Value
1	Yes	0.9572
2	Yes	0.9565
3	Yes	0.9574
4	Yes	0.9567
5	No	0.9736
6	No	0.9636
7	No	0.9732
8	No	0.9746
9	No	0.9673
10	No	0.9769
11	No	0.9736
12	No	0.9636
13	No	0.9735
14	No	0.9746
15	No	0.9736
16	No	0.9636
17	No	0.9735
18	No	0.9746

5.3   Results of Pre and Post-fault Oscillations of Rotor-Angle for the Given Disturbance

The simulation was done using Standard IEEE 18 Bus Test system using Matlab Simulink Model by building a MG consisting of four Generators. Three Phase fault is created on Transmission line. The fault was cleared after 3rd second, and the simulation was run for 5 s. Figure 10 presents graphical representation of Load angles of all Generator 1 in the MG. As we can see pre fault oscillations and fault oscillations are extremely irregular, whereas post fault oscillations are consistent in nature representing stability after the fault.

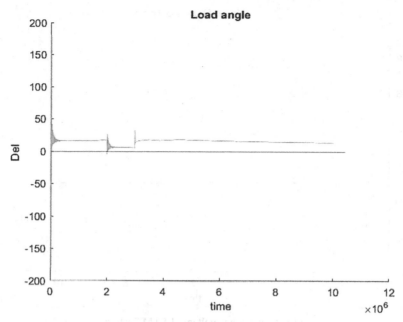

Fig. 7. Load Angle- LSTM Testing

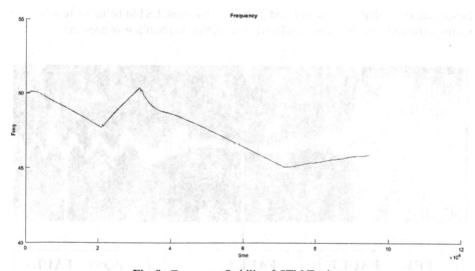

Fig. 8. Frequency Stability- LSTM Testing

To reduce pre fault and fault oscillations we had to find VCPI Index for each bus in the network, if VCPI Index was closer to 1 it means Stable bus, if it was closer to 0 it means it's a weak bus. After finding weak Buses Optimum decisions can be taken to bring back system to stability like that of Reactive power Injection. For this reason two of the ML Algorithms such as KNN and LSTM were considered to find the weak

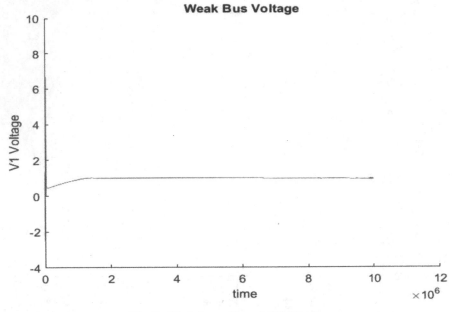

Fig. 9. Weak bus voltage- LSTM Testing

buses and also voltage, frequency and load angle statuses. LSTM being more advanced method showed most accurate results whereas KNN was half a way accurate.

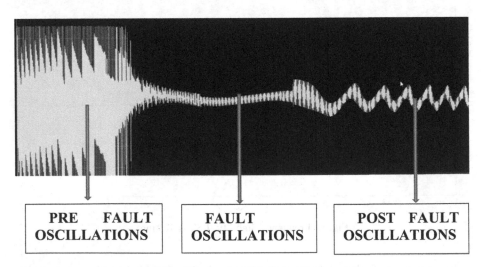

| PRE FAULT OSCILLATIONS | FAULT OSCILLATIONS | POST FAULT OSCILLATIONS |

Fig. 10. Load angle- Generator 1

6 Conclusion

In conclusion, design and Analysis of Micro Grid Stability was carried out using Machine learning and deep learning Approaches and has been implemented. To assess the state of the network, which includes Frequency, Voltage, Load angle, and the status of individual buses, a primary approach called KNN was explored alongside an advanced RNN method called LSTM. After the KNN and LSTM algorithms have been trained and tested, an exhaustive overview of stable and weak buses as well as a graphical depiction of frequency, small signal, and voltage stability are available. With the help of all these variables, we can identify stable and weak buses. In the event of instability, reactive power may be injected to restore stability, enhancing system reliability. Comparative investigation revealed that in terms of Accuracy, LSTM outperformed KNN.

Overall KNN is a simple, instance-based algorithm primarily used for tabular data and relatively small datasets, while LSTM is a deep learning algorithm designed for sequential data, making it suitable for tasks involving time series, text data, and other types of sequences. The choice between KNN and LSTM depends on the specific problem and the nature of data.

References

1. You, S., et al.: A review on artificial intelligence for grid stability assessment. In: 2020 IEEE International Conference on Communications, Control, and Computing Technologies for Smart Grids (SmartGridComm). IEEE (2020)
2. Xu, Y., et al.: A reliable intelligent system for real-time dynamic security assessment of power systems. IEEE Trans. Power Syst. **27**(3), 1253–1263 (2012)
3. You, S., et al.: Impact of high PV penetration on US eastern interconnection frequency response. In: 2017 IEEE Power & Energy Society General Meeting. IEEE (2017)
4. Liu, Y., et al.: Frequency response assessment and enhancement of the US power grids toward extra-high photovoltaic generation penetrations—an industry perspective. IEEE Trans. Power Syst. **33**(3), 3438–3449 (2018)
5. You, S., et al.: Impact of high PV penetration on the inter-area oscillations in the US eastern interconnection. IEEE Access **5**, 4361–4369 (2017)
6. Li, H., et al.: Analytic analysis for dynamic system frequency in power systems under uncertain variability. IEEE Trans. Power Syst. **34**(2), 982–993 (2018)
7. You, S., et al.: Comparative assessment of tactics to improve primary frequency response without curtailing solar output in high photovoltaic interconnection grids. IEEE Trans. Sustain. Energy **10**(2), 718–728 (2018)
8. Bashir, A.K., et al.: Comparative analysis of machine learning algorithms for prediction of smart grid stability. Int. Trans. Electri. Energy Syst. **31**(9), e127064 (2021)
9. Tang, Y., Li, F., Wang, Q., Xu, Y.: Hybrid method for power system transient stability prediction based on two-stage computing resources. IET Gener. Transm. Distrib. **12**(8), 1697–1703 (2017)
10. You, S., Guo, J., Kou, G., Liu, Y., Liu, Y.: Oscillation mode identification based on wide-area ambient measurements using multivariate empirical mode decomposition. Electr. Power Syst. Res. **134**, 158–166 (2016)
11. You, S., et al.: Disturbance location determination based on electromechanical wave propagation in FNET/GridEye: a distribution-level wide-area measurement system. IET Gener. Transm. Distrib. **11**(18), 4436–4443 (2017)

12. Zhang, X., et al.: Measurement-based power system dynamic model reductions. In: 2017 North American Power Symposium (NAPS), pp. 1–6. IEEE (2017)
13. Zhang, X., Xue, Y., You, S., Liu, Y., Liu, Y.: US Eastern Interconnection (EI) model reductions using a measurement-based approach. In: 2018 IEEE/PES Transmission and Distribution Conference and Exposition (T&D), pp. 1–5. IEEE (2018)
14. Zhang, C., Li, Y., Yu, Z., Tian, F.: Feature selection of power system transient stability assessment based on random forest and recursive feature elimination. In: Power and Energy Engineering Conference (APPEEC), 2016 IEEE PES Asia-Pacific, pp. 1264–1268. IEEE (2016)
15. Zhang, Y., Xu, Y., Dong, Z.Y., Xu, Z., Wong, K.P.: Intelligent early warning of power system dynamic insecurity risk: toward optimal accuracy-earliness tradeoff. IEEE Trans. Ind. Inf. **13**(5), 2544–2554 (2017)
16. Tong, N., et al.: Dynamic equivalence of large-scale power systems based on boundary measurements. In: 2020 American Control Conference (ACC), pp. 3164–3169. IEEE (2020)
17. Yuan, H., et al.: Machine learning-based PV reserve determination strategy for frequency control on the WECC system. In: 2020 Innovative Smart Grid Technologies, pp. 1–5. IEEE (2020)
18. Xiao, H., et al.: Data-driven security assessment of power grids based on machine learning approach. In: International Council on Large Electric Systems (CIGRE): Proceedings of the United States National Committee for Grid of the Future Symposium, CIGRE, pp. 1–5 (2019)
19. Cui, Y., You, S., Liu, Y.: Ambient synchrophasor measurement based system inertia estimation. In: 2020 IEEE Power & Energy Society General Meeting (PESGM), pp. 1–5. IEEE (2020)
20. Amraee, T., Ranjbar, S.: Transient instability prediction using decision tree technique. IEEE Trans. Power Syst. **28**(3), 3028–3037 (2013)
21. Amjady, N., Majedi, S.F.: Transient stability prediction by a hybrid intelligent system. IEEE Trans. Power Syst. **22**(3), 1275–1283 (2007)
22. Jafarzadeh, S., Genc, V.M.I.: Probabilistic dynamic security assessment of large power systems using machine learning algorithms. Turkish J. Electr. Eng. Comput. Sci. **26**(3), 1479–1490 (2018)
23. Kundur, P., et al.: Definition and classification of power system stability. IEEE Trans. Power Syst. **19**(3), 1387–1401 (2004)
24. Alazab, M., et al.: A multidirectional LSTM model for predicting the stability of a smart grid. IEEE Access **8**, 85454–85463 (2020)
25. Geeganage, J., Annakkage, U.D., Weekes, T., Archer, B.A.: Application of energy-based power system features for dynamic security assessment. IEEE Trans. Power Syst. **30**(4), 1957–1965 (2015)
26. James, J., Hill, D.J., Lam, A.Y., Gu, J., Li, V.O.: Intelligent time-adaptive transient stability assessment system. IEEE Trans. Power Syst. **33**(1), 1049–1058 (2018)
27. Ucar, F.: A comprehensive analysis of smart grid stability prediction along with explainable artificial intelligence. Symmetry **15**(2), 289 (2023)
28. James, J., Lam, A.Y., Hill, D.J., Li, V.O.: Delay aware intelligent transient stability assessment system. IEEE Access **5**, 17230–17239 (2017)
29. Lv, J., Pawlak, M., Annakkage, U.D.: Prediction of the transient stability boundary using the lasso. IEEE Trans. Power Syst. **28**(1), 281–288 (2013)
30. Liu, R., Verbič, G., Xu, Y.: A new reliability-driven intelligent system for power system dynamic security assessment. In: Universities Power Engineering Conference (AUPEC), 2017 Australasian, pp. 1–6. IEEE (2017)
31. Zhang, L., Hu, X., Li, P., Shi, F., Yu, Z.: ELM model for power system transient stability assessment. In: Chinese Automation Congress (CAC), pp. 5740–5744. IEEE (2017)

32. Sharifian, A., Sharifian, S.: A new power system transient stability assessment method based on Type-2 fuzzy neural network estimation. Int. J. Electr. Power Energy Syst. **64**, 71–87 (2015)
33. Tan, B., Yang, J., Pan, X., Li, J., Xie, P., Zeng, C.: Representational learning approach for power system transient stability assessment based on convolutional neural network. J. Eng. **2017**(13), 1847–1850 (2017)
34. Chu, X., Liu, Y.: Real-time transient stability prediction using incremental learning algorithm. In: Power Engineering Society General Meeting, pp. 1565–1569. IEEE (2004)
35. Chao-Rong, C., Yuan-Yin, H.: Synchronous machine steady-state stability analysis using an artificial neural network. IEEE Trans. Energy Convers. **6**(1), 12–20 (1991)
36. You, S., et al.: Non-invasive identification of inertia distribution change in high renewable systems using distribution level PMU. IEEE Trans. Power Syst. **33**(1), 1110–1112 (2017)
37. Mohammadi, M., Gharehpetian, G., Raoofat, M.: A new BVM based approach to transient security assessment. Eur. Trans. Electr. Power **20**(8), 1163–1176 (2010)
38. Teeuwsen, S.P., Erlich, I., El-Sharkawi, M.A., Bachmann, U.: Genetic algorithm and decision tree-based oscillatory stability assessment. IEEE Trans. Power Syst. **21**(2), 746–753 (2006)
39. Moulin, L., Da Silva, A.A., El-Sharkawi, M., Marks, R.J.: Support vector machines for transient stability analysis of large-scale power systems. IEEE Trans. Power Syst. **19**(2), 818–825 (2004)
40. Pannell, Z., Ramachandran, B., Snider, D.: Machine learning approach to solving the transient stability assessment problem. In: Texas Power and Energy Conference (TPEC), pp. 1–6. IEEE (2018)
41. Hang, F., Huang, S., Chen, Y., Mei, S.: Power system transient stability assessment based on dimension reduction and cost-sensitive ensemble learning. In: 2017 IEEE Conference on Energy Internet and Energy System Integration (EI2), pp. 1–6. IEEE (2017)
42. Soni, B.P., Saxena, A., Gupta, V.: Online identification of coherent generators in power system by using SVM. In: 2017 4th International Conference on Power, Control & Embedded Systems (ICPCES), pp. 1–5. IEEE (2017)

Video Analytics

Cloud-Based Real-Time Sign Language Detection and Voice Synthesis for Impaired Individuals Using Machine Learning

V. R. Monish Raman, Ganeshayya Shidaganti(✉), V. Aditya Raj, Shane George Shibu, and Roshan Ismail

Department of Computer Science and Engineering, Ramaiah Institute of Technology, Bangalore, Karnataka, India
ganeshayyashidagnti@msrit.edu

Abstract. Individuals with hearing and speech impairments find it harder to communicate in real time as they can primarily speak sign language and the general public usually requires a translator for them to understand. Therefore, there is a requirement for a system that translates the sign language gestures into audible speech in real-time, ensuring them an opportunity to communicate. This research paper presents a cloud-based solution that offers real-time sign language recognition and text-to-speech conversion websites leveraging a Random Forest classifier. The user can turn on their webcam to detect sign language in real-time and display each letter recognized from hand landmarks detected by the cloud-deployed Random Forest model and store it in a text file. Once the recording of the video is done, the user is immediately provided with an audio file of the converted text file, through an on-screen MP3 player, that is natural and audible enough for enabling smooth communication. Through extensive testing and experimentation, the Random Forest model was found to have an accuracy of 88.2% on testing data and made quite accurate predictions. In conclusion, the paper demonstrates an intuitive and reliable tool for effective communication for impaired individuals, by aiming to empower them with the means to participate fully in the digital age.

Keywords: Sign Language Detection · Text-to-speech · Cloud Computing · Amazon Web Services (AWS) · Elastic Computing (EC2) · Random Forest Classifier

1 Introduction

Access to effective communication is a very crucial aspect of one's life. Digital revolutions have brought in many changes in daily communication starting from translation apps to annotation apps that make communication between individuals who generally cannot communicate with each other. Individuals with hearing and speech impairments face unique challenges when it comes to effective communication in the digital age. Generally, for such individual's communication often relies on sign language that utilizes hand gestures, facial expressions, and body movements. Though sign language is a

V. N. M. Aradhya et al. (Eds.): CCIP 2023, CCIS 2044, pp. 93–107, 2024.
https://doi.org/10.1007/978-3-031-60725-7_8

very powerful means of conveying thoughts and ideas to individuals who are fluent in it, it can come across as difficult for a broader section of people. Most of the general public requires an interpreter for them to understand sign language, such dependency restricts the autonomy and spontaneity of individuals with hearing and speech impairment. Taking into account this communication gap, this paper presents an innovative cloud-based website that leverages the random forest classifier which has been meticulously trained on sign language gestures, to detect and translate sign language quickly and accurately.

The research is a fusion of computer vision, machine learning, and cloud computing mostly utilizing AWS EC2 instances to provide computational power, scalability, and reliability. The sign language recognition systems are primarily machine learning models such as the Support Vector Machine and the Convolution Neural Networks [1]. Machine learning in this research is built upon the random forest classifier that is trained extensively for each gesture representing an alphabet or a number. Recognizing Sign gestures requires a comprehensive dataset of sign gestures. The paper [2] discusses the data collection process, including the use of sensors or cameras. The model is trained with nearly 2000+ images to ensure accurate and instant recognition of the gestures. The model also employs computer vision [3] techniques to detect and track hand landmarks, recognizing the intricate gestures that constitute sign language. Following the identification of the alphabet, they are stitched together to make a meaningful sentence and stored in a text file. The paper [4] delves into the methods used to generate spoken language output or produce written text based on video inputs. The text file is then converted to speech by integrating a robust text-to-speech conversion mechanism using Google Text-to-Speech (gTTS), a Python library and a tool interface with Google Text-to-speech API, the conversion process transforms the recognized sign language gestures into clear, natural, and audible speech in real-time.

The creation of an intuitive and secure web interface is a critical component of the research as the user interface needs to be simple and easily understandable by anyone. The interface serves as the gateway through which users access and interact with the system's capabilities for real-time sign language recognition and text-to-speech synthesis. Moreover, it incorporates robust security measures, including dynamic key-pair authentication, to protect user data and privacy. The interface offers real-time feedback while recognizing sign language to increase user confidence. To achieve real-time recognition, it involves the continuous streaming and processing of sign language gestures [5]. The system dynamically displays the recognized letters or phrases on the user's screen as it recognizes and interprets sign language gestures, providing immediate visual confirmation. The flow is kept straightforward, minimizing the number of steps required to begin and end communication sessions. Hence, the research represents a significant advancement in enhancing communication accessibility for individuals with hearing and speech impairments in the digital age. The rest of this paper is organized as follows. Section 2 talks about other related works. In Sect. 3, we have discussed the System architecture of the model with relevant images. The methodology of the systems is clearly explained in Sect. 4. Followed by the results achieved by the research in Sect. 5. The paper ends with the Conclusion given in Sect. 6.

2 Literature Review

The advancement of technologies has led to various methodologies in developing dynamic sign language recognition techniques. The literature review sheds light on the foundation technologies of the recognition system and gives an idea about the wide range of methods that have been employed by other researchers. The review provides insights into novel approaches, challenges, and the potential impact of this technology on enhancing accessibility and inclusivity by examining a group of related works that add to the growing body of knowledge in the field of sign language recognition and translation.

The technical aspect of being able to capture hand and finger movements with precision by enabling the use of gloves that have sensors to capture the spatial data of hand and finger movements as users make sign language gestures [6]. In a similar approach, [7] brings in a novel idea that combines the Hue-Saturation-Value (HSV) colour model that separates colour information into distinct components, allowing for more robust recognition specifically for the recognition of American Sign Language (ASL). The integration of Convolutional Neural Networks (CNNs) and Recurrent Neural Networks (RNNs) to extract spatial features from images and capture temporal sequences respectively to understand the dynamics of ASL signs is shown in [8]. The paper also addresses how the gesture data can be pre-processed by image resizing, noise reduction and data augmentation. Similarly, [9] provides a reference point for designing and developing a system that facilitates ASL communication through advanced deep learning and computer vision techniques. The authors of [10] highlight the evolution of deep learning-based techniques, emphasizing their role in advancing the accuracy and robustness of sign language. The comprehensive analysis gives valuable insights into the latest trends and developments in this particular field.

The authors of [11] present benchmark datasets commonly used in sign language recognition research. The authors also explain the data augmentation techniques employed to expand training datasets that are crucial for enhancing the generalization capability of deep learning models, especially when dealing with limited data. The summary of the available sign language datasets that are currently accessible, including finger spelling motions and vocabulary items can act as an evaluation tool for learning sign languages [12]. In [13], the authors introduce Leap Motion technology which is a sensor technology that enables precise tracking of hand and finger motions in three-dimensional space, making it well-suited for applications related to gesture technology. In addition to this, the authors add enhancements to the existing Long Short-Term Memory (LSTM), such as the addition of extra layers, attention mechanisms, or specialized loss functions to better capture temporal dependencies and transitions between signs. A practical application of the sign language-to-speech conversion idea that uses Support Vector Machines to classify sign motions is implied by the presentation of the crucial feature of translating sign language gestures into spoken language in [14]. Convolutional Neural Networks (CNNs), which are highly suited for image-based tasks, are used in [15] to perform real-time translation of sign language motions into both text and speech. This allows for more accurate processing and classification of the video frames that are acquired.

Therefore, the literature review gives the technical advancements, challenges, and various methodologies applied in the sign language recognition field. Keeping these ideas in mind our research implements a real-time sign language recognition model using a random forest classifier that is cloud-deployed leveraging AWS EC2 instances that offer scalability and reliability, surpassing many localized solutions. The voice synthesis aspect is implemented by Google Translates text-to-speech API which ensures high-quality, natural-sounding speech synthesis, enhancing comprehension for users. Hence, the solution offered in this paper presents comprehensive and advanced solutions promoting effective communication for individuals with hearing and speech impairments.

3   System Architecture

The system architecture involves several interconnected components that enable real-time sign language detection and voice synthesis as shown in Fig. 1.

The main components of the architecture are as follows:

A. Random Forest Model: The most important part of the system is the Random Forest Model, which is meticulously trained to recognize sign language gestures It uses a dataset of sign language gestures, including multiple samples for each alphabet and number, to ensure accurate and instantaneous recognition.

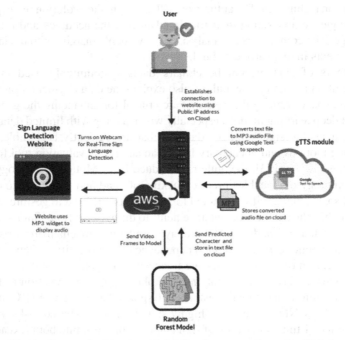

Fig. 1. System Architecture of the Sign Language Detection Website

B. gTTS module: Real-time speech synthesis is made possible by gTTS, ensuring that the transformed speech is immediately available following sign language recognition. The fluidity and spontaneity of communication must be maintained by this real-time component for users to have uninterrupted, natural discussions.

C. AWS EC2 Server: The AWS EC2 server provides significant computational power, enabling the efficient training and inference of the Random Forest Classifier. The system's scalability guarantees that it can manage a rising user base and a range of workloads without experiencing performance deterioration, hence improving system dependability and responsiveness. Virtual private clouds (VPCs), identity and access management (IAM), and network security groups are just a few of the strong security features offered by AWS. These protect user data and system resources and improve the system's overall security posture.

D. Sign Language Detection Website: The website's connection to the AWS EC2 server is smooth, allowing video data to be transmitted for text-to-speech conversion and sign language recognition. Through the website, users can start and stop video recording during communication sessions, as well as select choices for sign language recognition.

4   Methodology

In this section, we highlight the methodology of the research paper which is divided into 3 phases. The first phase is Initializing a secure connection between the running EC2 server instance on the AWS cloud to the deployed sign language detection website. The next phase involves the user interacting with the deployed website by turning on their webcam to use the real-time sign detection model to predict the letter using hand gestures and landmarks. The predicted characters are continuously stored in a text file to keep track of the word. The final phase involves using the Google Text to Speech (GTTS) Python module which converts the stored text file to an audio file that can be played by the MP3 widget on the website. The flow of these three phases is shown in Fig. 2.

4.1   Connection Between AWS EC2 Server and Sign Language Detection Website

Amazon Web Services provides cloud-based solutions such as EC2 instances are servers or applications of selected OS types. Here we have selected the Amazon Linux AMI 2 server to deploy our sign language detection website on a public IP address so that it can be accessed anywhere by anyone.

Figure 3 depicts the dashboard of the EC2 instance created on AWS cloud to deploy sign language detection. This displays important information about the Amazon Linux 2 AMI server like the public and private IP addresses assigned to the EC2 instance which can be used based on our needs. The dashboard also provides us with options to monitor incoming traffic and change security protocols according to the website's needs. For example, for our use case, we have changed security protocols to allow all incoming HTTP/HTTPS requests and also opened a custom TCP/IP port:8501 for specific use cases pertaining to our website. To transfer the Sign Language Detection project folder from the local system to The Amazon Linux server we have used "WinSCP Toolkit"

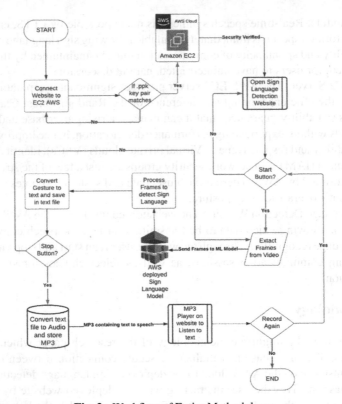

Fig. 2. Workflow of Entire Methodology

Fig. 3. Amazon Linux 2 AMI Instance in AWS Dashboard

which uses secure credentials of the EC2 instance like username, allowed Port number and ppk key-pair file is specific to each EC2 instance that acts as a password to provide a secure SSH connection between local system and server.

Fig. 4. WinSCP Toolkit UI to Transfer Files

Figure 4 shows the simple UI of "WinSCP Toolkit" where left side indicated the local system files and right side indicates the EC2 instance on the cloud. This software provides a seamless transfer of files between local system and cloud server which can be done by selecting the "Upload" option on selected folders. In parallel the Amazon Linux server gets updated to these changes that have been made in WinSCP sessions. Once the files are transferred to the server, we have to set up the server by creating a virtual environment to download all required dependencies and modules needed to run the project. Once all the modules are downloaded, we run the project, thereby establishing a secure connection between the website and cloud.

Fig. 5. Amazon Linux 2 Server running the website

Figure 5 shows the secure connection established between the server and the website. We can also see that a public IP address is assigned on Port:8501 as configured and can be accessed by anyone from any part of the world using a web browser.

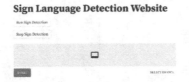

Sign Language Detection Website

Fig. 6. Sign Language Detection Website UI

Figure 6 shows the Sign Language Detection Website deployed on AWS cloud services with a user-friendly website that can be accessed by anyone with impairment to effectively communicate with others by converting the sign language to audio/speech.

4.2 Sign Language Detection Using Random Forest Classifier

Random Forest Classifier is a versatile and powerful ensemble learning technique widely used in the field of machine learning and data science. It is a robust and highly effective algorithm known for its versatility in solving a diverse range of problems, including classification, regression, and feature selection. Random Forest owes its popularity to its ability to produce accurate predictions, handle high-dimensional data, and mitigate overfitting, all while maintaining ease of use and interpretability. In this paper, we leverage

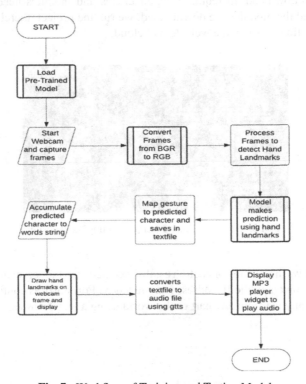

Fig. 7. Workflow of Training and Testing Model

the power of the Random Forest algorithm to develop a sign language detection system that recognizes and interprets hand gestures in real-time. By harnessing the capabilities of Random Forest, we aim to provide an effective and reliable tool for enhancing communication for individuals with hearing and speech impairments.

Figure 7 describes the entire workflow of the sign detection model. Now in the following text, we shall talk about the various steps involved in developing the sign detection model and its detailed working.

4.3 Dataset

For testing purposes, we have chosen to train our model using Indian Sign Language. We have made our own dataset as seen in Fig. 8, to train the model which consists of 100 burst images taken for each letter for the highest accuracy and better training the model. To be precise an overall of 3500 images have been used to train the model to identify the Indian sign language. The dataset employed in developing the sign detection model comprises an extensive collection of sign language gestures, carefully curated to ensure diversity and inclusivity. With a sample size of 3500 instances, the dataset is stratified to cover a broad spectrum of gestures, accommodating variations in hand movements, positions, and expressions. To enhance model generalization, the dataset is further partitioned into distinct training and validation sets, allowing for robust training and effective evaluation of the sign detection algorithm. Once these images are taken, we carry out with data pre-processing technique that is used to scale data within a specific range which is given by Eq. (1).

Fig. 8. Dataset Created for Training and Testing Model

$$normalized = \frac{(original - min_{value})}{(max_{value} - min_{value})} \tag{1}$$

This equation is applied separately to the 'x' and 'y' coordinates of hand landmarks to find the relative hand position within the image. Now we perform image conversion from BGR to RGB using the OpenCV python module and 'MediaPipe' module to process these images using Eq. (2).

$$rgb = cv2.cvtColor(img, cv2.COLOR_{BGR2RGB}) \tag{2}$$

Once the images are processed, we iterate through the hand landmarks detected using 'x' and 'y' coordinates for each landmark. 'data.aux' is a list used to collect the normalized coordinates for each hand landmark. Using this data.aux list we add corresponding labels to each character and maintain a labels list all stored in 'data.pickle'. The dataset contains meticulous representations of sign language gestures as features, with a primary focus on capturing significant aspects of hand movements and landmarks. The dataset is structured such that each instance fully captures the dynamic nature of sign language communication, including sequential frames, hand poses, and spatial information. The dataset, which makes use of computer vision techniques, captures the subtleties of a wide range of gestures, guaranteeing that the model can recognize and generalize across different signing expressions.

4.4   Training Random Forest Model with Dataset

After we save data.pickle file we train the Random Forest Model with this dataset. Once the dataset is loaded, we start padding the sequence to ensure all sequences have the same length. This is done by calculating 'max_sequence_length' and adding zeros to the sequence until the length becomes sane as 'maxlength'. Padding involves adding zeros to sequences. Mathematically, for a sequence X of length L, the padding adds zeros until the length becomes max_sequence_length. For each element X_i in the sequence, the padding is expressed as Eq. (3):

$$Padded(X_i) = X_i \ if \ i < L \ else \ 0 \tag{3}$$

After the sequence is padded with zeros to match max length, we perform data and data and label conversion. Convert the padded data and labels into NumPy arrays with a float data type for compatibility with scikit-learn. Once this is done, we perform Train-Test split to divide the dataset for training and splitting. This is shown in as Eq. (4):

$$x\_train, x\_test, y\_train, y\_test = train\_test\_split$$
$$(data, labels, test\_size = 0.2, shuffle = True, stratify = labels) \tag{4}$$

The dataset is split into training and testing sets, with 80% for training and 20% for testing. The shuffle and stratify options ensure data randomness and class balance in the splits. Now the dataset is ready to be used for training the Random Forest Model as seen in Eq. (5). Random Forest algorithm combines multiple decision trees, and each tree is trained based on the dataset. The model learns relationships between features and labels.

$$model = RandomForestClassifier()$$
$$model.fit(x_{train}, y_{train}) \tag{5}$$

Once the model is trained, we use the trained model to make predictions on the testing data and calculate the accuracy score to assess model performance. The accuracy score measures the ratio of correctly classified samples to the total number of samples in the test set. It's expressed in Eq. (6):

$$Accuracy = \frac{(Number \ of \ Correct \ Predictions)}{(Total \ Number \ of \ Predictions)} \tag{6}$$

We received an accuracy of 98.2% with testing data. Now the trained model is saved as a 'model.p' file to be used by the website to make sign language prediction on webcam video.

4.5   Cloud-Deployed Sign Language Detection Website

The AWS deployed Cloud Website consists of the Sign Language Detection model integrated with Webcam to enable real-time detection on the website which can be accessed by anyone using the Public IP address assigned by the EC instance server.

Fig. 9. Working of Sign Language Detection Website

Figure 9 shows the working of the Sign Language Detection which accurately detects the letter 'C' from hand landmarks detected on webcam in real-time. The Website is used to test a sign language detection model in real-time using a webcam. It captures video frames, detects hand landmarks, and predicts sign language letters using a trained Random Forest Classifier. The script starts by loading the trained sign language detection model from a pickle file. It initializes variables, including the webcam (VideoCapture), a flag to track letter addition, language settings for text-to-speech, and a variable to store detected words. After this we initialize MediaPipe python module for hand landmark detection to set confidence thresholds and styles for drawing hand landmarks. Now a dictionary is defined to map class labels to corresponding letters and its ground truth labels. Using the labels dictionary, MediaPipe processes each frame to detect hand landmark which makes a bounding box around the hand and then makes prediction based on these landmarks and maps the prediction to the labels that we have saved. Once this letter is predicted it is pushed to a word variable to keep track of the sentence and display and it on the frame so that users can keep track of the word they are trying to communicate. These words are constantly stored in a text file which is later converted to an audio file to speak the words out.

4.6   Text to Speech Using GTTS Module for Real -Time Voice Synthesis

Using the saved text file containing the letters predicted from the sign language detection model, we use Google Text to Speech python module which takes a text file as an input and converts it into an MP3 playable audio file. The conversion from text to speech happens using the inbuilt function given in Eq. (7)

$$myobj = gTTS(text = contents, lang = language, slow = False) \qquad (7)$$

5   Experimental Results and Discussions

In this Section, we present the outcomes of our research paper. Which explores the development of cloud-based solutions for real-time sign detection and text-to-speech synthesis. Communication plays an important role in day-to-day human interactions which can be quite challenging for impaired individuals. To bridge this gap, our research paper is focused on using Machine Learning algorithms for sign detection and AWS cloud services for efficiency and quicker deployment. Through this integration of cloud computing and secure web interface, our system empowers individuals with speech and hearing impairments to communicate effectively with other humans.in this section we dive into technical details, performance evaluation and user experience to provide a concise overview of the Cloud deployed Sign Language Detection Website.

First, the user navigates to the Cloud Deployed Sign Detection Website using the public IP address assigned to the EC2 Instance on AWS Cloud. Once the user is connected, A simple User Interface can be seen on the website as seen in Fig. 6. When the user is ready to utilize real-time sign language detection, they can click the run sign detection button which in turn turns on the inbuilt webcam to start real-time sign language detection as seen in Fig. 10(a).

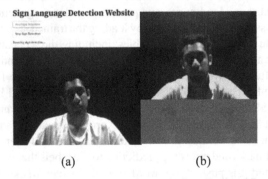

(a)   (b)

Fig. 10. Frames Extracted from Live Web-Cam Feed and Processed

Once the webcam is turned on, we extract each frame using OpenCV python module, with a fixed width and height that can be processed by the model. Using this Python module, the extracted frame is pre-processed and grayscales as seen in Fig. 10(b), to identify the hand landmarks and make predictions on the letters. This is how each frame is extracted and pre-processed to apply a sign detection model to detect sign language.

Figure 11 depicts how when the user makes a hand gesture for sentence 'ABC', bounding box was drawn in the frame around the hand landmarks detected to identify

Fig. 11. Prediction based on hand gestures and keeps track of letters

the gesture pattern and make required prediction on which letter the user is trying to show. As we can see the model correctly makes the prediction for the hand gesture to be letter 'A' which can be seen by the text depicted above the bounding box. The model also depicts and keeps track of the letters which are continuously stored in a text file to display the word created by user on the frame window. This text file is stored on the Amazon Linux 2 server as seen in Fig. 12(a).

(a)   **(b)**

Fig. 12. (a) Text file of predicted letters saved on cloud server (b) MP3 widget to play converted audio file

Once the user clicks stop sign detection button, the stored text file is converted to a playable MP3 audio file consisting of the text to speech audio. This happens with the help of Google Text to Speech python module (gTTS). Once the text file is converted to a playable MP3 audio file the website UI changes to display a MP3 widget to play the audio out aloud for communication purposes as seen in Fig. 12(b).

Figure 13(a) illustrates the training and testing accuracy that were achieved by our dataset. The Random Forest model was found to make highly accurate prediction over extensive training. Figure 13(b) illustrates the cost efficiency between many cloud providers and on-premise solutions. It can be clearly seen that Amazon Web Services and other cloud providers have higher performance scores compared to On-Premise solutions with a much cheaper cost making it a highly preferred method of website deployment.

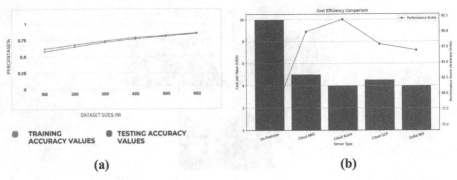

Fig. 13. (a) Training and Testing Accuracy of Model. (b) Comparison between Cost Efficiency of Cloud service with On-Premise Services

6   Conclusion

Communication plays a pivotal role in the daily lives of human beings as it shapes our interactions, relationships and experiences. Our Cloud-Deployed Sign Language Detection website provides a seamless interface that empowers users to communicate with ease and also includes impaired individuals into the digital era. Integrating Machine Learning Models like Random Forest Classifier and Cloud-Computing we have come up with an efficient and simple solution to detect sign language gestures in real-time and convert these predicted gestures to text and store them in a text file which is later converted to a playable audio file that can speak out the text thereby enabling impaired individuals with speech abilities to communicate. Through rigorous testing and experimentation, the accuracy of the model was found to be around 98.2% and the website was deployed on an Amazon Linux 2 AMI server with 8 GB RAM and 2 CPU cores for processing which helped deploy the website within 3 s. Hence this research paper has the potential to revolutionize the way impaired individuals communicate and with the added capabilities of Cloud Computing these solutions can be deployed and maintained at a cheaper cost, with the added benefit of universal accessibility.

References

1. Katoch, S., Singh, V., Tiwary, U.S.: Indian sign language recognition system using SURF with SVM and CNN. Array **14**, 100141 (2022)
2. Adithya, V., Vinod, P.R., Gopalakrishnan, U.: Artificial neural network based method for Indian sign language recognition. In: 2013 IEEE Conference on Information & Communication Technologies, pp. 1080–1085. IEEE (2013)
3. Oudah, M., Al-Naji, A., Chahl, J.: Hand gesture recognition based on computer vision: a review of techniques. J. Imaging **6**(8), 73 (2020)
4. Sonare, B., Padgal, A., Gaikwad, Y., Patil, A.: Video-based sign language translation system using machine learning. In: 2021 2nd International Conference for Emerging Technology (INCET), pp. 1–4. IEEE (2021)
5. Mariappan, H.M., Gomathi, V.: Real-time recognition of Indian sign language. In: 2019 International Conference on Computational Intelligence in Data Science (ICCIDS), pp. 1–6. IEEE (2019)

6. Shukor, A.Z., et al.: A new data glove approach for Malaysian sign language detection. Procedia Comput. Sci. **76**, 60–67 (2015)
7. Konwar, A.S., Sagarika Borah, B., Tuithung, C.T.: An American sign language detection system using HSV color model and edge detection. In: 2014 International Conference on Communication and Signal Processing, pp. 743–747. IEEE (2014)
8. Bendarkar, D., Somase, P., Rebari, P., Paturkar, R., Khan, A.: Web based recognition and translation of American sign language with CNN and RNN, pp. 34–50 (2021)
9. Bantupalli, K., Xie, Y.: American sign language recognition using deep learning and computer vision. In: 2018 IEEE International Conference on Big Data (Big Data), pp. 4896–4899. IEEE (2018)
10. Adaloglou, N., et al.: A comprehensive study on deep learning-based methods for sign language recognition. IEEE Trans. Multimed. **24**, 1750–1762 (2021)
11. Al-Qurishi, M., Khalid, T., Souissi, R.: Deep learning for sign language recognition: current techniques, benchmarks, and open issues. IEEE Access **9**, 126917–126951 (2021)
12. Zheng, L., Liang, B., Jiang, A.: Recent advances of deep learning for sign language recognition. In: 2017 International Conference on Digital Image Computing: Techniques and Applications (DICTA), pp. 1–7. IEEE (2017)
13. Mittal, A., Kumar, P., Roy, P.P., Balasubramanian, R., Chaudhuri, B.B.: A modified LSTM model for continuous sign language recognition using leap motion. IEEE Sens. J. **19**(16), 7056–7063 (2019)
14. Chandra, M.M., Rajkumar, S., Kumar, L.S.: Sign languages to speech conversion prototype using the SVM classifier. In: 2019 IEEE Region 10 Conference (TENCON), TENCON 2019, pp. 1803–1807. IEEE (2019)
15. Ojha, A., Pandey, A., Maurya, S., Thakur, A., Dayananda, P.: Sign language to text and speech translation in real time using convolutional neural network. Int. J. Eng. Res. Technol. (IJERT) **8**(15), 191–196 (2020)

Cognitive Computing and its Applications

Machine Learning Approaches for Analysing Sentiment in Reviews on Massive Open Online Courses

Apurva Jain[1]([✉]), Manisha[1], Basant Agarwal[2], and Parikshit Kishor Singh[3]

[1] Department of CSE, Indian Institute of Information Technology Kota, Kota 325003, Rajasthan, India
{2019kucp1098,2021kpad1004}@iiitkota.ac.in
[2] Department of CSE, Central University of Rajasthan, Ajmer 305817, Rajasthan, India
basant@curaj.ac.in
[3] Department of ECE, Indian Institute of Information Technology Kota, Kota 325003, Rajasthan, India
parikshit@iiitkota.ac.in

Abstract. With the advancement of online learning, it is observed that there is an exponential growth of data and information across the internet which leads the students to enroll for Massive Open Online Courses (MOOC) [25]. Regardless, users struggle with choosing the right course given its credibility and complementary aspects. Many MOOC sites provide a review option for users' feedback. Students generally opt for any course based on user ratings and feedback comments available on MOOC. Therefore, analyzing online reviews gives more exhaustive feedback of a course rather than assessing quantified ratings given by users. To predict the sentiment represented in a piece of text, we employed different machine learning models like convolutional neural networks (CNN), recurrent neural network (RNN), long short term memory (LSTM), etc. to perform comparative sentiment analysis by drawing an analogy between reviews and ratings data This paper provides insights for the user engagement and satisfaction and offers insightful analysis of MOOC learner's experience and recommendations for pertinent course selection.

Keywords: Massive Open Online Courses(MOOC) · Sentiment analysis

1 Introduction

E-learning, which symbolises the future of the teaching and learning processes, is a response to the changing educational needs of society and a significant development in information and communication technologies (ICT) [1, 2]. Due to the increase in digitalization and interactivity in higher education over the past several years, online education has become more common than ever. According to statistics, the online learning sector has risen by 900 percent since 2000 and is predicted to continue growing in the years to come. Over the years, the standard of online learning has increased, and as a result, so has its reputation.

V. N. M. Aradhya et al. (Eds.): CCIP 2023, CCIS 2044, pp. 111–122, 2024.
https://doi.org/10.1007/978-3-031-60725-7_9

The feedback remarks were mirrored in another study revealed the average sentiment expressed through online posts. Beginners, the MOOC's target audience, were more happy about the course than experienced participants, owing to the extra assistance they received. Many skilled participants expected to learn about issues outside the scope of the MOOC. According to the research, MOOC designers should think about employing sentiment analysis to analyse student input and inform MOOC structure [3]. The observations suggest that learners are extremely satisfied with the course educator, engagement, and course material, however they are dissatisfied with course evaluation and learning platform health. This study also reflects the need for real-time analysis of student feedback [4, 5]. Although MOOCs provide a lot of liberty in terms of learning, there are a few difficulties that students and course owners must deal with. Students face challenges such as a lack of incentive, time constraints, other commitments, difficulty levels, a lack of focus on forums, insufficient prior knowledge, mere shortage of time or disliking the course material, while tutors face issues such as a lack of responses in online discussions, monotonous teaching, or monetary demands [6].

These factors either result in the task not being completed or in falling out of the course. Despite MOOCs' widespread acceptance, their high attrition/drop rate continues to be a problem. With nearly 16,300 MOOCs, the majority of them may barely attract one or two thousand students annually, even on the best platforms [7]. Evaluating the opinions of learners taking the course is a crucial reason behind the high dropout rates. However, it is impossible to read and comprehend every remark due to the multitude of users present on MOOC [8]. Additionally, the star ratings provided in the feedback forms frequently differ from the actual feedback provided by users, which further obscures the true assessment of the MOOC. To tackle such an issue, there are many prediction techniques that have been implemented so that it is attainable to retain and attract new students.

Sentiment analysis can be utilised as a first step in identifying complicated emotions like excitement, frustration, or boredom [9]. Further, SA of discussion forum posts is utilised for collecting student feedback so that course administrators are aware of unsatisfied students. In order to extract these opinions, sentiment analysis of the forum posts is implemented which assists in helping MOOC owners understand the mindset of learners towards their course. Based on these extracted opinions, MOOC administrators can decide the next steps to take to try and reduce attrition. The concept of sentiment analysis is a component of Natural Language Processing (NLP) that allows sentimental applications to extract informative texts and facts. [10] The goal of Natural Language Processing (NLP) is to train machines to interpret human-written statements in common language. Hence, the NLP technique has been established to facilitate and satisfy communication with machines using natural language models [11].

2   Related Work

Baohua Su suggested a method to analyze the comments on online courses according to a hierarchical attention mechanism in [12] by using deep learning technology and beginning with the sentiment analysis of online course review text. The technique uses CNN to obtain local sentiment information and LSTM to get the text's hidden representation, enriching the extracted information. Then, the global information extracted by the

LSTM and by the CNN, respectively, are screened by gate mechanisms. The hierarchical attention mechanism lessens the impact of noise on emotional polarity judgements, as well as also lessens the interference of the words with intense sentiment information on the model judgement.

Additionally, Chen et al. (2020) used a cutting-edge structural topic modelling technique to examine 1,920 reviews of 339 computer science courses in order to identify the main issues the learners faced. From their data collection, they discovered that 64.2% of total reviews were rated five stars, while just 16.7% were rated four stars, demonstrating blatantly biased rating values [12, 13].

In the paper [14], opinion examination has been taken into account using either AI strategies or feeling dictionaries. The semantic direction of words, sentences, or phrases is still up for debate in dictionary-based opinion analysis for each sentence. Again, the AI method uses SVM and Naive Bayes calculations to organise the text. It has been shown that the WSD's W-Lexicon-based approach is more accurate [15].

Since sentiment categorization and sarcasm detection are connected, the authors of [16] suggested a multitask learning-based approach that uses a deep neural network. Only 800 or fewer samples of 1-2 sentences total were included in the dataset collection [17]. The 3W-CNN is a suggested combination of deep learning techniques and conventional feature-based techniques [18]. The quality of CNN results are categorised using a confidence divider component, and then the NB-SVM is used to recategorize predictions with low confidence.

Word embedding has recently been found to be helpful for online course reviews, according to researchers [19]. They demonstrated that embeddings taught on smaller specific resource online courses are more efficient than those educated on larger general resource online courses. The researchers in [20] assessed 6393 students who were enrolled in 249 MOOC courses from Class Central and their perception of (satisfaction) with the course. Based on the evaluation, it has been determined that the instructor, assessment methods, schedule, and content play significant roles in predicting students' satisfaction. Conversely, factors such as course duration, major, workload, and difficulty do not significantly contribute to students' perception of satisfaction.

The number of students that drop out each day and sentiment ratio, which was calculated according to daily forum posts, were found to be correlated by the author in [21]. The effect of sentiment on reduction over time on a user-level was assessed. Using a straightforward collective sentiment analysis, the author of this work found a substantial association between the sentiment expressed in course forum postings and the quantity of students who abandon the course. The author used sentiment analysis to analyze drop out behavior in three MOOCs. However, as one looks at practices for expressing sentiment inside that particular course environment, it has been observed that the association of sentiment with dropout within a certain course makes sense. Reports on sentiment may therefore be useful if they also give consumers instances of the ways the sentiment phrases are commonly used in that course.

A method to determine the polarity and denial of assertions has been proposed by the authors [22]. The user can form opinions based on the System's summary result. The sentiment orientation techniques outperformed the AIRC sentiment analyzer system. For people who have seen another person's review of a good or service, sentiment analysis is essential. This can be used by users to list the advantages and disadvantages of their goods or services.

Tan et al. [19] and Yulia Yu. Dyulicheva [23] analysed the use of the random forest and the linear regression model to look at how demographic data and family background factors, high school factors, academic achievement of students, and their non-cognitive behavior influence students' involvement in engineering learning choice.

3   Proposed Work

In this paper, we compare different machine learning models for expression of sentiments in reviews of Massive Open Online Course(MOOC). As shown in Fig. 1, the proposed work make use of the technique described below and multiple ML training models on Coursera datasets. We provide details of each of the step in detail in subsequent sections.

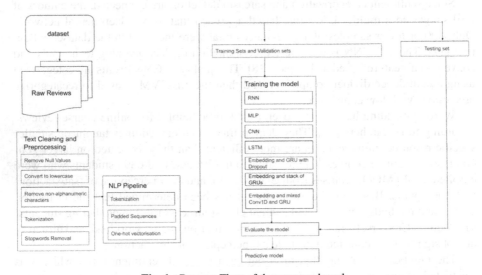

Fig. 1. Process Flow of the proposed work

3.1   Dataset

A comparative sentiment analysis using machine learning models was conducted on dataset acquired from two distinct data segment of Coursera courses, one consisting the reviews of Coursera and other listing all the courses available on the platform. These datasets contain information about courses offered on Coursera and the corresponding learner reviews. To perform a comprehensive analysis, the datasets were integrated based on the shared indexes. This enabled the association of each review with its respective course and facilitated a holistic examination of sentiment. Integrated dataset comprises eight columns, providing essential information about reviews, reviewers, review dates, ratings, course identifiers, names, institutions, and URLs.

Figure 1 illustrates the distribution of ratings observed in the dataset. Notably, reviews with a rating of 3 stars or lower constitute only 5.62% of the total, while 78.79% have 5-star ratings and 15.58% have 4-star ratings. This distribution indicates a significant bias toward positive ratings, with 95.4% of all reviews being highly positive. The prevalence of 5-star ratings reveals an imbalance and skew towards positive sentiments, emphasizing the need for alternative course selection models (Fig. 2).

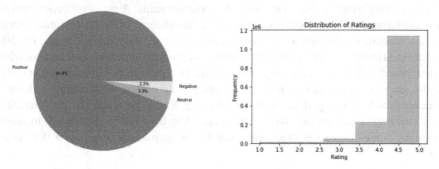

Fig. 2. Frequency analysis

3.2 Methodology

This section outlines the steps that were used to conduct the sentiment analysis research.

Data Cleaning and Preprocessing. The reviews underwent a number of vital data cleaning and preprocessing [24] processes before the sentiment analysis. In order to provide consistent analysis regardless of the letter case used in it, reviews were first transformed to lowercase. Thereafter, non-alphanumeric characters were eliminated from it since they can produce noise and do not significantly contribute to sentiment analysis. Transformed reviews were next subjected to the tokenization process, which divides the text into tokens, or individual words. Specific filtering criteria were used to verify the dataset's accuracy and reliability. The dataset was cleaned up by eliminating any rows with blank or incorrect ratings. This stage ensured a more thorough and reliable analysis by removing any incomplete or dubious reviews.

Stopword elimination was performed in order to improve the data's quality. Stopwords are often employed as words that have little or no significance in sentiment analysis (e.g., "and," "the," and "is"). Hence, these were eliminated, and more emphasis was placed on more crucial and sentimental words. Lemmatization and stemming methods were also used to further refine the data. Stemming, which entailed reducing words to their fundamental or root form, was helpful in minimising word variants. While, lemmatization attempted to return words to their dictionary or canonical form. Lemmatization and stemming ensured a more uniform representation of words, allowing for far more accurate sentiment analysis. Filtering the dataset allowed focusing on reviews exclusively with credible ratings, which raised the accuracy of the sentiment analysis results.

NLP Pipeline. Processing and analysis of text data are done using a set of stages called an NLP pipeline. The key process in this research's NLP pipeline was tokenization, which involved using the Keras library's Tokenizer class to turn textual data specifically, reviews into tokenized sequences of numbers. By assigning an integer value to each distinct token, the Tokenizer class made it easier to create a vocabulary. The text came across pre-processing, like lowercase conversion and the removal of non-alphanumeric letters, before tokenization. Next, Word tokenizer separated the text into individual words while removing frequent stopwords with no semantic value. A set of tokenized reviews that were represented as integer sequences were the outcome of the tokenization process [25]. Each number in the series was a unique token from the existing dictionary. The NLP pipeline used in our research was built on the basis of this numerical representation, which made it possible for later processing and analysis. Due to the inherent variation in review lengths, the next step sequence padding sought to guarantee uniform sequence lengths. Sequences were either padded or trimmed using Keras' to reach the predetermined maximum length. To maintain data integrity, padding involved adding tokens to shorter sequences while truncation made sure that longer sequences adhered to the desired length.

NLP pipeline's final phase, one-hot vectorization, included encoding categorical target labels as binary vectors, specifically ratings. This encoding aided the training of machine learning model. Each category, or set of ratings, was represented as a binary vector by one-hot vectorization. Ratings from 1 to 5 were represented in this study as binary vectors with a length of 5. Each binary vector had a value of 1, with all other elements set to 0, at the index corresponding to the rating. ML model was able to understand and handle classified ratings as numerical inputs due to this encoding approach. Next, the target labels or ratings were effectively transformed using Keras, into the corresponding one-hot vector representation in order to carry out one-hot vectorization. The obtained one-hot vectors were used as the target variable in ML model's training phase. The model was able to distinguish between different rating categories by encoding ratings as one-hot vectors, and it could use acquired information to use learnt patterns to produce precise predictions.

Model Architecture. An important aspect of sentiment analysis can be divided into two categories: lexicon-based approaches and corpus-based approaches. Lexicon- based methods typically employ a dictionary of sentiment words and phrases, as well as intensification and negation, to compute a sentiment score for each text.

Sentiment classification is treated by corpus-based approaches as a special case of the text categorization problem that makes use of machine learning [26].

We compare different model architectures for sentiment analysis such as CNN, RNN, LSTM, GRU, and variants of LSTM and GRU. The multi-layer perceptron (MLP) model is a simple multi-layer perceptron that ignores sequence information. To discover patterns related to sentiment in the reviews, it uses fully connected layers [27]. Convolutional Neural Network (CNN) is frequently used for text review sentiment analysis when taken into account the local patterns and sequential information contained within the text data [25]. Recurrent neural network layers are used by the RNN model to process sequential data. It should be appropriate for sentiment analysis since it captures temporal dependencies in the tokenized reviews. Based on the sequencing of the words, RNNs can discover patterns related to various sentiment labels [14]. The embedding layers used in the LSTM and GRU models, as well as their modifications, learn the semantic meaning of words from the reviews. Long-term dependencies and temporal information are exceptionally well captured and retained by these models. Moreover, the stacked GRU layers and combined Conv1D and GRU layers strive to combine all the advantages of both convolutional and recurrent layers.

Experimental Settings. The dataset was split into training, testing, and validation sets using a 60:20:20 ratio, respectively, to conduct the analysis. This division technique assures adequate data for models' training as well as facilitates fair evaluation and validation. The data splitting procedure entailed randomly mixing the dataset and then grouping it into three subsets: training, testing, and validation. 60% of the data were in the training set, whereas 20% of the data were in each of the testing and validation sets. To learn the patterns and relationships present in the data, the models were trained using the training set. The models' performance on unseen data was evaluated using the testing set suggesting an accurate evaluation of their ability for generalisation. Additionally, the models' hyperparameters were adjusted and optimised for performance using the validation set to give them the best possible outcomes. The use of this 60:20:20 data splitting technique allowed for a balanced distribution of data for training, testing, and validation while still ensuring an extensive and unbiased evaluation of the models' performance. Dropout is applied to improve regularisation while minimising overfitting, with a rate of 0.2. The Adam optimizer, which dynamically adjusts the learning rate during training to enhance convergence and weight updates, is employed to construct the models. Early prevention and model checkpoint callbacks are implemented to avoid overfitting and guarantee model generalisation. The early stopping callback keeps track of the model's effectiveness on a validation set and stops training if no progress is made after a predetermined number of epochs.

Model Evaluation. Model Evaluation. In order to determine the model's efficacy in sentiment analysis of MOOC reviews, its performance was thoroughly assessed using the testing data. Accuracy, loss, precision, recall, and F1 score were used as metrics to evaluate the model's performance comprehensively [28].

$$Accuracy = \frac{TP + TN}{TP + TN + FP + FN}$$

- TP is the number of true positive predictions
- TN is the number of true negative predictions
- FP is the number of false positive predictions
- FN is the number of false negative predictions

The precision, recall, and F1 scores were used to analyse the model's capability to classify reviews into the relevant sentiment categories [29].

$$Precision = \frac{TP}{TP + FP}$$

Recall, often referred to as sensitivity or true positive rate, is the ratio of the number of real positive instances that the model accurately identified. It can be calculated as the proportion of accurate positive predictions to all positive instances [28].

$$Recall = \frac{TP}{TP + FN}$$

The F1 score, which is a harmonic mean of precision and recall, offers a fair evaluation of the model's performance by taking into account both metrics. It provides a single metric that combines recall and precision, making it possible to conduct an in-depth analysis.

$$F1score = \frac{2 \cdot (Precision \cdot Recall)}{Precision + Recall}$$

4   Results and Discussions

In the paper, multiple model architectures for sentiment analysis of MOOC reviews were evaluated. The results of the experiments are shown in the following Table 1 and Figs. 3, 4 and 5.

Table 1. Performance of different models

Model	Accuracy	Precision	Recall	F1-score
RNN	0.90	0.89	0.90	0.89
MLP	0.93	0.93	0.93	0.93
CNN	0.90	0.90	0.90	0.87
Embedding and LSTM	0.89	0.89	0.88	0.89
Embedding and GRU	0.86	0.87	0.88	0.87
Embedding and GRU with dropout	0.88	0.87	0.88	0.86
Embedding and stack of GRUs	0.88	0.87	0.89	0.88
Embedding and mixed Conv1D and GRU	0.92	0.92	0.92	0.91

The MLP model got the greatest accuracy of 0.93 based on the experimental findings, indicating its efficacy in correctly categorizing the sentiment of MOOC reviews. A 0.90 accuracy was attained by the CNN model, which likewise performed well. These models use various strategies, with CNN using convolutional layers for pattern extraction and MLP concentrating on non-sequential data processing. Similar to the CNN model, the RNN model, which makes use of recurrent connections to determine sequential relationships, attained an accuracy of 0.90. This demonstrates how well RNN capture temporal information and contextual dependencies in tasks involving sentiment analysis. The accuracy of Embedding and LSTM model was 0.89, while that of the Embedding

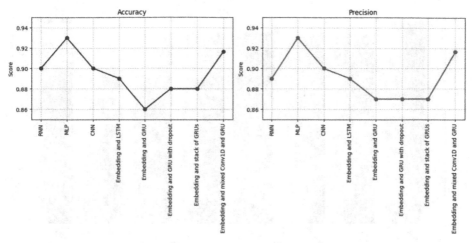

Fig. 3. Performance of different models with respect to Accuracy and Precision

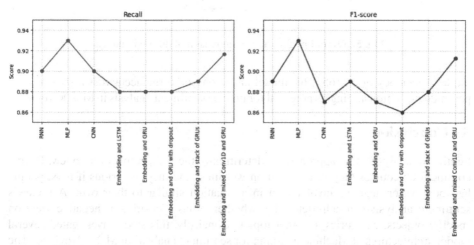

Fig. 4. Performance of different models with respect to Recall and F1 score

and GRU model was 0.86 among the models using recurrent architectures. These findings imply that, in comparison to GRU-based models, LSTM-based models may be more suitable for detecting long-term dependencies in sequential data. The results also show that dropout regularization caused the performance of both the Embedding and GRU with dropout model to somewhat degrade, with an accuracy of 0.88. This shows that in this particular job, the dropout strategy may not be as successful in preventing overfitting. Additionally, the accuracy of the embedding and stack of GRUs model was 0.88, highlighting the potential advantages of utilising several GRU layers to identify intricate patterns in textual data. Convolutional and recurrent layers are combined effectively for sentiment analysis, as shown by the Embedding and mixed Conv1D and GRU

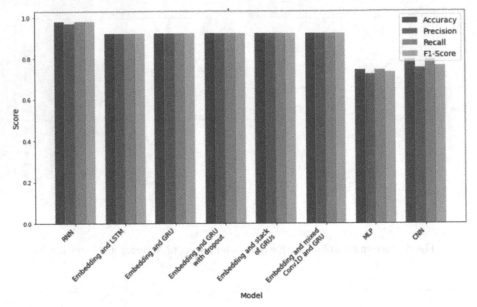

Fig. 5. Overall performance comparison of different models

model's accuracy of 0.9165. This model has strong performance across all assessment parameters, demonstrating its potential for precise sentiment analysis in MOOC reviews.

5 Conclusion

Sentiment analysis is an approach for determining the perspective of a review. People comment on courses they've attended on websites, and they're curious if most people had positive or negative involvement in a situation similar to their own. A review's sentiment analysis can help determine whether it has a positive or negative view on specific objects, categories, or other topics. Concisely, this study investigated several model architectures of Machine Learning for sentiment analysis of MOOC reviews. The experimental findings show that different model arrangements produce varying levels of performance, with the CNN, MLP and Embedding models, along with the combined Conv1D and GRU models.

Acknowledgement. This work was generously supported by RajComp Info Services Ltd (RISL), Government of Rajasthan under the project titled "Technology dissemination through massive open online courses for skill enhancement and supporting higher education with advanced learning analytics for effective teaching".

References

1. Bhat,M., Qadri, M., Beg, N.A., Kundroo, M., Ahanger, N., Agarwal, B.: Sentiment analysis of the social media response on the COVID19 outbreak. Brain Behav. Immun. https://doi.org/10.1016/j.bbi.2020.05.006

2. Nefedova,N.: Investigating MOOCs with the use of sentiment analysis of learners' feedback, p. 68 (2022)
3. Lundqvist, K., Liyanagunawardena, T., Starkey, L.: Evaluation of student feedback within a MOOC using sentiment analysis and target groups. Int. Rev. Res. Open Distrib. Learn. 21(3), 140–156 (2020)
4. Agarwal, B.: Financial sentiment analysis model utilizing knowledge-base and domain-specific representation. Multimedia Tools Appl. 82, 8899–8920 (2023). https://doi.org/10.1007/s11042-022-12181-y
5. Yan, X., Li, G., Li, Q., Chen, J., Chen, W., Xia, F.: Sentiment analysis on massive open online course evaluation. In: 2021 International Conference on Neuromorphic Computing (ICNC) (2021). https://doi.org/10.1109/ICNC52316.2021.9608255
6. Soukaina, S., El Miloud, S., Azzouzi, S., El Hassan, C.M.: Quality approach to analyze the causes of failures in MOOC. In: 5th International Conference on Cloud Computing and Artificial Intelligence (2020). https://doi.org/10.1109/CloudTech49835.2020.9365904
7. Li, L., Johnson, J., Aarhus, W., Shah, D.: Key factors in MOOC pedagogy based on NLP sentiment analysis of learner reviews: what makes a hit. Comput. Educ. 176, 104354 (2022). https://doi.org/10.1016/j.compedu.2021.104354
8. Marfani, H., Hina, S., Tabassum, H.: Analysis of learners' sentiments on MOOC forums using natural language processing techniques. In: 2022 3rd International Conference on Innovations in Computer Science & Software Engineering (ICONICS) (2022). https://doi.org/10.1109/ICONICS56716.2022.10100401
9. Moreno-Marcos, P.M., Alario-Hoyos, C., Muñoz-Merino, P.J., Estévez-Ayres, I., Kloos, C.D.: Sentiment analysis in MOOCs: a case study. In: Proceedings of 2018 IEEE Global Engineering Education Conference (EDUCON2018), 17–20 April 2018, Santa Cruz de Tenerife, Canary Islands, Spain, pp. 1489–1496 (2018). https://doi.org/10.1109/EDUCON.2018.8363409
10. Agarwal, B., Agarwal, A., Harjule, P., Rahman, A.: Understanding the intent behind sharing misinformation on social media. J. Exp. Theor. Artif. Intell. (2022). https://doi.org/10.1080/0952813X.2021.1960637
11. Xu, G., et al.: Chinese text sentiment analysis based on extended sentiment dictionary. IEEE Access (2019). https://doi.org/10.1109/ACCESS.2019.2907772
12. Singh, A.K., Kumar, S., Bhushan, S., Kumar, P., Vashishtha, A.: A Proportional sentiment analysis of MOOCs course reviews using supervised learning algorithms, pp. 501–506 (2021). https://doi.org/10.18280/isi.260510
13. Gomez, M.J., Calderón, M., Sánchez, V., Clemente, F.J.G., Ruipérez-Valiente, J.A.: Large scale analysis of open MOOC reviews to support learners' course selection. Expert Syst. Appl. 210, 118400 (2022)
14. Agarwal, B., Mittal, N.: Semantic feature clustering for sentiment analysis of English reviews. IETE J. Res. 60(6), 414–422 (2014)
15. Daniel, D., Meena, J.: Deep learning-based hybrid sentiment analysis with feature selection using optimization algorithm. Multimedia Tools Appl. 82, 1–24 (2023). https://doi.org/10.1007/s11042-023-14767-6
16. Deng, R., Benckendorff, P.: What are the key themes associated with the positive learning experience in MOOCs? An empirical investigation of learners' ratings and reviews 18, 9 (2021). https://doi.org/10.1186/s41239-021-00244-3
17. Kastrati, Z., Imran, A.S., Kurti, A.: Weakly supervised frame-work for aspect-based sentiment analysis on students' reviews of MOOCs. IEEE Access (2020). https://doi.org/10.1109/ACCESS.2020.3000739
18. Wen, M., et al.: Sentiment analysis in MOOC discussion forums: what does it tell us? In: Educational data mining 2014. Citeseer (2014)

19. Chen, X., Zou, D., Xie, H., Cheng, G.: What Are MOOCs learners' Concerns? Text analysis of reviews for computer science courses. In: Nah, Y., Kim, C., Kim, S.Y., Moon, Y.S., Whang, S.E. (eds.) Database Systems for Advanced Applications. DASFAA 2020 International Workshops. Lecture Notes in Computer Science(), vol. 12115. Springer, Cham (2020). https://doi.org/10.1007/978-3-030-59413-8_6

20. Chang, Y.C., et al.: Developing a data-driven learning interest recommendation system to promoting self-paced learning on MOOCs. In: 2016 IEEE 16th International Conference on Advanced Learning Technologies, pp. 23–25. IEEE (2016)

21. Majumder, N., Poria, S., Peng, H., Chhaya, N., Cambria, E., Gelbukh, A.: Sentiment and sarcasm classification with multitask learning. IEEE Intell. Syst. **34**(3), 38–43 (2019). https://doi.org/10.48550/arXiv.1901.08014

22. Gomez, M.J., Calderón, M., Sánchez, V., Clemente, F.J.G., Ruipérez-Valiente, J.A.: Large scale analysis of open MOOC reviews to support learners' course selection. Expert Syst. Appl. 210, 118400 (2022). https://doi.org/10.1016/j.eswa.2022.118400, https://doi.org/10.48550/arXiv.2201.06967

23. Dyulicheva, Y., Bilashova, E.: Learning analytics of MOOCs based on natural language processing. In: 4th Workshop for Young Scientists in Computer Science & Software Engineering, Kryvyi Rih, Ukraine (2021)

24. Enduri, M.K., et al.: Comparative study on sentimental analysis using machine learning techniques. Mehran Univ. Res. J. Eng. Technol. **42**, 207 (2023). https://doi.org/10.22581/muet1982.2301.19

25. Elrashidy, M., Gaffer, A., El-Fishawy, N., Aslan, H., Khodeir, N.: New weighted BERT features and multi-CNN models to enhance the performance of MOOC posts classification. Neural Comput. Appl. **35**, 1–15 (2023). https://doi.org/10.1007/s00521-023-08673-z

26. Zhang, Y., Zhang, Z., Miao, D., Wang, J.: Three-way enhanced convolutional neural networks for sentence-level sentiment classification. Inf. Sci. **477**, 55 (2018). https://doi.org/10.1016/j.ins.2018.10.030

27. Onan, A.: Sentiment analysis on massive open online course evaluations: a text mining and deep learning approach. Comput. Appl. Eng. Educ. **29**, 572 (2020). https://doi.org/10.1002/cae.22253

28. Wang, C., Huang, S., Zhou, Y.: Sentiment analysis of MOOC reviews via ALBERT-BiLSTM model. In: MATEC Web Conference, vol. 336, p. 05008 (2021)

29. Alsolami, F.J.: A hybrid approach for dropout prediction of MOOC students using machine learning. IJCSNS Int. J. Comput. Sci. Netw. Secur. **20**(5), 54–63 (2020)

Deep Belief Network Optimization Using PSOGAA Algorithm for Efficient Crop Recommendation

J. Madhuri[1]([⊠]) [iD], M. Indiramma[2] [iD], and N. Nagarathna[2]

[1] Department of Computer Science and Engineering, Bangalore Institute of Technology, Bangalore, India
madhurij@bit-bangalore.edu.in

[2] Department of Computer Science and Engineering, B.M.S. College of Engineering, Bangalore, India

Abstract. The agricultural sector plays a crucial role in the development of an emerging economy, providing employment to a significant portion of the population. Selecting the most suitable crops based on specific weather and soil conditions is vital to maximize yield and ensure profitability for farmers, contributing to global food security. In this context, this paper introduces a crop recommendation model utilizing Deep Belief Networks (DBN), fine-tuned by a hybrid optimization approach combining Genetic Algorithm (GA), Particle Swarm Optimization (PSO), and Adam optimization. To enhance the efficiency of DBN-based crop recommendation model, this paper proposes the PSOGAA algorithm, a novel hybrid optimization algorithm designed to optimize the DBN's network structure. Subsequently, genetic operators featuring self-adjusting crossover and mutation probabilities are applied to further refine the PSO and explore a global optimization solution. Ultimately, this global optimization solution is employed to construct the network structure of the crop recommendation model.

Experimental results demonstrate the superior performance of the proposed algorithm compared to other DBN optimization techniques, showcasing an average classification accuracy improvement of at least 2.3%. This emphasizes the effectiveness of the PSOGAA algorithm as an efficient DBN optimization technique.

Focusing on four major crops in India—rice, sugarcane, maize, and finger millet—the crop recommendation model's outcomes are compared with those of the DBN model optimized using alternative algorithms. The experimental findings highlight that the proposed hybrid optimization algorithm surpasses other optimizers, exhibiting enhanced accuracy in crop recommendations.

Keywords: Deep Belief Networks · Hybrid Optimization algorithms · Particle Swarm Optimization · Restricted Boltzmann Machines · Crop recommendation

1 Introduction

Agriculture sustainability is of great importance for global food production. Crop recommendation and yield prediction based on location-specific soil and weather characteristics are necessary for strengthening global food security [1]. Crop recommendation

V. N. M. Aradhya et al. (Eds.): CCIP 2023, CCIS 2044, pp. 123–137, 2024.
https://doi.org/10.1007/978-3-031-60725-7_10

is important because it helps farmers make informed decisions about what crops to grow, based on local climate, soil conditions, water availability, and market demand. Recommendations can improve crop yields, increase farmers' income, and reduce the risk of crop failure. Additionally, crop recommendations can help ensure food security by promoting the growth of crops well-suited to local conditions, and reducing dependence on imports [2]. Machine learning can analyze large amounts of data on weather patterns, soil conditions, and pest infestations to make predictions and inform decision-making processes. Machine Learning (ML) can also help detect and diagnose plant diseases, assist with precision farming, and improve supply chain management. ML techniques have enabled the creation of tools for recommendation systems, decision making systems, harvest predictions and various applications in agriculture sector [3, 4]. To create efficient agricultural applications there is a need to analyze the agricultural ecosystems by contantly monitoring different agricultural variables. This creates huge amounts of data that needs to be stored and processed in real time for some operations [5]. This data can be weather data collected on daily basis, soil data collected periodically, daily food price data. ML algorithms have been widely used in agriculture, and neural networks are one of the widely used algorithms as they can handle the relationship between the features more accurately [6]. Artificial Neural Networks(ANN) are used in agriculture to analyze large amounts of data and make predictions about various topics, such as crop yields, weather patterns, and pest infestations [7, 8]. But ANN architecture typically consists of two to three hidden layers, hence the capacity to establish the relationships between the different features is limited. Deep Learning(DL) is a more powerful form of machine learning that can automatically learn hierarchical representations from raw data without the need for manual feature engineering, making it particularly useful in applications where large amounts of data are available. DL is a subset of machine learning that uses artificial neural networks with multiple layers to extract hierarchical representations of data. Deep Belief Network (DBN) is a specific type of DL algorithm that use unsupervised learning to pretrain the layers of the neural network in a layer-wise manner. Once all the layers have been pretrained, the entire network is fine-tuned using supervised learning to perform the desired task. DBN is a form of ANN that uses a stacked generative model architecture with multiple layers of Restricted Boltzmann Machines (RBMs). With the increase in the number of RBMs in a DBN can fit any data distribution [9]. Once all the RBMs have been trained, the DBN can be fine-tuned using supervised learning techniques to perform classification or regression tasks [10–12]. Due to its stated benefits, including the quick interpretation and the capacity to represent higher-order network structures, the DBN has lately gained popularity in machine learning [13, 14].

One of the challenges associated with DBN architectures is the appropriate selection of their hyperparameters, such as the number of units per layer and the learning rate. The depth and quantity of neurons in each layer make up the network structure of DBN. Therefore, there are two ways to improve the DBN classifier's performance: by enhancing the network structure of DBN, which entails determining an appropriate DBN depth and the number of neurons in each layer. The complicated functions are approximated by learning a deep nonlinear network structure. These functions aim to increase classification and prediction accuracy [15]. There are fewer open documents for the DBN network structure optimization challenge. Since neural networks are most frequently used to solve non-convex problems, selecting an optimization technique to locate the global minimum in these networks is often difficult, since it requires estimating many of parameters in a high-dimensional search space. The traditional approach to hyper-parameter selection relies on trial and error, which leads to subjective interference, slow training, and lower classification accuracy and stability [16]. The significantly used update rule is Gradient Descent (GD) to update the weights associated with different layers when Backpropagation of error occurs in artificial neural networks and deep neural networks [17].

In recent research, appropriate parameters for such DL approaches has been attempted to be modeled as a metaheuristic optimization problem [18]. However, the field of DL based on meta-heuristic optimization is still in its embryonic stages in the context of providing optimal parameters [19]. In recent years, researchers have attempted to use swarm based metaheuristic algorithms and evolutionary algorithms to fine tune DBNs [20, 21]. Some studies in the literature have used nature-inspired metaheuristic methods. For example, [22] utilized the Gravitational Search Algorithm to optimize CNN hyper-parameters, while [23] used evolutionary optimization techniques to fine-tune recurrent networks. [24, 25] proposed Particle Swarm Optimization to select hyperparameters in RBMs, and [26] applied the Firefly Algorithm to fine-tune DBN hyperparameters. Similarly, [19] investigated various metaheuristic techniques for hyperparameter optimization in Deep Boltzmann Machines.

This study proposes a crop recommendation modelwhich is a combination of Adam optimization algorithm with Genetic algorithm and Particle Swarm Optimization (PSO-GAA) to optimize the hyperparameter of DBN such as number of layers, weights and biases, learning rate and batch size.

The contributions in the paper is as follows:

1. To build the Deep Belief Network (DBN) with optimized layers and weighted connection between layers to regularize the data flow to develop a crop recommendation model.
2. To fine tune DBN with evolutionary Genetic Algorithm (GA) and metaheuristic Particle Swarm Optimization (PSO) with Adam optimizer.
3. To compare the performance of proposed optimized recommendation system with other optimization algorithms.

The paper is organized as follows: Sect. 2 introduces the Restricted Boltzmann Machines (RBMs), DBNs, PSO, GA and gradient descent optimization. Sections 3 present the methodology, Sect. 4 discusses the experimental results, and Sect. 5 states the conclusions and future works.

2 Theoretical Background

2.1 Restricted Boltzmann Machine (RBM)

RBM is the variant of the Boltzmann machine developed by Paul Smolensk. RBM generally consists of two neural networks comprising a visible layer and hidden layers. Every unit in the visible layer consists of a symmetric weighted connection to the hidden layer units [27].

The purpose of the visible layer is to receive input data. In contrast, the purpose of the hidden layer is to detect input features of the data received based on weighted connections. The learning process of RBM is based on a contrastive divergence [28] training strategy to approximate the relationship of the network weight with its gradient. The gradient prioritizes the direction of learning to progress toward ideal network parameters. The input vectors of the visible layer and hidden layer are represented as v = {v_1, v_2, v_3 .....v_x} and h = { h_1, h_2, h_3 .....h_x} respectively. For the hyperparameter set $\theta = \{W, a_v, a_h\}$, the energy function can be given by,

$$E(h, v|\theta) = -\sum_{i=1}^{n} a_{vi} v_i - \sum_{j=1}^{m} a_{hj} h_j - \sum_{i=1,j=1}^{i=n,j=m} v_i h_j w_{ij} \tag{1}$$

where a_v and a_h are the bias values considered for the visible layer and hidden layer respectively, w_{ij} are the weights connecting the neurons in the visible layer and the hidden layer. The probability distribution function of the visible layer and hidden layer is given by,

$$P(v, h|\theta) = \frac{e^{-E(h,v|\theta)}}{\sum_{h,v} e^{-E(h,v|\theta)}} \tag{2}$$

The first part of RBM training starts with Gibbs sampling which is the most common method for probabilistic inference. Given the input vector v, the hidden values are calculated using,

$$P(h_j = 1|v, \theta) = \sigma(a_{hj} + \sum_{j=1}^{m} w_{ij} h_j) \tag{3}$$

Now with the hidden values, the new values for the visible layer are calculated using the,

$$P(v_i = 1|h, \theta) = \sigma(a_{vi} + \sum_{i=1}^{n} w_{ij} v_i) \tag{4}$$

$$\text{Where } \sigma(z) = \frac{1}{1 + e^{-z}} \text{ is the sigmoid function} \tag{5}$$

2.2 Deep Belief Networks

A Deep Belief Network (DBN) is constructed by stacking RBM layers [29]. Each RBM layer will be able to communicate with the previous layer as well as the following subsequent layers. DBN stacks multiple RBM with a simple calculation method that expresses the entire structure except for the last layer with conditional probability equation as shown in Eq. 6:

$$P(v, h_1, h_2 \ldots \ldots h_j) = \Pi(P(h_{j-1}|h_j)(P(h_{j-1}, h_j)) \tag{6}$$

where h_j represents the number of hidden layers.

Deep Belief Networks (DBN) are networks that consist of many two-layer networks, each layer of DBN performs the role of a hidden layer for the preceding node and as an

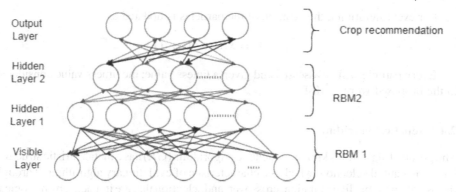

Fig. 1. Structure of DBN

input layer for the subsequent node except the first input layer and last output layer. The Deep Belief Network architecture is shown in Fig. 1.

DBN performs the pretraining that sequentially performs training from the input layer toward the upper layer. The weights of the DBN are initialized by the input data in the pretraining step. The fine-tuning of the weights in consecutive iterations is carried out with the Backpropagation algorithm (BP). The precision of the DBN model can be increased by defining the ideal weights between the connections of layers. Hence the subsequent layer is trained after the weights of the preceding layers are determined. BP adjusts the weights for the model for improved performance starting from the output layer towards the input layer.

2.3 Particle Swarm Optimization

Particle Swarm Optimization (PSO) is a heuristic optimization algorithm inspired by the movement patterns of birds flocking or fish schooling. PSO has been applied to optimize the weights of neural networks [30]. In PSO for neural network optimization, each particle represents a set of network weights, and the particle's velocity indicates the direction of weight update. The optimization process updates the velocity and position of each particle based on the particle's current position, and the best position seen by any particle in the swarm. All particles have velocities, which control the direction of particles, which are assessed by a fitness function to be optimized [31, 32]. To establish the most ideal particle features is to establish the best combination of weights.

The velocity of each particle is given by the Eq. 7

$$V(t + 1) = w * v(t) + c_1 r_1 \left(x' \text{pbest} - x(t) \right) + c_2 r_2 (\text{gbest} - x(t)) \qquad (7)$$

where r_1 and r_2 are the random weights assigned between 0 and 1 assisting in maintaining the magnitude of the steps; c1 and c2 are the cognitive and global components leading to convergence of the particles; and ω is the inertia weight, decreasing from 1 to nearly 0 linearly during training. Pbest is the personal best position of particle, gbest is the best position of the whole swarm.

For every iteration t, the position of the particles is updated as,

$$x(t + 1) = x(t) + v(t + 1)$$

Every particle will be assessed and given a fitness value; the fitness value considered in the proposed work is MSE.

2.4 Genetic Algorithm

The group of algorithms known as Genetic Algorithms (GA) has a metaheuristic structure based on natural selection, which is a characteristic of evolutionary algorithms. Through the use of operators like mutation, crossover, and selection that are impacted by biological evolution, GAs are utilized to produce optimal solutions to a variety of optimization and search issues [33, 34].

The problem of initializing weights of a DBN can be modeled using GA, where the individuals of the random population, will represent a possible solution. The population in GA consists of the following operators:

Selection:
This operator selects individuals from the current population to be used as parents for generating the next generation. By giving the population's weaker members the chance to participate in reproduction, which may aid in the discovery of fresh domains in the search space, this strategy ensures the effectiveness of global search.

Crossover:
Two members of the population participate in reproduction and create offspring through the genetic recombination of their chromosomes. The best characteristics of the parents are passed down to the offspring through genetic recombination, and because recombination is sometimes random, it may produce a better individual.

Mutation:
Mutation is a key factor in the introduction of abnormalities into the population during reproduction leading to benefit of the future population. The mutation operator in this model presents the fundamentals of global search, as the individual may be rated as either weaker or fitter based on their location in the search space.

2.5 Gradient Descent Algorithm (Adam)

Gradient descent optimization is used to find the minimum value error function based on an iterative technique. In supervised learning, gradient descent is also used to find the best parameter values. One of the best known optimizers in gradient descent is Adam, with the advantage of the change of the magnitudes of the parameter updates concerning the change of the gradient [35]. The Adam optimization algorithm is a gradient-based optimization method used in deep learning and other machine learning applications. It is an extension of the stochastic gradient descent (SGD) optimization method [36].

The Adam algorithm uses an adaptive learning rate, which changes dynamically during training based on the historical gradient information. The algorithm keeps track of an exponential moving average of the gradients and the squared gradients, and uses these averages to adjust the learning rate for each parameter. The equations for velocity, step magnitudes, and weight updating is shown in Eq. 8–10.

At each iteration t, update the first moment estimate m(t) and the second moment estimate v(t) as shown in Eq. 8 and 9 respectively:

$$m(t) = \beta 1 * m(t - 1) + (1 - \beta 1) * g \qquad (8)$$

$$v(t) = \beta 2 * v(t - 1) + (1 - \beta 2) * g^2 \qquad (9)$$

where $\beta 1$ and $\beta 2$ are hyperparameter that control the decay rates of the moving averages, and g is the gradient of the loss function with respect to the parameters. Weight update between the layers after each iteration is given by Eq. 10.

$$w(t) = w(t - 1) - \eta * \frac{m(t)}{\sqrt{v(t)} + \varepsilon} \qquad (10)$$

w(t) is the weight at each iteration t, η is the hyperparameter that controls the step size of the update, m(t) is the moving average of the gradient at t, v(t) is the moving average of the squared gradient at t, ε is a small constant added for numerical stability. These equations define the Adam optimization algorithm, which adjusts the learning rate for each parameter based on the historical gradient information.

3   Proposed PSOGAA Optimization Algorithm

In the DBN network structure, the number of neurons in the input layer depends on the number of attributes, and the number of neurons in the output layer depends on the output classes.

Optimizing hyper-parameters, in DBN construction is a crucial but challenging task that significantly impacts the performance of the DBN model. Genetic Algorithm (GA) is a biologically inspired optimization method that uses principles of evolution, such as selection, mutation, and crossover, to search for optimal solutions. Particle Swarm Optimization (PSO) is a swarm-based optimization technique that simulates the behavior of a swarm of particles moving in a search space to find optimal solutions. Particle Swarm Optimization (PSO) algorithm can converge faster in search spaces but can also lead to early convergence of models. However it does not provide gradient information needed to optimize the network parameters [37]. On the other hand, Adam optimizer is a gradient-based optimization algorithm that can effectively update the learning rate based on the gradients, but it may have slow convergence or get trapped in local minima. Therefore an optimization algorithm, hybrid of GA, PSO and Adam optimization known as PSOGAA has been proposed with the goal of discovering the most optimal hyperparameters. With the advantages of PSOGAA, such as efficient global search, fast convergence, and strong adaptability, the method optimizes the hyperparameter: neural unit bias, weight between the layers, the learning rate and batch size to expedite network training and improve the classification performance of the DBN model.

3.1 Proposed PSOGAA Optimization

Step 1: Begin by populating the initial set with N individuals.

Step 2: Assess the fitness of each individual in the population.

Step 3: Retain the best individual in the population as the personal best (pBest).

Step 4: Repeat until the stopping criterion is met:

    a. Select individuals for crossover using genetic operations.

    b. Apply crossover and mutation to create new offspring and enhance genetic diversity.

    c. Evaluate the fitness of the offspring.

    d. Update pBest if the offspring outperforms the previous best.

    e. Utilize Particle Swarm Optimization (PSO) to refine the parameters of the offspring.

    f. Implement Adam optimization to adapt the learning rate for the offspring:

$$m(t) = \beta1 * m(t-1) + (1-\beta1) * g$$
$$v(t) = \beta2 * v(t-1) + (1-\beta2) * g^2$$
$$w(t) = w(t-1) - \eta* m(t) / (sqrt(v(t)) +\varepsilon)$$

    g. Update the velocity of the offspring using PSO

$$v(t+1) = w * v(t) + c1 * rand * (pBest - x(t)) + c2 * rand * (gBest - x(t))$$

    h. Update the position of the offspring using PSO

$$x(t+1) = x(t) + v(t+1)$$

    i. Update pBest if the new position surpasses the previous best.

    j. Replace the least fit individuals in the population with the offspring.

Step 5: Conclude by returning pBest as the solution.

The proposed PSOGAA optimization algorithm is employed to determine the optimal parameters for a Deep Belief Network (DBN).

1. Initialize the population with N individuals.

    The population comprises diverse hyperparameter configurations for the DBN, encompassing factors such as the number of hidden layers, neurons in each layer, learning rate, and regularization strength.

2. Assess the fitness of each individual in the population.

    Individual fitness is determined by training the DBN with the hyperparameters represented by that individual, gauging its performance on a validation dataset using a suitable metric.

3. Record the best individual in the population (pbest).

    The individual with the highest fitness in the population is stored as the present optimal hyperparameter configuration (pbest).

4. Iterate until the stopping criterion is satisfied

    The algorithm iteratively generates new offspring by applying genetic operations like crossover and mutation to the best individuals in the population. These offspring undergo optimization using PSO to identify the optimal hyperparameters. Adam optimization is employed to dynamically adjust the learning rate during training.

    The velocity of the offspring is updated via PSO, and their position is adjusted accordingly. The best offspring is then compared to pbest, and if superior, pbest is updated. The weakest individuals in the population are replaced by the offspring to maintain the population size.

5. Conclude by returning pbest as the solution

4 Methodology

In this section we present the methodology to evaluate the performance of proposed PSOGAA optimization regarding hyperparameter selection for DBN and it is applied to build the crop recommendation model (Fig. 2).

4.1 DBN Model Selection

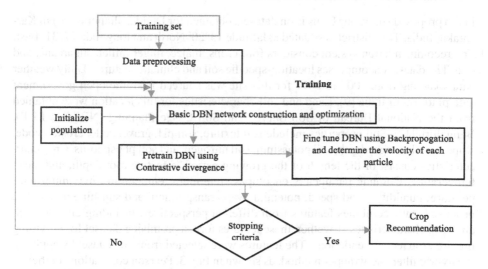

Fig. 2. Hybrid PSOGAA optimization based crop recommendation system

1. Initialize the GA population with a set of hyperparameter
2. Selection of fitness function: The fitness function used is mean square error between the actual value and predicted value.
3. Evaluate the fitness of each chromosome in the population by training and testing the DBN with those hyperparameters
4. Generate new candidate solutions by applying genetic operators such as crossover and mutation to the selected chromosomes
5. Evaluate the fitness of the new candidate solutions
6. Repeat the steps 3–5 until the termination criterion is met or the maximum number of generations is reached
7. Initialize the PSO swarm with a set of weight and bias parameters
8. Update the velocity and position of each particle based on its own best position and the best position of the swarm
9. Evaluate the fitness of the new particle positions
10. Repeat steps 8–9 until the termination criterion is met or the maximum number of iterations is reached
11. Select the best DBN obtained from the GA and PSO phases

12. Fine-tune the selected DBN using Adam optimization algorithm
13. Return the optimized DBN as the final solution.

The soil parameters, weather parameters and crop characteristics are the input to the DBN where the crop recommendation results are the output.

5 Experimentation and Results

5.1 Dataset and Evaluation Indicators

In the proposed study, our focus is on datasets obtained for Doddaballapur (dist.) in Karnataka, India. This district is situated at latitude $13°20'$ North and longitude $77°31'$ East. The recommendation system considers four crops: maize, finger millet, sugarcane, and rice. The dataset encompasses location-specific soil and climatic features. Daily weather data spanning from 2007 to 2017 for this site was sourced from the open government data platform in India [9]. Land and soil characteristics for this location were obtained from the National Bureau of Soil Survey and Soil Usage Planning (NBSS & LUP), Bengaluru [12]. Soil properties include soil texture, soil pH, gravel code, erosion code, slope, soil drainage, depth, soil potassium, soil nitrogen, and soil phosphorus. Crop characteristics consist of the length of the growing period, effective root depth, and mean temperature. Climatic parameters encompass minimum temperature, maximum temperature, humidity, wind speed, potential evapotranspiration, and sunshine hours. The proposed study combines features from different perspectives, including climate, soil, and crop characteristics. Together, these features form a promising dataset for providing precise crop recommendations. The features were selected from the dataset by applying the hybrid filter and wrapper method, as shown in Fig. 3. Pearson correlation coefficient for correlation-based feature selection filters out the features with low correlation. The filtered data is subjected to backward elimination wrapper method that selects the significant features based on p-value. The optimal dataset is obtained after being subjected to a hybrid feature selection [38].

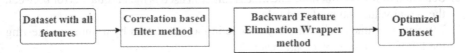

Fig. 3. Hybrid feature selection method

The optimal dataset obtained is segmented into three parts: a training dataset, a validation dataset, and a test dataset, streamlining the effective development of the recommendation model. In our investigation, climate data spanning the years 1972–2000 were integrated with soil and crop parameters for the training dataset. For the validation dataset, climate data from 2000–2010 were combined with corresponding soil and crop parameters, while the testing dataset involved climate data from 2010–2020 along with the respective soil and crop parameters.

In the context of the crop recommendation system, accuracy and Mean Square Error (MSE) serve as key indicators for evaluation. The classifier's performance is assessed using metrics such as true positive (TP), true negative (TN), false positive (FP), and false negative (FN) values obtained from the testing data. The classification accuracy of the model is computed by defining the ratio of correct predictions to the total number of predictions, as illustrated in Eq. 11.

$$Accuracy = \frac{TP}{TP + TN + FP + FN} \tag{11}$$

Mean Square Error (MSE) is a commonly used metric for evaluating the performance of classification model. It measures the average of the squared differences between the predicted and actual values for a set of data points as follows.

$$MSE = \frac{\sum_{t=1}^{n} (r_t - r_{pred})^2}{n} \tag{12}$$

5.2 Results

To validate the outcomes of the Deep Belief Network (DBN) constructed using the PSO-GAA optimization algorithm proposed in this paper, a comparative analysis is conducted against experimentation results obtained from DBN models optimized with Adagrad, Adam, and traditional PSO algorithms. For the evaluation of various optimization algorithms applied to DBN models using a crop recommendation dataset, we employed five distinct algorithms to train models on the training set and subsequently tested them on the testing set.

Tests were conducted on four DBN recommendation models to validate the enhancement in crop recommendation achieved by the proposed algorithm. Initial analysis using crop recommendation results from DBN with the Adam optimizer indicated a significant change in Mean Square Error (MSE) after 300 iterations. Consequently, the stopping criteria for training were set at N = 800 iterations and an error tolerance of ε = 0.001. Table 1 presents MSE values obtained for various optimization algorithms, along with the iterations required to reach the minimum MSE according to the stopping criteria. The PSOGAA optimizer achieves the minimum MSE after 580 iterations. These optimization algorithms involve an iterative improvement process.

Table 2 provides a summary of the average training time and accuracy of DBN models optimized by the PSOGAA algorithm. In comparison to other DBN optimization algorithms, the PSOGAA algorithm extended the average training time while enhancing accuracy.

The quality and accuracy of the model are influenced by the number of iterations, enabling particles to explore a sufficient number of positions to determine the optimal solution. The diverse crops included in the recommendation process are Rice, Maize, Sugarcane, and Fingermillet. A set of testing samples is randomly chosen to feed into the four types of DBNs. The accuracy of the crop recommendation results achieved through various optimization algorithms is presented in Table 3.

For further verification, tests are carried out with for groups of samples covering the different types of crops considered. The confusion matrices depicted in Fig. 4 are employed to assess the classification capability of crop recommendation results. The

Table 1. Accuracy and MSE values of optimization algorithms

Optimization Algorithm	Iterations	MSE values
Adagrad DBN	800	0.022
Adam DBN	780	0.017
GA DBN	750	0.011
PSO DBN	720	0.012
PSOGAA DBN	580	0.010

Table 2. Average Training time and accuracy values

Optimization Algorithm	Training Time (s)	Accuracy values(%)
Adagrad DBN	1.15	72.2
Adam DBN	1.79	78.6
GA DBN	3.34	80.2
PSO DBN	3.90	85.5
PSOGAA DBN	5.84	93.2

Table 3. Accuracy value obtained for crop recommendation results

	Adagrad DBN	Adam DBN	PSO DBN	PSOGAA DBN
Rice	0.718	0.781	0.894	0.911
Maize	0.733	0.730	0.875	0.923
Sugarcane	0.773	0.830	0.864	0.937
Fingermillet	0.682	0.733	0.822	0.896

recommendation accuracy of PSOGAA exceeds 90% for all crops except for fingermillet. The performance gaps in Adagrad DBN, Adam DBN, PSO-DBN is mainly observed for rice, sugarcane and fingermillet.

Hence, based on the experimental findings, it can be inferred that the proposed approach presents a notable edge in terms of both recommendation accuracy and computational efficiency when contrasted with alternative Deep Belief Network (DBN) recommendation models.

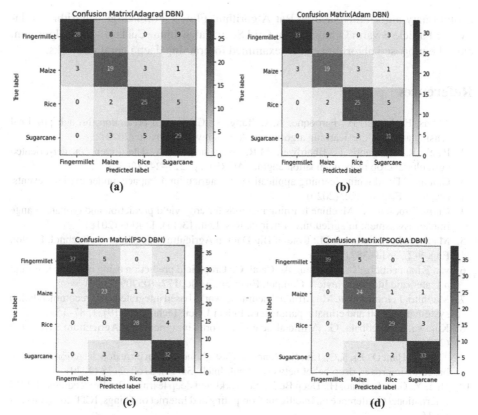

Fig. 4. Confusion matrix of crop recommendation. (a) Adagrad DBN (b) Adam DBN (c) PSO-DBN (d) PSOGAA DBN.

6 Conclusion

The agriculture sector holds a crucial place in the growth of any developing economy and supports the livelihood of a large portion of the population through its contribution to income and employment. A major challenge faced by small and marginal farmers is selecting the appropriate crops to cultivate in order to achieve maximum benefits. Considering this the paper proposes a crop recommendation model built with Deep Belief Networks trained with hybrid of Adam- Particle swarm- Genetic Algorithm Optimization (PSOGAA). Further the efficiency of the proposed work is evaluated by comparing the MSE and accuracy with the model was trained with Adagraxd optimization, Adam Optimization, Particle Swarm Optimization. With the analysis of the experimental results, our proposed PSOGAA Optimization performed better over the other optimization algorithms. Though the MSE obtained for both PSO and PSOGAA optimization is smaller, PSOGAA converged to minimum MSE value with lesser number of iterations but the training time was more compared to other optimization algorithms.

The new PSOGAA optimization can be tested with other real-world challenges such as prediction, forecasting, classification, etc. Further analysis can be carried out with evolutionary algorithms such as Bat Algorithm, Flower Pollination Algorithm, Relativistic Particle Swarm Optimization, Grid Search algorithm, Cuckoo search algorithm, etc. The proposed algorithm can be examined for training deep neural networks.

References

1. Abbas, F., Afzaal, H., Farooque, A.A., Tang, S.: Crop yield prediction through proximal sensing and machine learning algorithms. Agronomy **10**(7), 1046 (2020)
2. Patel, R., Enaganti, I., Bhardwaj, M.R., Narahari, Y.: A data-driven, farmer-oriented agricultural crop recommendation engine (ACRE), pp. 227–248 (2022)
3. Gaitán, C.F.: Machine learning applications for agricultural impacts under extreme events, no. 2015. Elsevier Inc. (2020)
4. Crane-Droesch, A.: Machine learning methods for crop yield prediction and climate change impact assessment in agriculture. Environ. Res. Lett. **13**(11), 114003 (2018)
5. Madhuri, J., Indiramma, M.: Role of Big Data in Agriculture. Int. J. Innov. Technol. Explor. Eng. **9**(2), 3811–3821 (2019)
6. van Klompenburg, T., Kassahun, A., Catal, C.: Crop yield prediction using machine learning: a systematic literature review. Comput. Electron. Agric. **177**, 105709 (2020)
7. Madhuri, J., Indiramma, M.: Artificial neural networks based integrated crop recommendation system using soil and climatic parameters. Indian J. Sci. Technol. **14**(19), 1587–1597 (2021)
8. Kujawa, S., Niedbała, G.: Artificial neural networks in agriculture. Agriculture **11**(6), 497 (2021)
9. Tian, Q., Han, D., Li, K.C., Liu, X., Duan, L., Castiglione, A.: An intrusion detection approach based on improved deep belief network. Appl. Intell. **50**(10), 3162–3178 (2020)
10. Hua, Y., Guo, J., Zhao, H.: Deep Belief Networks and deep learning. In: Proceedings of 2015 International Conference on Intelligent Computing and Internet of Things, ICIT 2015, pp. 1–4 (2015)
11. Senthilnath, J., et al.: DRBM-ClustNet: a deep restricted Bltzmann-Kohonen architecture for data clustering. IEEE Trans. Neural Netw. Learn. Syst. **35**, 2560–2574 (2022)
12. Hinton, G.: A practical guide to training restricted Boltzmann machines a practical guide to training restricted Boltzmann machines. Computer (Long. Beach. Calif) 9(3), 1 (2010)
13. Tamilselvan, P., Wang, Y., Wang, P.: Deep belief network based state classification for structural health diagnosis. In: IEEE Aerospace Conference Proceedings (2012)
14. Zhong, G.Q., Wang, H.Y., Zhang, K.Y., & Jia, B.Z.: Fault diagnosis of Marine diesel engine based on deep belief network. In: Proceedings - 2019 Chinese Automation Congress CAC 2019, pp. 3415–3419 (2019)
15. Zhang, C., Tan, K.C., Li, H., Hong, G.S.: A cost-sensitive deep belief network for imbalanced classification. IEEE Trans. Neural Networks Learn. Syst. **30**(1), 109–122 (2019)
16. Gai, J.; Zhong, K., Du, X., Yan, K., Shen, J.: Detection of gear fault severity based on parameter-optimized deep belief network using sparrow search algorithm. Measurement **185**, 110079 (2021)
17. Haji, S.H., Abdulazeez, A.M.: Comparison of optimization techniques based on gradient descent algorithm: a review-Palarch's. J. Archaeol. Egypt/Egyptol. 18(4), 2715–2743 (2021)
18. Roder, M., De Rosa, G.H., Passos, L.A., Papa, J.P., Rossi, A.L.D.: Harnessing particle swarm optimization through relativistic velocity. In: 2020 IEEE Congress on Evolutionary Computation CEC 2020 - Conference Proceedings (2020)
19. Roder, M., Passos, L.A., de Rosa, G.H., de Albuquerque, V.H.C., Papa, J.P.: Reinforcing learning in deep belief networks through nature-inspired optimization. Appl. Soft Comput. **108**, 107466 (2021)

20. Papa, J.P., Scheirer, W., Cox, D.D.: Fine-tuning deep belief networks using harmony search. Appl. Soft Comput. **46**, 875–885 (2016)
21. Ali, M.A., et al.: Classification of glaucoma based on elephant-herding optimization algorithm and deep belief network. Electronics **11**(11), 1763 (2022)
22. Fedorovici, L.O., Precup, R.E., Dragan, F., David, R.C., Purcaru, C.: Embedding gravitational search algorithms in convolutional neural networks for OCR applications. In: SACI 2012 - 7th IEEE International Symposium on Applied Computational Intelligence and Informatics, Proceedings, pp. 125–130 (2012)
23. Chung, H., Shin, K.S.: Genetic algorithm-optimized long short-term memory network for stock market prediction. Sustainability **10**, 3765 (2018)
24. Tan, X., Su, S., Zuo, Z., Guo, X., Sun, X.: Intrusion detection of UAVs based on the deep belief network optimized by PSO. Sensors **19**(24), 5529 (2019)
25. Wen, Y., Wang, Y., Liu, J., Cao, B., Fu, Q.: CPU usage prediction for cloud resource provisioning based on deep belief network and particle swarm optimization. Concurr. Comput. Pract. Exp. **32**(14), e5730 (2020). https://doi.org/10.1002/CPE.5730
26. Rosa, G., Papa, J., Costa, K., Passos, L., Pereira, C., Yang, X.S.: Learning parameters in deep belief networks through firefly algorithm. In: Schwenker, F., Abbas, H., El Gayar, N., Trentin, E. (eds.) Artificial Neural Networks in Pattern Recognition. ANNPR 2016. Lecture Notes in Computer Science(), vol. 9896, pp. 138–149. Springer, Cham (2016)
27. Zhang, N., Ding, S., Zhang, J., Xue, Y.: An overview on restricted Boltzmann machines. Neurocomputing **275**, 1186–1199 (2018)
28. Hinton, G.E.: Computation and undefined 2002. "Training products of experts by minimizing contrastive divergence," ieeexplore.ieee.org. Accessed 29 Sep 2022
29. Hu, S., Xiang, Y., Huo, D., Jawad, S., Liu, J.: An improved deep belief network based hybrid forecasting method for wind power. Energy **224**, 1–30 (2021)
30. Veerachamy, R., Ramar, R.: Agricultural irrigation recommendation and alert (AIRA) system using optimization and machine learning in Hadoop for sustainable agriculture. Environ. Sci. Pollut. Res. **2021**, 1–20 (2021)
31. Clerc, M., Kennedy, J.: The particle swarm—explosion, stability, and convergence in a multidimensional complex space. IEEE Trans. Evol. Comput. **6**(1), 58–73 (2002)
32. Poli, R., Kennedy, J., Blackwell, T.: Particle swarm optimization. Swarm Intell. **11**(1), 33–57 (2007). https://doi.org/10.1007/S11721-007-0002-0
33. Holland, J.H.: Genetic algorithms. Sci. Am. **267**(1), 66–72 (1992)
34. Mirjalili, S.: Genetic algorithm. Stud. Comput. Intell. **780**, 43–55 (2019)
35. Llugsi, R., El Yacoubi, S., Fontaine, A., Lupera, P.: Comparison between Adam, AdaMax and Adam W optimizers to implement a weather forecast based on neural networks for the Andean city of Quito. In: ETCM 2021 - 5th Ecuador Technical Chapters Meet (2021)
36. Dogo, E.M., et al.: Optimization algorithms on convolutional neural networks. In: 2018 International Conference on Computational Techniques, Electronics and Mechanical Systems, pp. 92–99 (2018)
37. Liu, L., Moayedi, H., Rashid, A.S.A., Rahman, S.S.A., Nguyen, H.: Optimizing an ANN model with genetic algorithm (GA) predicting load-settlement behaviours of eco-friendly raft-pile foundation (ERP) system. Eng. Comput. **36**(1), 421–433 (2020)
38. Madhuri, J., Indiramma, M.: Hybrid filter and wrapper methods based feature selection for crop recommendation, pp. 247–252 (2022)

A Practical Solution Towards Development of Real-Time Face Attendance System

D. L. Shivaprasad[1]([⊠]) [iD], D. S. Guru[1] [iD], and R. Kavitha[2] [iD]

[1] Department of Studies in Computer Science, University of Mysore, Manasagangotri, Mysuru, India
shivaprasaddl143@gmail.com, dsg@compsci.uni-mysore.ac.in
[2] School of Computer Science and IT, JAIN Deemed to be University, Bangalore, India
kavitha.rajamanii@gmail.com

Abstract. Face recognition is an interesting and familiar research area in biometric with many more applications. Face recognition-based attendance system is one of the effective applications in the area of biometrics. Marking the attendance manually is a difficult task for a large corpus, identifying unconnected persons and also poses many challenges. The proposed work is an effective solution to overcome those problems by the way of developing a real-time face attendance system. It subsequently combines the process of classification and then matching for the person identification. Through the experimentation, minimal sample requirement for each person and suitable learning algorithm is identified for the proposed work. The respective samples are found out by an effective clustering algorithm. Also, proposed a novel method to compute the matching threshold. Comparative study is done with existing state of the art result face attendance systems. The proposed system is evaluated with 200 students of age ranging from 21–25 years for a semester long and noticed that the system outperforms with identifying unconnected people with 100% True Acceptance Rate with a matching threshold of 0.43. Finally, the proposed system maintains entire tasks of attendance management, generates reports and notifies to the admin in a dashboard.

Keywords: Face Attendance System · YOLOv5 · FaceNet · K-Means · K-Medoid · True Acceptance Rate · False Acceptance Rate

1 Introduction

Face recognition is a process to identify a person using facial features in order to compare against existing faces. The face recognition in real-time scenario includes series of steps; detecting face from frames, extracting the facial features, and identifying the faces. The major challenges in face recognition are illumination, occlusion, facial expression, and face pose variation. One of the interesting applications in face recognition is Real-time Face Attendance System (FAS), which comprises of face recognition and attendance marking system. Here, the outcome of face recognition is considered for marking the attendance.

The significance of FAS is to reduce the manual intervention in such a way that time is reduced for marking attendance for a large corpus in an accurate way and to

V. N. M. Aradhya et al. (Eds.): CCIP 2023, CCIS 2044, pp. 138–153, 2024.
https://doi.org/10.1007/978-3-031-60725-7_11

generate attendance reports without any error in a lesser period of time compared to manual preparation. The face attendance system aids in solving the issues that may occur in traditional attendance marking such as mismarking the attendance to the absentee student, mismarking when there is a similar name in a large population. It is useful for personal authentication to avoid the usage of fake identity cards and there is no need to remember the login password also. Particularly this system does not require any other document to authenticate the person as it needs only face image. This system reduces the burden of the teachers to mark attendance in the classroom and helps them by providing more time for delivering the content; hence it is beneficial to all educational institutions. Also, it helps the police department by identifying the thief using their face data. Because of regulations, people do not have access to biometric device for authentication during the covid-19 pandemic situation where the FAS can play a major role.

Though many attempts have been done towards implementing the FAS, still it needs to be addressed as they fail to declare 'unconnected' for a new person face data during classification and also they fail to declare generalized threshold for unknown person identification. An effective model is proposed to fill this gap by identifying the unknown people to avoid misclassification and provide a novel method to compute global threshold. The proposed system is a novel approach in FAS because it is accomplished by both classification and matching techniques. Only classification technique is not supportive to identify the unknown samples as it is mapped to any known person. Also, only matching technique consumes expensive time to match in a large carpus of data which is not feasible. Hence, a combination of these two techniques by a pipeline of classification yielding to matching for person identification is proposed. Our proposed FAS works on real-time scenario as the face detector uses a popular deep architecture to detect faces accurately in all environmental conditions to achieve accurate results. Not only marking the attendance, but also managing the entire process of attendance system is done by the proposed FAS. The overall objectives of the proposed work are:

- To design an effective face detector having capability to detect faces in all environmental conditions.
- To examine the suitable learning algorithm for classification and analyses the minimal sample requirement of each person to the proposed FAS.
- To develop an accurate and effective FAS.
- To address comparative analysis of proposed work with existing FAS.

The second section reviews the recent works held in the area of FAS. The third section discusses about the architecture of the proposed work and the fourth section de-scribes the hardware requirement to develop the FAS. The fifth section explains in detail about the experimentation and performance analysis. Finally, the sixth section provides the conclusion.

2 Literature Review

In recent days, Face Recognition (FR) is a well-known human biometrics research area, and it started its journey at past twenty years ago and gradually evolved with huge research activities [9]. But it is still a challenging research area [6]. The state-of-the-art result achieved is 99.83% [1, 7]. A FR system is developed [2] but still it provides an ineffective solution, because of major challenges of occlusion, pose variation, facial expression, low illumination, and resolution [1, 7]. Especially, in real-time scenarios, the motion blur loses facial data [9]. The FR is solved by the traditional machine learning techniques, using feature extraction techniques such as Gabor [5, 9], PCA [11, 13, 19], LBP [9], HOG [22], SIFT[23] and feature transformation techniques PCA [24, 25] and LDA [13]. Also, Using deep learning, Alexnet stands first subsequently followed by FaceNet [3], GoogleNet, MobileNet, MobileFaceNet, etc., in gradually improving the FR system [7] with different challenges like recognizing the faces with a mask [4] which was very much essential in covid-19 pandemic situation, FR in partial faces [26], FR using face components [29], encoding based face recognition [28], FR using subspace methods [30], NIR based FR [27] and many more attempts is done to recognize the human face, Using these, one of the major applications of FR is Face Attendance System (FAS), marking attendance by identifying faces from all enrolled faces stored in the database [10].

Table 1. Recent work held in Face Attendance System.

	Face Detection Algorithm	Feature Extraction Architecture	Recognition Model	Type of Prediction
Al-Amoudi et al., [3]	MTCNN	FaceNet	Softmax	Classification
Arsenovic, M et al., [15]	MTCNN	FaceNet	SVM	Classification
Fu, R. et al., [21]	MTCNN	ResNet-101	Softmax	Classification
Yang, H., & Han, X. [10]	Viola-Jones	Gabor feature, PCA, LDA	SVM	Classification
Khan, S. et al., [11]	YOLOv3	DNN	Softmax	Classification
Winarno, E. et al., [13]	CNN 3d Model	PCA	Mahalabis Distance	Matching
Jadhav, A. et al., [17]	Viola-Jones (Histogram Equalisation)	PCA	SVM	Classification
Patil, A. and Shukla, M. [19]	Viola-Jones (Histogram Equalisation)	PCA and LDA	Euclidian Distance	Matching
Sunaryono, D. et al., [8]	Viola-Jones (Laplacian Filtering)	Gray Scale Image	Logistic Regration, LDA and KNN	Classification
Wagh, P. et al., [18]	Viola-Jones	PCA	Euclidian Distance	Matching
Kar, N. et al., [20]	Viola-Jones	PCA	Euclidian Distance	Matching
Sawhney, S. et al., [12]	Viola-Jones (Histogram Equalisation)	PCA and LDA	CNN	Classification
Bhattacharya, S. et al., [14]	Viola-Jones (Laplacian Filtering)	CNN		Classification

During last few years, FAS becomes a well-known application to everyone and many researchers worked with different modalities such as; QR scanner to collect face data using smartphones [1, 8], FAS only in frontal faces [19], allowing pose angle of 30^0 for left and right sides [17], sharpening techniques for better classification [13], Eigenface based FAS [12], FAS with class strength [11]. It was found from review that the deep learning techniques are performing well for FR. But lightweight and robust models are required to handle large data carpus. The other requirement is handling face images/frames with the challenges of low-resolution, noisy, expression in real-time. Some of the existing popular face attendance systems are tabulated in Table 1 with parameters used for implementation. From the survey it is noticed that, the person identification task in all existing FAS takes only classification [5, 8, 12–17, 20] or only matching [10, 11, 17, 18]. These tasks are pictorially represented in Fig. 1.

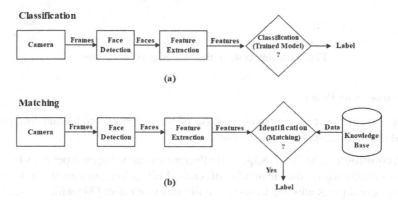

Fig. 1. Person identification held by (a) Classification or (b) Matching.

These two methods have their own drawbacks. One is misclassification will happen by increasing the number of classes and another is time complexity will increase by matching with an enrolled large corpus of data. Also, no one can accomplish the identification of unknown person in an effective way and no method is there to fix a matching threshold other than ROC. Similarly, no one is addressed about the minimal sample requirement for the FAS. Hence it motivated us to overcome these problems by proposing the deployable effective FAS by combining both the methods and also designed a novel generalized method to compute the matching threshold to achieve effective and accurate FAS with less time complexity for real-time scenarios. In Biometrics, the threshold fixing and performance measure are based on the ROC curve. In that, FAS performance is evaluated using TAR and FAR.

3 Proposed FAS

The proposed face attendance system consists of two phases: one is Enrollment phase and another is Attendance Marking phase. The proposed system consists of two databases, one is to store all person's relevant information called as Knowledge base (KB), and another is to store all attendance reports called as Attendance Base (AB). Each step of our proposed FAS is explained below in detail and the architecture is given in Fig. 2.

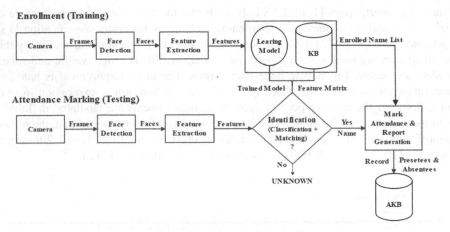

Fig. 2. Architecture of the Face Attendance System.

3.1 Enrollment Phase

The enrollment phase is the training phase of the proposed model and this phase is divided into five sub-phases as explained below.

Data Acquisition. The data is acquired in the form of capturing each person's face video data individually with sufficient number of poses. While collecting data, the Holomorphic Filtering technique is adopted to solve the illumination effect [31] which is very much faster than Histogram Equalization.

In general, 'M' samples of each person's face data are collected. If there are 'N' number of people enrolled then there are NM number of samples totally.

Face Detection. In each video sample, faces are detected and extracted using a face detector. The face detector is a model that has the capability to identify face region in given video frames and also, it is able to detect faces in real-time challenges like different poses, occlusions and environment conditions. Deep learning based face detector is well performing in handling the low quality video frames. Hence, the proposed FAS uses a deep learning based face detector by training faces of all categories of people. The extracted faces are resized to required standard input size of the architecture.

Feature Extraction. After face detection, the deep features are extracted from all the pre-processed faces and represented in a vector form. These feature vectors are used for further person identification and also stored into the KB.

In general, d-number of features are extracted from deep architecture from Hence, the feature matrix has the dimension of $N \times M \times d$.

Face Recognition Model Building. Initially, the numerosity reduction is applied so that sample space can be reduced. The correlated samples are removed from each class by using a clustering technique. Each person's samples are clustered and the representatives are taken into account as training samples, which is shown in Fig. 3. It helps to train a model without outliers. It yields better performance and reduces the training time.

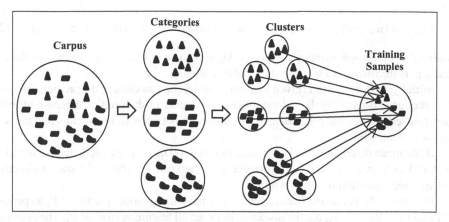

Fig. 3. Numerosity reduction representation using a clustering technique.

In general, each person's samples are clustered into 'K' clusters and the resultant feature matrix of 'N' people have the dimension N × K × d, where K << M. The learn-ing model is trained by using this feature matrix. The trained model is also stored in the KB. The already stored feature matrix and this learned model play an important role in person identification and attendance marking.

This enrollment phase is a one-to-one communication system where a system collects facial data from a single person at the time as enrollment.

3.2 Attendance Marking Phase

After the completion of enrollment, the person identification is done using the stored feature matrix and the learned model in KB. It is followed by attendance marking and managing whole records related to the attendance system. Here, face detection and feature extraction techniques are similar to the enrollment phase. This phase is divided into three sub-phases as explained below.

Test Data Acquisition. The face image is captured through real-time cameras similarly to the above as explained in Data Acquisition sub section; detection and extraction of faces from frames using the face detector are done. Then, the deep features are extracted and represented as a test feature vector.

Person Authentication. Person Authentication is done by considering the decision of two combined techniques, one is classification for identification and the other is matching for verification. The verification is done with the support of a matching threshold named as Decision_threshold (D_{th}).

Hence, a novel method to compute Dth is also proposed. It is computed by summing up the mean and standard deviation of the list generated by taking the sum of mean and standard deviation of intra-class distances from all classes as in Eq. 1 and 2.

$$\mu = \frac{\sum_{i=1}^{k} D_i}{K} \text{ and } \sigma = \frac{\sqrt{\sum_{i=1}^{k} (D_i - \mu)}}{K} \quad (1)$$

$$L_{intra} = [\mu_1 + \sigma_1, \mu_2 + \sigma_2, \ldots, \mu_{Pc} + \sigma_{Pc}] \text{ and } D_{th} = \mu(L_{intra}) + \sigma(L_{intra}) \qquad (2)$$

where P_c is the total number of classes, D_i is the intra-class mean distance of the ith class, μ is the mean and σ is the standard deviation.

Initially, the test vector is given as input to the learned model and the predicted person id is recognized partially. By taking all feature vectors of the predicted person id from the knowledge base, the mean distance of distances between all the vectors and the test vector is computed.

If the mean distance value is less than or equal to D_{th} then the predicted person id is declared as 'correct' otherwise it is declared as 'unknown'. This technique is effective towards identification of unknown faces.

In general, F_t is the test feature vector. Let the trained model predicted F_t as person id P_i and $D_1, D_2, \ldots, D_M$ are the distances between all feature vectors of P_i. The decision is taken as follows in Eq. 3.

$$\textbf{Person id} = \begin{cases} \text{if } \frac{\sum_{i=1}^{M} D_i}{M} \leq \textbf{D}_{th}, & \text{then } \textbf{P}_i \\ \text{otherwise} & \text{UNKNOWN} \end{cases} \qquad (3)$$

Report Generation and Communication. Attendance is marked once the person identification is done using the predicted person id and produces the present and absentee list. The present list will be generated by the collection of identified persons and the absentees will be generated by taking the set difference between the enrolled people list and the present list. Both lists are stored to Attendance Base (AB).

In general, the present set is $P_L = \{P_1, \ldots, P_h\}$, where $1 \leq h \leq N$, then Absentees set is $A_L =$ set of all enrolled person id - P_L, where $A_L \cap P_L = \Phi$.

Using an absentee list, the proposed model is set to send a message to their parents to inform the absenteeism. Also, a report of regular absentees and a monthly attendance report for each person is made. Finally, all information are stored in ADB and notified as an everyday report to Admin using a dashboard.

This proposed model is designed and developed with Graphical User Interface (GUI) and the necessary interface hardware. The hardware details needed for the proposed system are given in detail in Sect. 4.

4   Hardware Requirement for Productization

The Hardware required for FAS are categorized into three parts as an input device, a processor unit, and an output device. The requirements and functions of each category are explained below.

4.1   Input Hardware

In FAS, a camera is the input hardware to capture the video frames in real-time. The proposed work uses the Arducam 12MP HQ Camera as the input hardware. It is shown in Fig. 4(a).

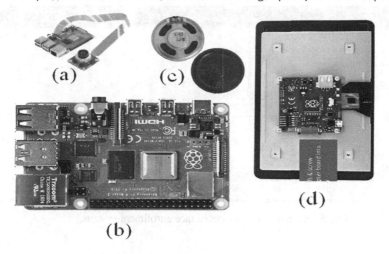

Fig. 4. Hardware images of proposed FAS.

4.2 Processing Unit

The processing unit is a combination of different hardware such as Raspberry Pi, Cooler, and power supply. The Raspberry Pi is an electrical circuit board that can do multi-tasks like a CPU. The processing unit handles all tasks of FAS. The proposed work uses 4 GB RAM Raspberry Pi 4, a small fan, a heat sink for cooler, and a battery as a power supplier. The Raspberry Pi board is given in Fig. 4(b).

4.3 Output Hardware

The proposed FAS has two output hardware; one is a touchscreen display and the other is a speaker. The touchscreen display works as both an input and output device. It is used as an input device only during the enrollment and as an output device to display face attendance marking by calling their names out. The proposed work uses Raspberry Pi 7″ Touch Screen Display and a Wired Speaker. Both the hardware are shown in Fig. 4(c) and 4(d) respectively.

5 Experimentations and Results

For experimentation, 200 people (N) face data in real-time are collected and stored. For each person, 25 samples (M) are collected with different poses for enrollment (training). Faces are detected and extracted using a face detector. Also, a camera is fixed into entry gate in our department to capture face data for testing. It is done in random count on different timings and days. To measure the performance of FAS, 3000 samples for recognition are used. The screen shot of enrollment page of the proposed work is given in Fig. 5.

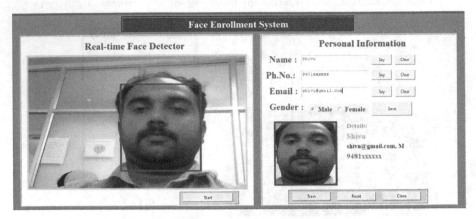

Fig. 5. Screenshot of proposed face enrollment system.

5.1 Face Detector

Face detector is essential in real-time face recognition. The existing face detector is not that much capable in detecting the faces in complex background and low intensity images/frames. To overcome this problem, a face detector is developed by training a well-known deep architecture namely YOLOv5 with 3000 images containing faces of the age ranging from 3–80 years. This performs well with 92% mAP score of detection and it is faster than other face detector like MTCNN, Faster-RCNN, etc.

5.2 Feature Extraction

The extracted faces are passed into a deep architecture FaceNet to extract the deep features to get feature vectors of 128-dimension. The training feature matrix has the dimension of 5000×128, and testing feature matrix has the dimension of 3000×128.

After feature extraction, the focus is towards in identifying a suitable classifier for person identification and the minimum number of samples required to the proposed FAS. Five different conventional classifiers such as Support Vector Machine classifier (with Linear (Ln), Polynomial (Poly), Radial Basis Functions (RBF), and Sigmoid (Sig) kernels), K-Nearest Neighbors classifier (KNN), Decision Tree classifiers (DT), Random Forest classifiers (RF) and Gaussian Naive Bias classifiers (GNB) are considered for model training. Experimentation is done with 25 trials for comparative analysis and then it is noticed that the SVM with Poly kernel is providing better classification result compared to all other classifiers with the highest average accuracy of 99.88%. Subsequently, SVM with RBF kernel and KNN are providing 99.74% and 99.55% average accuracy respectively.

In terms of time complexity, the SVM with Poly kernel is taking more time in training and testing compared to SVM with RBF kernel and KNN. KNN does not require training time and it will take less time for testing when compared to both the kernels of SVM classifiers as mentioned. Out of this experimentation it is found that two learning models (SVM with Poly and RBF Kernels) and KNN are fit for our proposed work but will finalize with further experimentations.

Then, experimentation is done to know the minimum number of samples required for the proposed work. Hence, initially one sample from each person from trainset is considered and then performance of all classifiers via recognition accuracy are checked and noticed. Similarly, experimentation is done by increasing samples with count 2 in each and consolidating the results.

In this experimentation, it is observed that the proposed system is well performing with minimum of 7 samples that is required from each person. KNN classifier is performing well with this sample count compared to other classifiers. The consolidated results are given in Table 2. Also, observed that SVM with Poly kernel is giving highest result, but also it is noticeable that after 7 samples count, the results are not much increasing effectively but with only increase in the range of 0.37%. With the support of this evidential study, it is concluded that the proposed work requires minimum 7 samples for recognition and KNN classifier is the suitable learning algorithm. In this experimentation, samples have been chosen randomly but it is not the right way of choosing. Hence, a clustering based sampling technique is adopted to choose highly discriminative samples from the given corpus (Numerosity reduction). The technique is to cluster the samples into 7 clusters and then select the cluster representatives as training samples as explained in the Sect. 3.1.

Table 2. Consolidated results of sample requirement analysis.

Samples	Average Accuracy	Average F-measure	Effective Classifier
1	95.90	96.74	SVM (RBF)
3	98.61	98.95	SVM (RBF)
5	98.96	99.24	KNN
7	**99.36**	**99.51**	**KNN**
9	99.37	99.56	KNN
11	99.41	99.55	KNN
13	99.46	99.61	KNN
15	99.51	99.65	SVM (Poly)
17	99.62	99.71	SVM (Poly)
19	99.76	99.82	SVM (Poly)
21	99.82	99.85	SVM (Poly)
23	99.82	99.86	SVM (Poly)
25	**99.85**	**99.88**	**SVM (Poly)**

Highly discriminant samples are extracted when compared to random sampling while adopting this technique. For experimentation purpose, two well-known clustering algorithms such as K-Means clustering algorithm and K-Medoid clustering algorithm are applied. The performance of both the algorithms in the proposed FAS is evaluated and the results are tabulated in Table 3. It is observed that, The K-Means clustering algorithm out performs the K-Medoid clustering algorithm. Also, it is evident that KNN is providing highest F1_score and Accuracy with less training and testing time compared to other classifiers.

Table 3. Comparative results of clustering algorithms.

Classifiers	K-Means Clustering				K-Medoid Clustering			
	Training time	Testing time	F1_Score	Accuracy	Training time	Testing time	F1_Score	Accuracy
SVM (Lin)	1.86	2.31	99.45	99.25	3.64	2.28	99.32	98.94
SVM (Poly)	1.92	2.62	99.44	99.28	3.06	2.34	99.29	98.91
SVM (RBF)	2.17	4.81	99.55	99.40	3.26	4.73	99.32	98.98
SVM (Sig)	1.93	2.47	99.45	99.24	3.05	2.43	99.26	98.87
KNN	0	0.27	99.72	99.62	0	0.56	99.40	99.21
RF	21.08	0.62	90.45	87.58	27.12	0.64	77.92	70.10
DT	4.43	0.02	41.72	31.86	5.66	0.01	33.55	25.14
GNB	0.03	1.06	83.97	80.41	0.03	1.06	63.86	56.06

The reason behind this is that K-Medoid choses a sample as the centroid and also it avoids the outlier samples of the class. But, in proposed work, the features are extracted from faces of different poses and some of the feature dimensions may vary as it causes samples into outlier. The K-Means clustering considers the mean point of the cluster as centroid, also it holds the relationship of all samples in the cluster. Hence the K-Means clustering is well performing when compared to K-Medoid clustering.

Also, it is noted that the result of clustering based sampling is better than random sampling and hence this method causes considerable reduction in sample space. Finally, from above experimentations obtained a new feature matrix of dimension 1400 × 128. These features are used for training the chosen KNN classifier for person classification. The comparative analysis of classifiers are shown in Fig. 6.

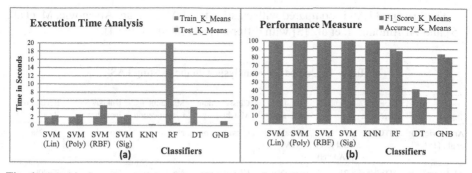

Fig. 6. Graphical representation of classifiers comparison with respect to (a) Execution time and (b) Performance analysis using K-Means clustering technique.

Another major phase in FAS is matching where the proposed work identifies the person with the combination of two modalities as recognition and matching as discussed in Sect. 3.2. The test vector of dimension 3000×128 is tested with the trained KNN classifier. The predicted name is considered partially correct, and then all enrolled samples of that predicted name from the trainset (25 samples) are selected. The distances between all samples with test sample are computed and mean of those distances is calculated. If the mean value is less than Decision_threshold (Dth), then it is declared that the predicted name in recognition is correct else it is declared that the test sample is 'Unknown'. This proposed work used Euclidean distance measure to calculate the distance between two samples.

In the real-time FAS, the False Positive Rate should reach towards zero as it computes the rate that some person is identified as 'P' who is not 'P' which is unbearable. The proposed system declares a person as 'Unknown' which is better than misidentification. To examine the scenario, an experimentation has been done.

The samples are partitioned into 'known' and 'unknown' class for experimentation purpose randomly. 1000 and 1447 sample face images are considered for 'known' and 'unknown' class respectively. The proposed model is built on this and the model accuracy is 94.85%. The confusion matrix is given below:

		Predicted	
		Known	Unknown
Actual	Known	874	126
	Known	0	1447

It is clearly evident that the False Positive is zero which is very much needed in real time FAS. Also, the samples belong to 'unknown' class are classified as 'unknown' only and it are not misidentified as a known person. This shows the good performance of the proposed model.

The proposed FAS is compared with existing two FAS such are Arsenovic, M. et al., [15] and Al-Amoudi, I. et al., [3] with different parameters (Table 4).

Table 4. Comparative analysis with the existing FAS.

	Face Detection	Dataset	Feature Extraction	Classification/ Matching	Matching + Classification	Unknown Identification	Recognition Rate
Arsenovic, M. et al., [15]	MTCNN	5 Subjects (Adults)	FaceNet + SVM	Classification	No	No	95.02%
Al-Amoudi, I. et al., [3]	MTCNN	21 Subject (Adults)	FaceNet + Softmax	Classification	No	No	87.20%
Proposed System	**YOLOv5**	**200 Subjects (Adults)**	**FaceNet + KNN**	**Classification and Matching**	**Yes**	**Yes**	**100%**

The compared studies used same deep architecture for feature extraction but worked with very less population and failed to recognize the unknown faces. Also, the results are comparative with our proposed FAS. Hence, our proposed system is achieved State-Of-The-Art result with 100% recognition rate. It means the system has 100% TAR and 0% of FAR with a Decision_threshold (D_{th}) value is 0.45 which is computed as explain in above section Person Authentication.

In other words, the proposed work has 100% specificity with 0% alpha error. The execution time of the proposed model for classification is < 0.05 s and for matching it is < 0.005 s. In this, the classification time is directly proportional to the number of classes (CT $\propto$ N). If the number of classes increases the classification time also increases and visa verse. But the matching time remains constant for all conditions.

Fig. 7. Screenshot of real-time face identification in proposed FAS.

This proposed work contributes a solution for a real-time face attendance system. A screen shot of person identification in proposed FAS is shown in Fig. 7. The entire proposed work is designed and developed with the support of Graphical User Inter-face (GUI) and Python programming language. The Comma Separated Value (CSV) files are stored in KB and AB. The Pickle library is used to store trained models. The complete model is well organized.

6 Conclusion

The proposed work performs well on successive attempts towards video based at-attendance system, maintains all needed records of attendance, sending messages to the absentee's parents, and notifying all reports to the administrator. For storage two databases are maintained. YOLOv5 is used as the face detector. The proposed FAS used the combination of classification and matching concepts for person identification. Also, the minimal number of samples required for person identification and the respective samples are identified by a novel method which uses a clustering approach. It is evident from the experimentation that no person is misidentified as other person but declared as unknown person which is mostly recommended in real time FAS. Surely this system will help teachers to deliver more content for students by limiting the time taken for effective attendance marking and management. In future, this system will be upgraded by adding other features like person's gait, pose, and height. Also, in surveillance, to monitor the student activities, especially alertness for kidnapping and any criminal activity on the campus could be implemented.

Acknowledgment. The first author of this work would like to thank the Government of Karnataka, for having sponsored the fellowship DST-Steps.

References

1. Gheisari, M., et al.: Automation attendance systems approaches: a practical review. BOHR Int. J. Internet Things, Artif. Intell. Mach. Learn. 1(1), 23–31 (2022). https://doi.org/10.54646/bijiotr.003
2. Lin, C.L., Huang, Y.H.: The application of adaptive tolerance and serialized facial feature extraction to automatic attendance systems. Electronics 11(14), 2278 (2022). https://doi.org/10.3390/electronics11142278
3. Al-Amoudi, I., Samad, R., Abdullah, N.R.H., Mustafa, M., Pebrianti, D.: Automatic attendance system using face recognition with deep learning algorithm. In: Isa, K., et al. (eds.) Proceedings of the 12th National Technical Seminar on Unmanned System Technology 2020. Lecture Notes in Electrical Engineering, vol. 770. Springer, Singapore, pp. 573–588 (2022). https://doi.org/10.1007/978-981-16-2406-3_44
4. Jeevan, G., Zacharias, G.C., Nair, M.S., Rajan, J.: An empirical study of the impact of masks on face recognition. Pattern Recogn. 122, 108308 (2022). https://doi.org/10.1016/j.patcog.2021.108308
5. Dalvi, J., Bafna, S., Bagaria, D., Virnodkar, S.: A survey on face recognition systems. arXiv preprint: arXiv:2201.02991 (2022). https://doi.org/10.48550/arXiv.2201.02991

6. Ali, N.S., Alhilali, A.H., Rjeib, H.D., Alsharqi, H., Al-Sadawi, B.: Automated attendance management systems: systematic literature review. Int. J. Technol. Enhanced Learn. **14**(1), 37–65 (2022). https://doi.org/10.1504/ijtel.2022.120559

7. Du, H., Shi, H., Zeng, D., Zhang, X.P., Mei, T.: The elements of end-to-end deep face recognition: a survey of recent advances. ACM Comput. Surv. (CSUR) **54**(10s), 1–42 (2022). https://doi.org/10.48550/arXiv.2009.13290

8. Sunaryono, D., Siswantoro, J., Anggoro, R.: An android based course attendance system using face recognition. J. King Saud Univ.-Comput. Inf. Sci. **33**(3), 304–312 (2021). https://doi.org/10.1016/j.jksuci.2019.01.006

9. Wang, M., Deng, W.: Deep face recognition: a survey. Neurocomputing **429**, 215–244 (2021). https://doi.org/10.1016/j.neucom.2020.10.081

10. Yang, H., Han, X.: Face recognition attendance system based on real-time video processing. IEEE Access **8**, 159143–159150 (2020). https://doi.org/10.1109/ACCESS.2020.3007205

11. Khan, S., Akram, A., Usman, N.: Real time automatic attendance system for face recognition using face API and OpenCV. Wireless Pers. Commun. **113**, 469–480 (2020). https://doi.org/10.1007/s11277-020-07224-2

12. Sawhney, S., Kacker, K., Jain, S., Singh, S.N., Garg, R.: Real-time smart attendance system using face recognition techniques. In: 2019 9th International Conference on Cloud Computing, Data Science & Engineering (Confluence), pp. 522–525) (2019). IEEE. https://doi.org/10.1109/CONFLUENCE.2019.8776934

13. Winarno, E., Al Amin, I.H., Februariyanti, H., Adi, P.W., Hadikurniawati, W., Anwar, M.T.: Attendance system based on face recognition system using CNN-PCA method and real-time camera. In: 2019 International Seminar on Research of Information Technology and Intelligent Systems (ISRITI), pp. 301–304. IEEE (2019). https://doi.org/10.1109/ISRITI48646.2019.9034596

14. Bhattacharya, S., Nainala, G.S., Das, P., Routray, A.: Smart attendance monitoring system (SAMS): a face recognition based attendance system for classroom environment. In: 2018 IEEE 18th International Conference on Advanced Learning Technologies (ICALT), pp. 358–360. IEEE (2018). https://doi.org/10.1109/ICALT.2018.00090

15. Arsenovic, M., Sladojevic, S., Anderla, A., Stefanovic, D.: FaceTime—deep learning based face recognition attendance system. In: 2017 IEEE 15th International Symposium on Intelligent Systems and Informatics (SISY), pp. 000053–000058. IEEE (2017). https://doi.org/10.1109/SISY.2017.8080587

16. Puthea, K., Hartanto, R., Hidayat, R.: A review paper on attendance marking system based on face recognition. In: 2017 2nd International Conferences on Information Technology, Information Systems and Electrical Engineering (ICITISEE), pp. 304–309. IEEE (2017). https://doi.org/10.1109/ICITISEE.2017.8285517

17. Jadhav, A., Jadhav, A., Ladhe, T., Yeolekar, K.: Automated attendance system using face recognition. Int. Res. J. Eng. Technol. (IRJET) **4**(1), 1467–1471 (2017)

18. Wagh, P., Thakare, R., Chaudhari, J., Patil, S.: Attendance system based on face recognition using Eigen face and PCA algorithms. In: 2015 International Conference on Green Computing and Internet of Things (ICGCIoT), pp. 303–308. IEEE (2015). https://doi.org/10.1109/ICGCIoT.2015.7380478

19. Patil, A., Shukla, M.: Implementation of classroom attendance system based on face recognition in class. Int. J. Adv. Eng. Technol. **7**(3), 974 (2014)

20. Kar, N., Debbarma, M.K., Saha, A., Pal, D.R.: Study of implementing automated attendance system using face recognition technique. Int. J. Comput. Commun. Eng. **1**(2), 100–103 (2012)

21. Fu, R., Wang, D., Li, D., Luo, Z.: University classroom attendance based on deep learning. In: 2017 10th International Conference on Intelligent Computation Technology and Automation (ICICTA), pp. 128–131. IEEE (2017). https://doi.org/10.1109/ICICTA.2017.35

22. Chandrakala, M., Devi, P.D.: Two-stage classifier for face recognition using HOG features. Mater. Today: Proc. **47**, 5771–5775 (2021). https://doi.org/10.1016/j.matpr.2021.04.114
23. Bagla, K., Bhushan, B.: A novel approach for face recognition using hybrid SIFT-SVM. In: 2016 IEEE 1st International Conference on Power Electronics, Intelligent Control and Energy Systems (ICPEICES), pp. 1–6. IEEE (2016). https://doi.org/10.1109/ICPEICES.2016.785 3661
24. Sumithra, R., Guru, D.S., Manjunath Aradhya, V.N., Anitha, R.: Transfer learning for children face recognition accuracy. In: Smys, S., Tavares, J.M.R.S., Bestak, R., Shi, F. (eds.) Computational Vision and Bio-Inspired Computing: ICCVBIC 2020, pp. 553–565. Springer Singapore (2021). https://doi.org/10.1007/978-981-33-6862-0_44
25. Sumithra, R., Guru, D.S., Aradhya, V.M., Raghavendra, A.: Face Verification Using Single Sample in Adolescence. In: Singh, S.K., Roy, P., Raman, B., Nagabhushan, P. (eds.) Computer Vision and Image Processing: 5th International Conference, CVIP 2020, Prayagraj, India, December 4–6, 2020, Revised Selected Papers, Part II 5, pp. 354–366. Springer Singapore (2021). https://doi.org/10.1007/978-981-16-1092-9_30
26. Elmahmudi, A., Ugail, H.: Deep face recognition using imperfect facial data. Futur. Gener. Comput. Syst. **99**, 213–225 (2019). https://doi.org/10.1016/j.future.2019.04.025
27. He, R., Li, Y., Wu, X., Song, L., Chai, Z., Wei, X.: Coupled adversarial learning for semi-supervised heterogeneous face recognition. Pattern Recogn. **110**, 107618 (2021). https://doi.org/10.1016/j.patcog.2020.107618
28. Shakeel, M.S., Lam, K.M.: Deep-feature encoding-based discriminative model for age-invariant face recognition. Pattern Recogn. **93**, 442–457 (2019). https://doi.org/10.1016/j.patcog.2019.04.028
29. Boussaad, L., Boucetta, A.: An effective component-based age-invariant face recognition using discriminant correlation analysis. J. King Saud Univ.-Comput. Inf. Sci. **34**(5), 1739–1747 (2022). https://doi.org/10.1016/j.jksuci.2020.08.009
30. Rao, A., Noushath, S.: Subspace methods for face recognition. Comput. Sci. Rev. **4**(1), 1–17 (2010). https://doi.org/10.1016/j.cosrev.2009.11.003
31. Fan, C.N., Zhang, F.Y.: Homomorphic filtering based illumination normalization method for face recognition. Pattern Recogn. Lett. **32**(10), 1468–1479 (2011). https://doi.org/10.1016/j.patrec.2011.03.023

Ancient Kannada Handwritten Character Recognition from Palm Leaf Manuscripts Using PyTesseract-OCR Technique

Parashuram Bannigidad[ID] and S. P. Sajjan[✉][ID]

Department of Computer Science, Rani Channamma University, Belagavi 571159, India
parashurambannigidad@gmail.com, sajjanvsl@gmail.com

Abstract. Ancient Kannada character recognition is a strenuous task since the Kannada language evolved over various decades, expanding and diversifying the character set. In this research, it is attempted to extract and recognize ancient palm leaf characters using the PyTesseract-OCR engine. The PyTesseract engine is used to denote the optical character recognition (OCR). It can "read" text that has been created into images—a wrapper for the Tesseract optical character recognition (OCR) engine written in Python. Tesseract-OCR uses Google's text-to-speech voice engine to facilitate optical character recognition. In the present paper, the captured image is further digitized and required to pre-process the ancient inscriptions to recognize the Kannada handwritten characters. The binarization process is used as a processing technique to improve image quality. In the next step, segmentation is carried out with the blob technique, and regional zoning is applied to create the character level. The efficiency of the processed character segmentation strategy as an accuracy of F1-score is 88.3%. Finally, character recognition is carried out, and its precision is above 82.3%. The outcome of this research is being done to contribute to the development of natural language processing research and development in the form of a comprehensive Kannada database.

Keywords: Palm leaf manuscripts · PyTesseract · OCR · Segmentation · Kannada Scripts · Binarization

1 Introduction

Character digitization and recognition are some of the vital applications of Computer vision. Computer vision and pattern recognition have many applications in various fields. Automation of Kannada handwritten character recognition will play an important role, especially in historical manuscripts, since Kannada scripts are an old Dravidian language, and we can understand the history and cultural customs of Kannada language people. This paper uses the PyTesseract-OCR engine to recognize historical Kannada handwritten palm leaf characters. In the literature, the previous research on OCR techniques has concentrated mainly on modern languages such as English, Arabic, Tamil and Chinese, etc., with minimal success an ancient letter. Little research has been investigated in OCR approaches for ancient Kannada character recognition from palm leaf

V. N. M. Aradhya et al. (Eds.): CCIP 2023, CCIS 2044, pp. 154–162, 2024.
https://doi.org/10.1007/978-3-031-60725-7_12

manuscripts. The use of machine learning techniques for recognizing historical Kannada handwritten characters has been proposed by Bannigidad, P., and Gudada, C [1], it has been observed from their study is that the difficulties due to the scripts intricacy, fading ink, and variances in handwriting styles. Sagar, B. M., et al. [2]. Have presents a case study on optical character recognition (OCR) using the open-source OCR programme Tesseract was accomplished by Patel, C., Patel, A., and Patel, D [3]. Which was used in order to recognize characters on the word level from ancient manuscripts. By Menon A. S., et al. [4]. The Tesseract engine is an open-source optical character recognition (OCR) system that facilitates the offline recognition of handwritten Chinese characters and was investigated by Li, Q., An, et al. [5]. A system that can read written Kannada text by looking at the letters. The wavelet features and a two-stage multi-network classification method was described by Kunte, R. S., and Samuel, R. S. [6]. The offline character recognition based on handwritten Kannada characters that have been divided was developed by Joe, K. G., et al. [7]. The Android app has been changed to use Tesseract with the Japanese script target for optical character recognition, which was proposed by Robby, G. A., et al. [8]. Using image processing combined with Tesseract for scene-text detection and recognition was proposed by Zacharias, E., et al. [9]. An innovative approach to optical character recognition (OCR) based on image recognition with application to the classification of ancient Tamil inscriptions found in temples has been invented by Giridhar, L., et al. [10]. The OCR conversion of printed Kannada text into a format that may be edited by machine using a database-driven technique was invented by Sagar, B. M., et al. [11]. Using multiple image enhancement techniques, an ancient Kannada handwritten palm leaf manuscript was restored, as described by Bannigidad, P., and Sajjan, S. P. [12]. Tesseract is an open-source optical character recognition engine that was used to recognize handwritten Roman numerals. Was developed by S. Rakshit et al. [13, 14]. The Historical Handwritten Scripts of the Kannada Recognition System, which uses Line Segmentation in combination with LBP characteristics, were described by Bannigidad, P., and Gudada, C. [15]. The application of a machine learning technique to recognize old handwritten Kannada characters has been proposed by Bannigidad, P., and Gudada, C. [1].

2 Proposed Method

The primary goal of this research is to recognize Halagagannada characters written on ancient Kannada palm leaf through the digitization process. The proposed task is categorized into three distinct portions, specifically: preprocessing, segmentation, and recognition. During the pre-processing stage, the input image performs a conversion procedure to transform it into a binary image, with the purpose of eliminating any noise or outliers present in the image, image segmentation is subsequently a fundamental computer vision technique used to divide an image into multiple segments or regions, each of which corresponds to a meaningful portion of the image. The next step is the detection and recognition of optical characters. PyTesseract-based OCR method is used to recognize the extracted characters from the image. Finally, Google's Tesseract-OCR, an open-source OCR engine, is used to identify the characters extracted from an ancient Kannada handwritten palm leaf manuscripts.

The flow diagram of the modeled architecture is shown in Fig. 1 is a character recognition system designed specifically for the Kannada language. The system has been developed to process an input image containing Kannada handwritten characters from palm leafs. It performs several operations such as binarization, segmentation, and utilizes the PyTesseract-OCR approach to accurately recognize and output the characters present in the image. The subsequent procedures delineate the progression of the system:

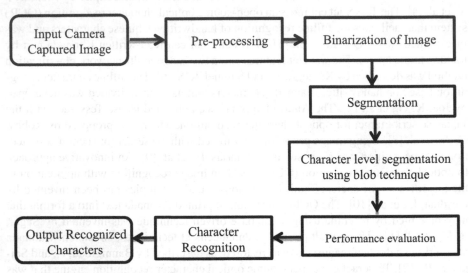

Fig. 1. The flow diagram of the modeled architecture

Pre-processing and segmentation are necessary for character recognition from a binaries image. Optical Character Recognition (OCR) is the last step, and it involves identifying and recognizing the restored characters in the image using a program like PyTesseract. Detailed descriptions of each phase are as follows:

a. **Pre-processing:** In order to enhance the quality of images, reduce noise, account for variations in the environment, and extract essential features, pre-processing is commonly utilized as the first step. The proposed adaptive threshold holding method is implemented by converting them to binary pictures where pixels are either converted to 0 or 255, the proposed method aids in pre-processing by categorizing image as black-and-white, depending on a threshold value. To better deal with changes in lighting and contrast, the suggested technique modifies the threshold value of each pixel in the image based on its near neighborhood. Thus, the proposed approach aids in removing document flaws such as irregular lighting, ink bleed, and smudges.

b. **Character Segmentation:** Character segmentation is a widely used technique in optical character recognition (OCR) systems, wherein it involves the separation of individual characters from a given text image. This method enables the extraction of text from images, facilitating subsequent processing. Character segmentation is important in several applications, such as handwritten text recognition, document analysis, and text-based image retrieval. The retrieval of characters is achieved by employing a bounding box approach in the provided method. The bounding box approach is a frequently employed technique in character segmentation, which aims to identify and precisely locate individual characters inside an image. The bounding box is a spatial region within a picture that delineates the boundaries of the topic. The determination of the geographic extent of the character region can be achieved through a bounding box technique. The retrieved data is retained for potential future utilization in evaluation and teaching.

c. **Optical Character Recognition:** This is the final process before the text that was extracted from the images can be used. It's a way to take a image with written letters and turn it into text that a computer can read, alter, search, and analyses. The PyTesseract model is used in the proposed approach to OCR development. The Google text-to-speech voice engine is built into the optional PyTesseract -OCR character recognition engine. The proposed method improves image quality through image binarization as the blob approach and regional zoning perform a processing technique and character-level segmentation. The suggested model recognizes and transforms images into editable text by first examining the extracted characters with the training model, then storing the recognized characters, and finally assessing the extracted words, as illustrated in Fig. 4.

3 Experimental Results and Discussion

The historical Kannada a handwritten manuscript written on palm leafs has been collected on by the e-Sahithya Documentation Forum located in Bangalore. The experimentation is performed on a Windows machine equipped with a 2.30 GHz Intel i5 CPU, 8 GB of RAM, and a 4 GB graphics processing unit (NVIDIA GeForce GTX 1050 Ti), with the Anaconda3 Distribution, Spider, and Python 3.7. Furthermore, the system is outfitted with 8 gigabytes of graphics memory. The camera captured a collection of medieval Kannada handwritten palm leaf manuscripts, which is given in Fig. 2(a). The

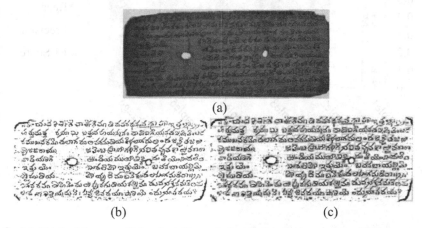

(a)

(b)   (c)

Fig. 2. (a) Original image of historical Kannada handwritten manuscripts, (b) Pre-processed image, (c) Segmented image.

Fig. 2(b) is an image that has been undergone pre-processing; In Fig. 2(c) illustrates the outcome of segmented image into individual characters.

The evaluation of the PyTesseract-OCR model includes the assessment of various standard metrics, including character segmentation. In Table 1 demonstrate, that the proposed technique exhibits notable levels of performance measure approaches; Accuracy, Recall, Precision, F1-score, and PSNR in the context of character segmentation. The quality of image segmentation is determined by higher values of PSNR, Precision, and F1-score and lower values of Recall are indicated as good quality of image (Fig. 3).

Table 1. Accuracy of Character Segmentation

Images	Accuracy	Recall	Precision	F1 Score	PSNR
Sample1	0.815	0.815	0.999	0.896	15.33
Sample2	0.830	0.830	0.998	0.905	15.65
Sample3	0.811	0.811	0.999	0.893	15.37
Sample4	0.821	0.821	0.998	0.864	15.71
Sample5	0.821	0.821	0.999	0.860	15.63
Average	**0.819**	**0.819**	**0.998**	**0.883**	**15.53**

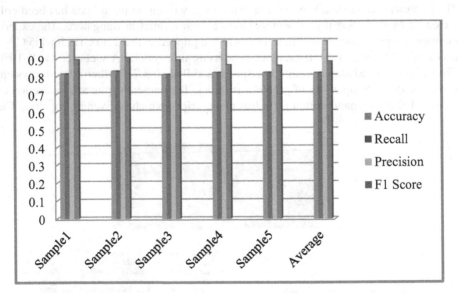

Fig. 3. A graphical representation of the effectiveness of the proposed results.

Finally, we executed a character recognition Python function is the PyTesseract-OCR technique, this function calculated the Precision and time taken to character recognition in milliseconds (ms). The Table 2 demonstrates the proposed methods in terms of Precision value as low as 0.783 and as high as 0.823, and the time taken to recognize characters is shown in column 4. Figure 4 shows the sample output of the Python program for character recognition.

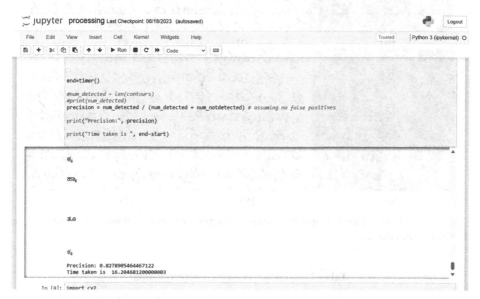

Fig. 4. Python program output of character Recognition

The sample images medieval Kannada handwritten palm leaf manuscripts are shown in Fig. 5. In Fig. 5(a) and (d) are original sample Palm leaf manuscripts, In Fig. 5(b) and (e) Binarized images and In Fig. 5(c) and (f) segmented images.

In this research, in the context of PyTesseract OCR, other methods were compared to the proposed method for segmentation, and recognition. The metrics employed to evaluate the effectiveness of the segmentation method, including PSNR, Accuracy, Precision, Recall, and F1-score, are used as quality measurements for character segmentation in Palm leaf manuscripts. Finally, we perform character recognition and evaluate its accuracy. Additionally, when measuring Precision for character recognition, we obtained a minimum of 0.783 and a maximum of 0.823. The experimental results will prove that the recommended strategy is more effective. The proposed method provides the best results in terms of character recognition, with a Precision value of 0.823. This is given in below Table 2.

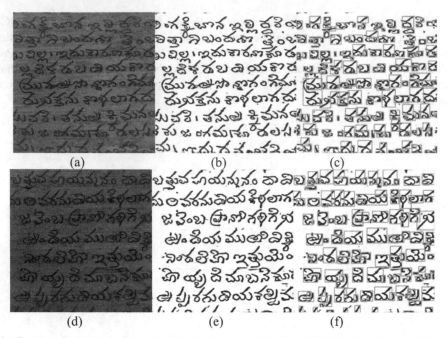

(a)   (b)   (c)

(d)   (e)   (f)

Fig. 5. (a) and (d) Original sample Palm leaf manuscripts, (b) and (e) Binarized images, (c) and (f) Segmented images.

Table 2. Accuracy of character Recognition.

Sample images of palm leafs manuscripts	Total No. of Characters	No. of characters recognized	Precision recognised characters	Time for Recognition (ms)
1	350	283	0.8230	15.40
2	250	170	0.7971	11.05
3	435	314	0.8001	16.71
4	550	440	0.7887	18.94
5	375	332	0.7839	16.58

The effectiveness of the proposed technique for successful binarization, segmentation, and recognition of Kannada manuscripts is represented by the accomplishment of segmentation accuracy, F1-score 88.3% and recognition Precision greater than 82.3%. The findings shown in Table 3 demonstrate that the suggested method achieves the highest accuracy rate of 88.3% when applied to diverse language datasets, specifically Arabic, Tamil, and Chinese.

Table 3. Prominent Literature Reviews

Sl. No	Author(s)	Dataset Method	Accuracy
1	Mansoor A. Ai Ghamdi	Arabic	77.3%
2	Lalitha Giridhar, et al.	Tamil	77.7%
3	Qi Li, Weihua An, et al.	Chinese	88.0%
4	Proposed method	Kannada	88.3%

4 Conclusion

The aim of this research presents the PyTesseract-OCR method for reading ancient Kannada scripts on palm-leaf manuscripts. The experimental results demonstrate the potential for classification and digitizing cultural literature from the past. Improved OCR technology for ancient writings would be a massive benefit to the preservation and accessibility of a wide range of linguistic and cultural heritage. The present study includes conducting a performance evaluation of different segmentation methods applying degraded images of Kannada handwritten palm leaf manuscripts. Accuracy, Precision, Recall, and F1-score were computed from these images to assess the effectiveness of the proposed methods. PSNR, Accuracy, Precision, Recall, and F1-score often fall within the range of 15.53, 0.819, 0.998, and 0.883, respectively. The minimum measured Precision for character identification was 0.783, and the maximum value is 0.823. In the literature, it is learning that the quality of the image is determined by the ratio of PSNR, Precision, and F1-score. The efficiency of the proposed method proves the completeness of the given method. To enhance the recognition of ancient Kannada characters, ideas for further research may involve using deep learning models and neural networks.

References

1. Bannigidad, P., Gudada, C.: Historical Kannada handwritten character recognition using a machine learning algorithm. In: Abraham, A., et al. (eds.) Proceedings of the 12th International Conference on Soft Computing and Pattern Recognition (SoCPaR 2020). Advances in Intelligent Systems and Computing, vol. 1383, pp. 311–319. Springer, Cham (2021). https://doi.org/10.1007/978-3-030-73689-7_30
2. Sagar, B.M., Shobha, G., Kumar, P.R.: Complete Kannada optical character recognition with syntactical analysis of the script. In: The 2008 International Conference on Computing, Communication, and Networking, pp. 1–4. IEEE (2008)
3. Patel, C., Patel, A., Patel, D.: Optical character recognition by the open-source OCR tool tesseract: a case study. Int. J. Comput. Appl. **55**(10), 50–56 (2012)
4. Menon, A.S., Sreekumar, R., Nair, B.B.: Character and word level recognition from ancient manuscripts using tesseract. In: the 2023 International Conference on Inventive Computation Technologies (ICICT), pp. 1743–1749. IEEE (2023)
5. Li, Q., An, W., Zhou, A., Ma, L.: Recognition of offline handwritten Chinese characters using the tesseract open-source OCR engine. In: 2016, the 8th International Conference on Intelligent Human-Machine Systems and Cybernetics (IHMSC), vol. 2, pp. 452–456. IEEE (2016)

6. Kunte, R.S., Samuel, R.S.: An OCR system for printed kannada text using a two-stage multi-network classification approach employing wavelet features. In: International Conference on Computational Intelligence and Multimedia Applications (ICCIMA 2007), vol. 2, pp. 349–353. IEEE (2007)
7. Joe, K.G., Savit, M., Chandrasekaran, K.: Offline character recognition on segmented handwritten Kannada characters. In: the 2019 Global Conference for Advancement in Technology (GCAT), pp. 1–5. IEEE (2019)
8. Robby, G.A., Tandra, A., Susanto, I., Harefa, J., Chowanda, A.: We implement optical character recognition using Tesseract with the Japanese script target in the Android application. Procedia Comput. Sci. **157**, 499–505 (2019)
9. Zacharias, E., Teuchler, M., Bernier, B.: Image processing-based scene-text detection and recognition with Tesseract. arXiv preprint: arXiv:2004.08079 (2020)
10. Giridhar, L., Dharani, A., Guruviah, V.: A novel approach to OCR using image recognition-based classification for ancient Tamil inscriptions in temples. arXiv preprint: arXiv:1907.04917 (2019)
11. Sagar, B.M., Shobha, G., Kumar, R.P.: OCR for printed Kannada text into machine editable format using a database approach. WSEAS Trans. Comput. **7**, 766–769 (2008)
12. Bannigidad, P., Sajjan, S.P.: Restoration of ancient Kannada handwritten palm leaf manuscripts using image enhancement techniques. In: Haldorai, A., Ramu, A., Mohanram, S. (eds.) 5th EAI International Conference on Big Data Innovation for Sustainable Cognitive Computing. BDCC 2022. EAI/Springer Innovations in Communication and Computing, pp. 101–109. Springer, Cham (2022). https://doi.org/10.1007/978-3-031-28324-6_9
13. Rakshit, S., Kundu, A., Maity, M., Mandal, S., Sarkar, S., Basu, S.: Recognition of handwritten roman numerals using the tesseract open-source OCR engine. In: Proceedings of the International Conference on Advances in Computer Vision and Information Technology, pp. 572–577 (2009)
14. Rakshit, S., Basu, S., Ikeda, H.: Recognition of handwritten textual annotations using tesseract's open source OCR engine for information just in time (iJIT). In: Proceedings of the International Conference on Information Technology and Business Intelligence, pp. 117–125 (2009)
15. Bannigidad, P., Gudada, C.: Historical Kannada handwritten scripts recognition system using line segmentation with LBP features. In: Alliance International Conference on Artificial Intelligence and Machine Learning (AICAAM) (2019)

Image Analysis

Anisotropic Guided Filtering and Multi-level Disintegration Method for NIR and Visible Image Fusion

Lokesh Gopinath ⓘ and A. Ruhan Bevi[(✉)] ⓘ

Department of Electronics and Communication Engineering, SRM Institute of Science and Technology, Kattankulathur, Chengalpattu, Tamil Nadu, India
`ruhanb@srmist.edu.in`

Abstract. The fusing of near-infrared and visible images holds substantial research relevance within the domain of image fusion. This paper presents a novel approach for fusing near-infrared and visible images, utilizing prospective multi-level disintegration and Anisotropic Guided Filtering (AnisGF). The proposed process involves using a Multi-level image Disintegration method based on Latent Low-Rank Representation (MDLatLRR) to carry out the multi-layer disintegration procedure, enabling the extraction of detailed data from the source images. Additionally, it softens the image to collect global image data. AnisGF provides good edge protection, reducing halo artifacts. When MDLatLRR and AnisGF are fused, the fused image reveals near-infrared heat and visible texture. The results of our experiment demonstrate that our approach surpasses five other established methodologies in terms of qualitative and quantitative measurements.

Keywords: Anisotropic guided filtering · Multi-level Disintegration · Image fusion · Near-infrared image · Visible image

1 Introduction

Near-Infrared (NIR) and visible image fusion improves the recognition of images and data content by combining data from many visible and NIR sensors. Various sensors often capture distinct ranges of images for a specific scene. However, a solitary sensor is limited by its physical limits to gather specified data about such a scene. Images taken by visible light sensors are made up of optical impulses that are perceptible to the human visual system. NIR images are made up of infrared radiation emitted by objects and captured by NIR sensors. In low-light circumstances, thermal photography, and nighttime driving, NIR images can be employed for target detection, among other applications. One reason for their heightened sensitivity to surface temperature variations is their thermal radiation characteristics. However, visible images can reveal more specific details about the object, such as its shape and color. Therefore, merging pictures from two wavelength bands can improve resolution and detection by offsetting each other's drawbacks.

Image fusion aims to take many images and fuse the most critical details from each image. The vital and fuse details in the final product of NIR and visible image fusion

V. N. M. Aradhya et al. (Eds.): CCIP 2023, CCIS 2044, pp. 165–175, 2024.
https://doi.org/10.1007/978-3-031-60725-7_13

include high contrast and detailed texturing. A multitude of NIR and visible fusion techniques have been proposed by researchers. Approaches such as NIR and visible image fusion utilizing saliency analysis and local edge-preserving multiscale disintegration, as well as fusion methods based on visual saliency map and Weighted Least Square (WLS) optimization [1], sparse representation [2], anisotropic diffusion filter [3], weighted anisotropic diffusion filter [4] and the application of generative adversarial examples for infrared and visible image fusion like FusionGAN [5], DenseFuse [6], DDcGAN [7], and RFN-Nest [8] exemplify various techniques in this field. The focus of our attention is on the research conducted by [9], which introduces MDLatLRR, A Novel Decomposition method for Infrared and visible image fusion. The proposed methodology involves decomposing the original image into its constituent parts, namely the essential and the elemental components. The improvement of extracting picture edge data was further advanced by proposing AnisGF [10]. The present research primarily addresses the difficulty of effectively managing detailed halo artifacts and uneven patterns observed in prior versions of guided filters.

This paper proposes a novel image fusion technique integrating a multi-scale transform-based method with the Latent Low-Rank Representation (LatLRR) [11] and an anisotropic guided filter. The aim is to enhance the fusion effect and get more satisfactory results. To commence, the texture data of the original image is partitioned into three distinct groups: edge texture, global texture, and base texture. An anisotropic-guided filter facilitates the extraction of edge texture data and the underlying image's base data. Conversely, a low-rank transform extracts global texture data and the image's base data. The data is subsequently integrated through various methodologies, with each approach customized to suit the particular characteristics of the data being utilized. A weighted average method is used for the edge texture and underlying data. The optimization of global texture data is achieved by using a WLS approach. The ultimate composite image is generated by combining the data from these three sub-images using carefully chosen weights to accentuate the most significant characteristics. Based on the experiment results, it can be inferred that this particular strategy demonstrates superiority over the other five extant methodologies, as indicated by purely aesthetic impacts and quantitative evaluations.

The remaining sections of this work are structured as follows. Image fusion is discussed in more detail in Sect. 2. Section 3 is a comprehensive explanation of the methodology that has been devised to integrate NIR and visible images. A quantitative, qualitative evaluation of the algorithm and the findings are presented in Sect. 4.

2   Related Work

2.1   Multi-scale Image Disintegration

LatLRR is a concept that allows for extracting low-rank and salience structures from the input data. The Latent Low-Rank Representation is a straightforward method for obtaining the projection matrix. Essential data, such as the image's detail portion and base part, can be extracted by applying the matrix to the image that has to be decomposed. In particular, the LatLRR is formulated as:

$$\underset{L,P,N}{\text{Min}} \|L\|_* + \|S\|_* + \lambda \|N\|_1$$

$$\text{s.t., } X = XL + SX + N \tag{1}$$

Balance coefficient $\lambda > 0$, nuclear norm (the sum of the matrix's singular values) denoted by $|| \cdot ||_*$ and $|| \cdot ||_1$ is l_1-norm. The observed data is represented by the matrix X, the low-rank coefficients by L, the salient coefficients matrix by P, and the sparse noisy matrix N. The salient coefficient PX is calculated by solving Eq. 1 using an approximation based on the Augmented Lagrangian Multiplier (ALM) method.

2.2 Anisotropic Guided Filter

AnisGF emerged in 2020 as an improved version of the Guided filter which enhances the benefits of mitigating gradient inversion artifacts and offering time-dependent complexities. The general aim of AnisGF is described as.

$$\underset{w_i}{\arg\min} \sum_{j \in N(i)} \left(W_{ij} \sigma_{gj}^2 \right)^2 + \in \sum_{j \in N(i)} \left(1 - W_{ij} \right)^2 \tag{2}$$

$N(i)$ is the area surrounding pixel i, and notation σ_{gj}^2 represents the variance of g_j and $\bar{g}_j$, where g_j is the individual pixel values and $\bar{g}_j$ represents the average value of the patch. This expression is used to determine the importance of a region centered on a given i, denoted by W_{ij}

$$W_{ij} = w_j = \frac{\in}{\sigma_{gj}^{2\alpha} + \in} \tag{3}$$

where α represents a standard deviation with an exponential weight. Due to the consistency of weights, W_{ij} can be quickly calculated using box filter. Replace variance with α to gain control over the objective. This leads to the following proximity of the objective function:

$$\underset{w_i}{\arg\min} \sum_{j \in N(i)} \left(W_{ij} \sigma_{gj}^\alpha \right)^2 + \in \sum_{j \in N(i)} \left(1 - W_{ij} \right)^2 \tag{4}$$

Due to their adaptability, the final weights for a central pixel must be normalized to 1.

3   Proposed Method

This paper proposes a novel approach for fusing NIR and visible images using a multi-scale transform-based technique. This approach combines the advantages of multi-level disintegration and AnisGF to achieve superior fusion results.

Figure 1 shows the overview of the proposed model. The initial step involves the application of individual AnisGF to the input image to extract the essential features and textures. Subsequently, the initial layer of fundamental data is inputted, followed by three low-rank disintegrations to derive the base and texture data pertaining to each case. The last base data acquired from input image processing is utilized to fuse base data, gained through the most recent low-rank disintegration. Upon extracting data from the original image, we fuse similar types of data from a collection of photos using a range of fusion criteria. A weighted average technique was utilized to aggregate the underlying data.

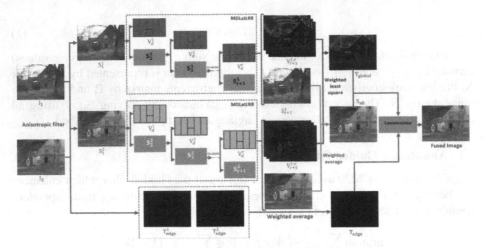

Fig. 1. Overview of the proposed model

3.1 Multi-scale Image Disintegration

Maximum diffusion, as described by [8], is achieved through weighted averaging, which lessens the visibility of detail halo artifacts in the guided filter without compromising the sharpness of the image's edges. The optimization of weights based on the variance within the local neighborhood enables efficient implementation of anisotropic filtering, while avoiding any additional computational load on the original bootstrap filter.

To obtain the multi-level data of an image, the MDLatLRR algorithm uses LatLRR to learn the projection matrix, and it is employed to extract the essential elements of the image.

AnisGF offers better edge protection capabilities than the LatLRR and guided filtering methods. In contrast, the MDLatLRR algorithm performs global softening operations to the image, resulting in a blurred overall appearance due to the extraction of texture data.

By fusing the benefits of both filters, we employ the method of integrating global data with localized data, which allows the merged image to retain a crisp edge outline while containing additional texture data of the source image. To initiate the process, the AnisGF algorithm is employed to apply a filtering technique on the source image. This filtering operation allows for the extraction of the edge texture data and the acquisition of some initial global data.

$$S_1 = \text{AnisGF}(I) \tag{5}$$

$$T_{edge} = I - S_1 \tag{6}$$

S1 is the foundational data, AnisGF is the anisotropy-guided filter and T_{edge} describes the edge texture.

The preliminary base data is smoothed three times using the multi-scale low-rank disintegration algorithm, with the resulting texture and base data being obtained after each smoothing. The steps of this procedure are as follows:

$$S_i = MDLatLRR(S_{i-1}) \tag{7}$$

$$T_i = I - S_i \tag{8}$$

where, MDLatLRR is a low-rank disintegration algorithm that works on multiple scales. S_i represents the elemental data, i represents the disintegration level and T_i represents the extracted global data.

3.2 Fusion of Base Data

The base data typically capture the image's global structure and total illumination. First impressions of an image's content are heavily influenced by the elemental data, which reveals the broad contours of the items in the image. The final fusion result pays more attention to the overall framework of the image, which is reflected by the image's base data, where pixel values are more consistent. Our proposed approach uses frequency distribution to determine weights and integrates the base data via the weighted average technique. This methodology enables a more precise depiction of the diverse rates of pixel value fluctuations across different geographical regions. The intended use of this is as follows:

$$S = W1 \cdot S_{ir} + W2 \cdot S_{vis} \tag{9}$$

where, W1 represents the Infrared image and W2 the visible image. The terms in question are defined in the following manner:

$$W1 = (0.5 + 0.5 * (SF(I_1) - SF(I_2))) \tag{10}$$

$$W2 = (0.5 + 0.5 * (SF(I_2) - SF(I_1))) \tag{11}$$

$SF(\cdot)$ is the function used to determine spatial frequencies.

3.3 Fusion of Texture Data

The texture data extracted in our proposed image fusion method is categorized into two categories: data on the texture's global appearance and data on the texture's edges. Consequently, we aim to integrate diverse textures by employing various fusion techniques. The WLS-based fusion algorithm is utilized for the integration of global data. The integration of this algorithm enables improved discernibility of intricate textural details. The following is the intended usage for it:

$$W^k = \begin{cases} 1, & |d_1^k| > |d_2^k| \\ 0, & \text{otherwise} \end{cases} (k = 1, 2, \ldots N) \tag{12}$$

where d^k refers as the global data. Upon incorporating extreme recurrence, the equation becomes:

$$T_h = W_{max} \times d_2^k + (1 - W_{max}) \times d_1^k \tag{13}$$

W_{max} is the maximum weight, d_1^k and d_2^k are the level data and T_h is the initial global texture data. Subsequently, it is possible to acquire comprehensive global texture data, as previously defined as

$$T_{global-all} = WLS(T_h, T_{i-ir}, T_{i-vis}) \tag{14}$$

The function WLS(·) represents the mathematical computation for the method of least squares. The integration of edge data is achieved by employing a fusion algorithm that utilizes a weighted mean and it is represented as

$$T_{edge-all} = W1 \cdot T_{edge-ir} + W2 \cdot T_{edge-vis} \tag{15}$$

The variable W1 denotes the Infrared image, while W2 represents the visible image. These variables are defined in the following manner:

$$W1 = (0.5 + 0.5 * (SM(I_1) - SM(I_2))) \tag{16}$$

$$W2 = (0.5 + 0.5 * (SM(I_2) - SM(I_1))) \tag{17}$$

The function SM(·) is utilized to compute the data content of a significant graph. Ultimately, the fusion image F is obtained.

$$F = \alpha * S + \beta * T_{global-all} + \lambda * T_{edge-all} \tag{18}$$

the hyperparameter α, β, and λ are defined as 0.7, 1.5, and 4, respectively.

4 Experiments

To assess the efficacy of this approach, a comparative analysis between the conventional fusion algorithm and the newly introduced fusion algorithm is conducted. The trial outcomes were evaluated both subjectively and objectively.

4.1 Datasets

The TNO dataset [12] and the real-time dataset were chosen as the test subjects to evaluate the effectiveness of the proposed method thoroughly. The TNO dataset comprises many pre-aligned pairs of NIR and visible images. Most image within the dataset predominantly capture military-related aspects, such as military bases, airplanes, and jet aircraft. To experiment, a set of thirty image pairs was chosen from the TNO dataset, and all the images were resized to a uniform size of 256×256 pixels. This resizing was done to facilitate the evaluation of multi-scale transformations. Thirty TNO picture pairings were tested on a laptop with 16 GB RAM and an 11th-generation Intel Core i7 processor.

Figure 2 exhibits three groups of testing images from the TNO dataset, featuring NIR images at the top and visible images at the bottom. Similarly, Fig. 3 exhibits three groups of testing images from the real-time dataset, featuring NIR images at the top and visible images at the bottom.

Fig. 2. Three test image pairs from TNO dataset

Fig. 3. Three test image pairs from the real-time dataset

4.2 Image Fusion Quality Metrics

The proposed Algorithm's fusion performance has been examined using six objective assessment measures. They are

Multi Scale_Structural similarity index measure: MS_SSIM is a way to measure the quality of an image or video based on how similar its structures are at different scales. A higher MS_SSIM score means that the similarity or quality is better.

Average Gradient: The AG quality metric evaluates the perceptual clarity of an image by analyzing its texture and contrast characteristics. The evaluation assesses how much the fused image effectively maintains the details and edges in the source images. A higher AG value is indicative of superior perceptual image quality.

FMI_w, FMI_{dct} and FMI_{pixel}: Feature Mutual Information (FMI) in wavelet, discrete cosine transforms, and pixel, respectively.

Improved assessment of fusion impacts: The N_{abf} index quantifies the level of noise or artifacts present in the fused image resulting from the fusion process.

4.3   Evaluation Against Rival Algorithms Using TNO Dataset

The validity of the proposed strategy is confirmed by the utilization of the TNO dataset. Figure 4 displays the Fusion results of the Kaptein_1123 source image, which portrays a person standing by the door. The viewable image displays intricate features such as homes, trees, and grass. Nevertheless, the NIR has high sensitivity to thermal radiation and is capable of capturing and storing this information. The fusion performance of the proposed technique was evaluated using both qualitative and quantitative approaches.

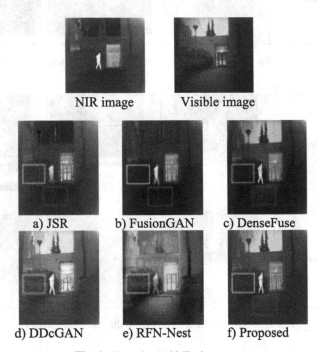

NIR image   Visible image

a) JSR   b) FusionGAN   c) DenseFuse

d) DDcGAN   e) RFN-Nest   f) Proposed

Fig. 4. Kaptein_1123 Fusion output

From a subjective standpoint, it can be observed that the fused image acquired through JSR (Fig. 4a) exhibits subpar visual quality and is deficient in various features present in the visible image. The fused images obtained through the utilization of Fusion-GAN exhibit a general blurriness, characterized by unclear boundaries and a significant amount of noise (Fig. 4b). This degradation in edge data hinders the visibility of the scene within the house, thereby posing challenges in its observation. The DenseFuse algorithm exhibits a lack of consistency in maintaining uniform brightness levels, as observed in the case of the road surface (Fig. 4c). Additionally, it can be observed that the output generated by DDcGAN (Fig. 4d) exhibits a certain level of haziness. At the same time, the results produced by RFN-Nest (Fig. 4e) appear to be dim. The proposed methodology exhibits superior contrast in detecting salient targets compared to all other methodologies. It is evident that the fused image produced by the proposed methodology effectively showcases rich textures of plants within the designated red box, as well as distinct ground patterns within the designated blue box.

Table 1. Multiple approaches averaged from TNO dataset

Size	MS_SSIM	AG	FMI_w	FMI_{dct}	FMI_{pixel}	N_{abf}
JSR	0.4595	3.2451	0.2852	0.2990	0.7564	0.1001
FusionGAN	0.6888	2.7355	0.3754	0.3565	0.8889	0.0131
DenseFuse	0.9078	5.0094	0.4252	0.3612	0.8741	0.0847
DDcGAN	0.5820	4.9214	0.4114	0.3863	0.8760	0.1016
RFN-Nest	0.6477	5.3171	0.2976	0.2897	0.9032	0.0114
Proposed	0.9004	5.4102	0.4414	0.3719	0.9100	0.0005

Table 1 represents the objective evaluation indices like MS_SSIM, AG, FMI_w, FMI_{dct}, FMI_{pixel}, and N_{abf}. This finding demonstrates that the proposed methodology exhibits superior capability in retaining the feature data inherent in the input images compared to alternative approaches. Consequently, the fused image acquired through the proposed method exhibits enhanced detail levels and superior visual effects.

4.4 Evaluation Against Rival Algorithms Using Real-Time Dataset

The Basler acA2040-25gmNIR recorded NIR images in real-time, whilst the HIKVISION 6MP IP Camera collected visible images. As a result of the image's different dimensions, it is resized to a smaller size of 256×256 and converted to grayscale. The fusion performance of the proposed technique was evaluated using both qualitative and quantitative measures.

The fusion results of the source image Architect_1111, which portrays an architectural structure constructed from truck tires in front of trees, are presented in Fig. 5. The visible image displays intricate features of buildings, trees, and grass. Nevertheless, the NIR exhibits a high sensitivity to thermal radiation and effectively captures and stores this data.

The utilization of crates in the FusionGAN and DDcGAN techniques yields outcomes that are characterized by haziness. The amalgamated visuals are disconcerting and devoid of realism. The FusionGAN (Fig. 5b) can achieve exceptional fusion performance. In addition, the DenseFuse (Fig. 5c) fails to accurately represent the beauty of the grass and ground, as depicted by the green and blue rectangles. RFN-Nest (Fig. 5e) appears to be in a condition of low brightness. The proposed method (Fig. 5f) enhances the brightness of the thermal radiation object, improves the clarity of the ground texture, and increases the overall brightness of the dim grass.

Table 2 shows average values for six objective evaluation metrics applied to a dataset in real-time, with the greatest values emphasized in the color red. The results indicate that, except FMIdct, the proposed algorithm attained the maximum achievable scores, confirming its superior fusion capability.

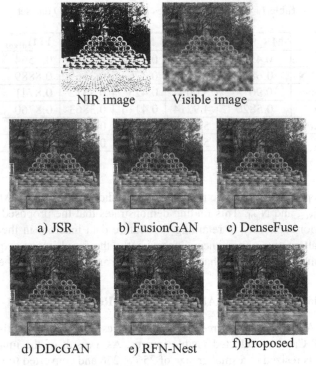

Fig. 5. Architect_1111 Fusion output

Table 2. Multiple approaches averaged from real-time datasets

Size	MS_SSIM	AG	FMI$_w$	FMI$_{dct}$	FMI$_{pixel}$	N$_{abf}$
JSR	0.4251	3.2414	0.2911	0.2777	0.8100	0.1822
FusionGAN	0.6430	2.7299	0.3169	0.3565	0.8889	0.0131
DenseFuse	0.7100	5.0081	0.3711	0.2855	0.8914	0.0098
DDcGAN	0.5820	4.9112	0.3499	0.3863	0.8760	0.1016
RFN-Nest	0.6820	5.2911	0.2737	0.2897	0.9032	0.0114
Proposed	0.7218	5.2998	0.3982	0.3719	0.9100	0.0004

5 Conclusion

This paper proposes a novel algorithm for fusing multi-scale near-infrared and visible images. The proposed method utilizes AnisGF and multi-level disintegration techniques. AnisGF has demonstrated commendable efficacy in preserving edges in image data extraction. Consequently, we employ this technique to recover edge texture data from the image. The multi-scale disintegration algorithm possesses the capability to enhance the overall smoothness of an image effectively. It is commonly employed to extract intricate image details and obtain comprehensive global texture data. The ultimate fundamental data, which encompasses the benefits of both techniques, is acquired by multi-scale disintegration. In image fusion, many fusion techniques are employed to integrate diverse forms of data. The weighted average method combines edge texture data with elemental data, while the WLS technique handles the global texture data. Summating all the constituent components obtains the fusion result. The findings from both the qualitative and quantitative analyses indicate that the suggested method outperforms the other five algorithms. In subsequent endeavors, ongoing efforts will enhance this methodology and further experiment and evaluation in other image fusion applications.

Acknowledgment. This research work is funded by SRM Institute of Science and Technology, Kattankulathur, under Selective Excellence Research Initiative.

References

1. Ma, J., Zhou, Z., Wang, B., Zong, H.: Infrared and visible image fusion based on visual saliency map and weighted least square optimization. Infrared Phys. Technol. **82**, 8–17 (2017). https://doi.org/10.1016/j.infrared.2017.02.005
2. Zhang, Q., Fu, Y., Li, H., Zou, J.: Dictionary learning method for joint sparse representation-based image fusion. Opt. Eng. **52**, 057006 (2013). https://doi.org/10.1117/1.oe.52.5.057006
3. Vasu, G.T., Palanisamy, P.: Multi-focus image fusion using anisotropic diffusion filter. Soft. Comput. **26**, 14029–14040 (2022). https://doi.org/10.1007/s00500-022-07562-2
4. Vasu, G.T., Palanisamy, P.: Gradient-based multi-focus image fusion using foreground and background pattern recognition with weighted anisotropic diffusion filter. Signal Image Video Process. **17**, 2531–2543 (2023). https://doi.org/10.1007/s11760-022-02470-2
5. Ma, J., Yu, W., Liang, P., Li, C., Jiang, J.: FusionGAN: a generative adversarial network for infrared and visible image fusion. Inf. Fusion **48**, 11–26 (2019). https://doi.org/10.1016/j.inffus.2018.09.004
6. Li, H., Wu, X.J.: DenseFuse: a fusion approach to infrared and visible images. IEEE Trans. Image Process. **28**, 2614–2623 (2019). https://doi.org/10.1109/TIP.2018.2887342
7. Ma, J., Xu, H., Jiang, J., Mei, X., Zhang, X.P.: DDcGAN: a dual-discriminator conditional generative adversarial network for multi-resolution image fusion. IEEE Trans. Image Process. **29**, 4980–4995 (2020). https://doi.org/10.1109/TIP.2020.2977573
8. Li, H., Wu, X.J., Kittler, J.: RFN-Nest: an end-to-end residual fusion network for infrared and visible images. Inf. Fusion **73**, 72–86 (2021). https://doi.org/10.1016/j.inffus.2021.02.023
9. Li, H., Wu, X.J., Kittler, J.: MDLatLRR: a novel decomposition method for infrared and visible image fusion. IEEE Trans. Image Process. **29**, 4733–4746 (2020). https://doi.org/10.1109/TIP.2020.2975984
10. Ochotorena, C.N., Yamashita, Y.: Anisotropic Guided Filtering. IEEE Trans. Image Process. **29**, 1397–1412 (2020). https://doi.org/10.1109/TIP.2019.2941326
11. Liu, G., Yan, S.: Latent low-rank representation for subspace segmentation and feature extraction. In: 2011 International Conference on Computer Vision, pp. 1615–1622 (2011). https://doi.org/10.1109/ICCV.2011.6126422
12. Toet, A.: The TNO multiband image data collection. Data Brief **15**, 249–251 (2017). https://doi.org/10.1016/j.dib.2017.09.038

An Approach for Detecting and Restoring Tampering in Digital Image Watermarking

Pavan A. C.$^{(\boxtimes)}$ ⓘ and M. T. Somashekar

Department of Computer Science and Applications, Bangalore University, Bengaluru, India
shyam2712.pavan@gmail.com

Abstract. In addition to ensuring image authenticity, watermarking aids in the recovery of digital images that have been altered or tampered with during transmission. Although many techniques have been developed for embedding the watermark that results in recovering itself of photos, they only effectively work in the uncompressed multiple domains, leaving images vulnerable to attacks on image compression, such as noise addition. In order to effectively detect tampered areas and assure self-recovery of JPEG images, we offer a solution to address these issues in the JPEG domain. Source code compresses the original image, while channel code protects it from tampering. As a result, the image will be compressed and then used as the watermark which is embedded. The approach proposed is successfully combined with these JPEG images, producing increased image quality as well as strong performance against noise attacks.

Keywords: Digital image watermarking · LDPC · Detection of tampering · SPIHT · JPEG Image Compression

1 Introduction

Data provided in any format, including photos, music, and video that is freely accessible online and may then be edited or altered by a range of image processing applications. Therefore, it is in order to halt the alterations and to recover this original pictorial content of the tampered communication, we apply the practice of watermarking plays as a crucial picture authentication strategy. Typically, the image is validated and checked before being used for image verification. The areas which are tampered are localised by some detection of error technique if any type of manipulation is found in the surveyed digital image. Finally, the pieces of the simulated image are recovered based on the altered area.

This tamper detection and picture recovery procedure requires the watermark to be processed using both of the source and channel coded bits. An effective image compression approach is used to synthesise source coded bits, improving recovered image quality and lowering PSNR. Parity check bits are also included in the watermark bits. To detect altered image content, these check bits also function as error detection bits. In order to both identify tampering and retrieve the image's damaged contents, these watermarking techniques insert a watermark into the image. Despite the fact that several

V. N. M. Aradhya et al. (Eds.): CCIP 2023, CCIS 2044, pp. 176–187, 2024.
https://doi.org/10.1007/978-3-031-60725-7_14

strategies and approaches have been developed for embedding watermarks that can be used for image self-recovery [1], they have only been effective in the uncompressed domain. In order to implant a watermark, the conventional procedure is to replace each picture block's least significant bits (LSB) with bits generated from that block's most significant bits (MSB). However, these methods are ineffective against noise assaults, which hinder authentication since noise attacks might damage the image's LSB content. Additionally, when JPEG compression is used, the LSB content is once more damaged. According to research, the majority of systems struggle to handle JPEG compression while inserting watermarks. As a result, it is necessary to create a new method using a self-recovery system [11] for watermarking compressed photos.

An established image compression technique is used to accomplish and code the first image compression. The altered source and channel-coded checking bits are combined in a watermark created by channel coding the source coded bits. The existing JPEG-compressed image [12, 13] then contains this output bit stream embedded within it. As a result, this watermark embedding technique can be appropriately adjusted to the image's JPEG compression model.

We have the original image's distorted version on the receiver side. From this distorted image, the watermarked bit stream is extracted via inverse quantization. In order to construct the compressed image, channel- decoding and source- decoding are applied at the received output bit stream. Nevertheless, IDCT produces a lossy received image for the other output bits. To identify the tampered area, these two photos are compared. The tampered zone [15] can now be retrieved to obtain the original rectified image if it extends beyond a calculated limit.

2 Literature Work

Many techniques have already been used to establish a image based watermark that potentially could enable the altered version of the required image to self-recover to the originality of the image. We have discovered that in Fridrich's more recent and ongoing efforts, the quantized DCT values as well as the low_depth version of the actual image which can be possibly used as significant feature for creating the reference [2]. Its self-recovery is being proposed using a variety of unique and cutting-edge algorithms and schemes that were established for image synthesis and representation [3–5]. These techniques generated good results, but they were only meant to be used to the uncompressed JPEG domain, not the compressed versions of the photographs.

The majority of the current methods are useless since choosing the JPEG domain changes the LSB information. However, there aren't many algorithms created for use in the compressed JPEG image domain. In paper [5], it is also demonstrated how to insert a watermark while also creating a reference bit utilising DCT coefficients, fountain coding, and hashing, which results in the JPEG domain images being able to recover themselves.

The suggested repair identifies the modification as a source coding issue before producing a watermark that may enable the affected image to self-heal. This notion was first created in the manner advised for the uncompressed form of images [6, 7]. The technique entails efficiently shrinking the actual image while utilising source coding and the SPIHT [8] algorithm. LDPC codes [9, 10], which also facilitate the identification of tampering maps, are utilised to build the H-matrix for channel coding. The compromised image can be recovered with the use of combined source-channel decoding.

3 Preliminaries

The suggested method makes use of blocks that employ different algorithms. Each subject covers a separate algorithm for successfully completing a certain task, including coding of source and coding of channel.

1. Compression of Lossy Data:

JPEG compression is used to recover the watermarked images at the sender/transmitter and, in essence, reverse its modified type/version at the receiver, subject to some restrictions. Throughout the JPEG-image process that is encoding and decoding process, the image is separated into 8×8 image blocks, as shown in the flowchart in Fig. 1. Every pixel is level-shifted by subtracting it by 128 and then applying the DCT transform. The 8 $\times$ 8 quantization matrix is then used to further quantize the resulting DCT coefficients. Depending on the required level of quality, the quality may fluctuate. The quantized coefficients are then delivered as a compressed and encoded bit stream after that has been encoded using the algorithm of a lossless compression which is like run-length or Huffman coding. The coefficients of quantized parts like $C_{i,j}$ are defined by (1):

$$C_{i,j} = \left[\frac{I_{i,j}}{Q_{i,j}} \right], i,j \in \{0, 1, 2, \ldots, 7\} \tag{1}$$

where $Q_{i,j}$ is the quantization-matrix and $I_{i,j}$ is the actual image. Inverse of quantization is used at the receiver side to retrieve the changed DCT coefficient values:

$$I'_{i,j} = C'_{i,j} \times Q_{i,j} \tag{2}$$

where $C'_{i,j}$ indicates the modified values of quantized DCT coefficients and $I'_{i,j}$ stands for recovered pixel values.

In order to incorporate the suggested method used into the JPEG compression, the following factors must be taken into account. It is well known that the quantization matrix and quality factor used by the JPEG domain to describe compression quality. However, because to the trade-off among both quality and compression rate, watermarking in high- and low-frequency zones poses issues with quality and durability, which prompts us to select some embedding for intermediate frequencies. For the domain that is compressed, the watermark's size must also be constrained. If we restricted the watermark size in comparison to the uncompressed domain approaches, the recovered image's quality would suffer. As a result, the error recovery is not particularly successful. Another issue in addition to this raises the problem of inserting the watermark. This is controlled by altering specific JPEG quantization steps.

2. Algorithm for SPIHT

After a few parameter tweaks, the SPIHT "Set Partitioning in Hierarchical Trees" algorithm [8] was determined to be the best compression method for coding of source at the transmitter. Because there is a finite amount of watermarking capacity, we must reduce the rate of SPIHT algorithm bits below unit bits/pixel.

3. LDPC Codes

The complete image is impacted by image recompression and noise addition in the actual original image. For such situations, a suitable channel method that can actively identify/detect the problem and subsequently enable bit-by-bit image retrieval is necessary. Low density parity checking (LDPC) [9, 10] codes were chosen as a good coding of channel technique because they needed fewer error - correcting bits and had a reduced bit error rate. Thus, the channel codes are being employed by LDPC, the applied scheme is strengthened and the propagation of little bit errors is stopped. The permutation [6] has the advantage of giving these codes significant performance sensitivity, making them more efficient than other error-correcting codes used in other watermarking techniques, even though it is not a required step. As a result, the ensuing bitstream is extended when LDPC codes are used to the origin coded output bitstream.

4. Embedding of Watermark

The quantization step is somewhat modified to integrate into the JPEG standard. Therefore, the updated equations for quantization that are used to embed watermarked bitstream can be expressed as follows:

$$C_{i,j} = C_f, \ if \ C_f\%2 = input \ bit \tag{3}$$

$$C_{i,j} = C_c, \ if \ C_c\%2 = input \ bit \tag{4}$$

$$C_{i,j} = C_r, \ if \ there \ is \ no \ input \ bit \tag{5}$$

In which,

$$C_f = \frac{I_{i,j}}{Q_{i,j}}, \ C_c = \frac{I_{i,j}}{Q_{i,j}}, \ C_r = \left[\frac{I_{i,j}}{Q_{i,j}}\right] \tag{6}$$

By changing the solution of reverse quantized during the compression of JPEG of the main image, we similarly use the inverse technique to extract the packed final bit stream at the receiving end. Run-length coding is used to finish off the remaining steps of the JPEG process.

5. Restoration of an Image

When the source & channel decoding are done correctly, the receiver produces two outputs: a lossy compressed JPEG and an extracted SPIHT algorithm compressed image from the lossy compressed image that was received. When comparing these two photos, the altered pixels may be seen. On some processes, the altered pixels create the tampered area. Thresholding, erosion, and dilation are the three phases used to complete this operation. The received/obtained tampered image pixels are swapped out with SPIHT pixels to produce the final recovered image when it detects the final map. So, the likely original version is reinstated.

6. Tampering Detection

The ultimate tampering map needed to aid in recovering the original image is created by comparing the two photos after we have both of them. We do this by employing three different comparison methods. Dilation, erosion, and thresholding are a few of these activities. When employing the SPIHT version of the image, the lossy image is originally thresholded. The area of the visible elements in both photos is then made obvious. Then the opening procedure is finished. By applying erosion to all of the values in its 5×5 neighborhoods and setting the value of every pixel that is less than 14 to zero, our method creates a tampering map. When the image is subsequently dilated, each pixel in its 15×15 neighborhood with a value greater than one is provided as one. The resulting tampering map is thus produces threshold image when performed an opening operation.

4 Methodology

A. Algorithm for Watermark Embedding (Sender side)

The steps that follow integrate the embedding process [16–18] within the JPEG standard to show how watermark embedding flows. It is shown in Fig. 1 as well.

- I - the original image, passes through two processes concurrently. JPEG compression is one of the processes.
- On eight by eight blocks of the original image, DCT is applied.
- The I's source code is being generated simultaneously as a second operation. The formula is then used to determine total no. of bits produced by coding of source from the full image is $N_s = N_p \times n_s$, where N_p is the no. of pixels in the image. The actual image is source coded at a rate of n_s bits per pixel (bpp).
- Correction of errors now the source coded bit-stream is channel coded in order to detect errors. As a result, the output bitstream is lengthened by bpp. It results in $N_c = N_p \times n_c$ being the total no. of coding channels bits for the considered image.
- A secret key is used to apply permutation on the output bitstream.
- Permuted bits are eventually incorporated using the watermark embedding method.
- The standard JPEG compression process is used. The sole change to the procedure is the replacement of the Jpg compression's quantized step with the revised quantization with regard to the input bit-stream. A watermarked image I_w is produced as a result of the overall watermark embedding process.

B. Algorithm for Watermark Embedding (Receiver Side)

We execute tamper detection and picture recovery from the likely attacked image, $I'w$, at the receiver end. As seen in Fig. 2, the following phases in picture restoration are involved:

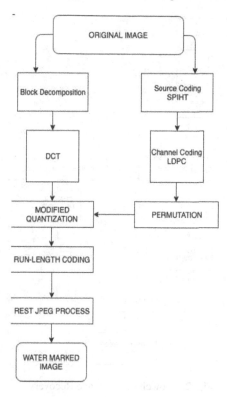

Fig. 1. Embedding flowchart

- On the received image I'w first, the JPEG decompression procedure is carried out first.
- Then, modified inverse quantization is used. The block-level DCT coefficients and the embedded watermark bitstream are its two outputs.
- The inverse DCT is used to recover image I".
- Using the secret key, inverse permutation is applied to the retrieved watermark bit-stream.
- To create the source coding output bit-stream, error correction channel decoding is used.
- To extract the source-coded image, source decoding is applied to the channel decoding output.
- Consequently, the received image is now available in two variants.
- To identify the changed pixels, two photos are examined.
- The source-coded picture is then used to replace the tampered image's pixels to create the reconstructed image.

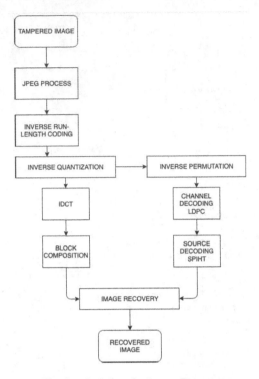

Fig. 2. Flowchart for Image Recovery

5 Experimental Results

This section displays the outcomes that were obtained after implementing each module to create the final watermarked image. The recovered picture I'' and a tampering map are then obtained from the altered image I'w. Figure 3's 8-bit 512 × 512 greyscale image of Lena is used to test the proposed technique.

JPEG is used to compress the test image at various quality factor levels. Under the quality factor of 75, the results are seen to have great quality since the PSNR of the generated images is low due to increased recovery after compression. Therefore, as we proceed with the other components of our approach, we use JPEG compression with a Quality factor value of 75. The reconstructed image is then obtained by performing SPIHT, as illustrated in Fig. 4 with the corresponding PSNR values.

Fig. 3. Original Image

In this case, the output bitstream of the SPIHT algorithm is truncated at ns = 0.1236bpp. As a result, the output of the compression is bs = 32,400 bits, and the average PSNR recovery quality is 30.15 dB. Additionally, LDPC is used so that it helps in adding error correcting code. Here, at a rate of 12, LDPC codes are utilised with input data of 32,400 bits to achieve notable performance for error correction (LDPC(64,800, 32,400)), resulting in a watermark signal of 64,800 bits. same when decoding the bitstream to obtain SPIHT bits. A higher quality compressed image can be produced with a lower PSNR value for a quality factor of 75 and an SPIHT compression rate of 0.1236bpp. Therefore, as we move on in the following phases, we use the SPIHT at a rate of 0.1236bpp for watermarking.

Fig. 4. PSNR = 30.15db and SPIHT = 0.1236bpp

Figure 5 depicts a watermarked image, and Fig. 6 shows the tampered image that was received after it had been transmitted. Now, in order to detect the altered regions in the obtained image, a thresholding step is applied, followed by the opening of morphological operations. Opening is a procedure in which the subject image is first eroded, and then enlarged. Figure 7(a) and (b) demonstrate the results of thresholding and opening, respectively (b).

Fig. 5. Watermarked image

The tampering map that was later developed and helped with the successful restoration of the original image is shown in Fig. 8. The results resisted modification and attacks like recompressing the received image and adding noise well.

The final watermarked image, as illustrated in Fig. 5, is subsequently obtained and sent in the direction of the receiver end. The broadcast image could potentially be assaulted at any time. Only 17.2% of the watermarked image is tampered [19] with, according to our experiments, which involved watermarking it. The watermark contained in the image is used to recover the original image if the amount of tampering is less than this value.

At the receiving end, the two output images are compared to produce the final image which is restored. There is a very high likelihood that the restored image and the original image are identical. The robustness of this technique in detecting and recovering tampering by embedding a watermark in Jpeg format is demonstrated by experimental findings [12] (Fig. 9).

Fig. 6. Received tampered image

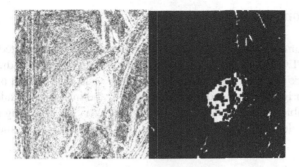

Fig. 7. a. Thresholding b. Opening aspect of result

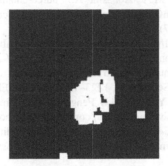

Fig. 8. Tampering Map

Fig. 9. Image after Recovery

The results are resistant to manipulation, noise addition, and recompression attacks on the received image. This proposed method can restore the original image as long as the watermarked image has been altered by 17.2% or less due to manipulation and these extra attacks.

6 Conclusion

In this paper, a tamper-proof watermark embedding method is suggested. Regarding the conventional JPEG compression chain, it has been appropriately modified. The length of the watermark string that is included in the image has a big impact on how easy it is to recover the original. Since compression reduces the image's redundancy and limits the space available for watermark insertion, the recovery of tampering is likewise only up to a certain tolerable rate. Plans to increase this acceptable rate could be made.

References

1. Sarreshtedari, S., Akhaee, M.A., Abbasfar, A.: Source-channel coding-based watermarking for self-embedding of JPEG images, pp. 107–116. Electrical and Computer Engineering. University of Tehran (2017)
2. Fridrich, J., Goljan, M.: Images with self-correcting capabilities. In: Proceedings of the International Conference on Image Processing, vol. 3, pp. 792–796 (1999)
3. Qian, Z., Feng, G.: Inpainting assisted self-recovery with reduced embedding data. IEEE Trans. Inform. Forensics Secur. 6(4), 1223–1232 (2011). IEEE Figure 6: Received altered picture X. Zhang, Z. Qian, Y. Ren, and G. Feng, Water-marking with adjustable self-recovery quality based on compressive sensing and compositional reconstruction
4. Korus, P., Biaas, J., Dziech, A.: Towards practical self embedding for JPEG-compressed digital images. IEEE Trans. Multimed. 17(2), 157–170 (2015). https://doi.org/10.1109/TMM.2014.2368696
5. Sarreshtedari, S., Akhaee, M.A.: A source-channel coding approach to digital picture protection and self-recovery. IEEE Trans. Picture Process. 24(7), 2266–2277 (2015). https://doi.org/10.1109/TIP.2015.2414878 can be found here
6. Sarreshtedari, S., Akhaee, M.A.: Discuss using a source-channel coding technique to create tamper proof images. In: The 2014 IEEE International Conference on Acoustics, Speech and Signal Processing (ICASSP), pp. 7435–7439 (2014). https://doi.org/10.1109/ICASSP.2014.6855045,
7. Pearlman, W., Said, A.: A novel, quick, and efficient image codec based on set partitioning in hierarchical trees. IEEE Trans. Circuits Syst. Video Technol. 6(3), 243–250 (1996)
8. Gallager, R.: Low Density Parity-Check Codes. MIT Press, Cambridge (1963)
9. Pavan, A.C., Lakshmi, S., Somashekara, M.T.: An improved method for reconstruction and enhancing dark images based on CLAHE. Int. Res. J. Adv. Sci. Hub 5(02), 40–46 (2023). https://doi.org/10.47392/irjash.2023.011
10. Chen, B., Wornell, G.W.: Quantization index modulation: a class of provably good algorithms for digital watermarking and information embedding. IEEE Trans. Inform. Theory 47(4), 1423–1443 (2001). https://doi.org/10.1109/18.923725
11. Zhao, X., Wang, H., Ho, A.T.S.: Digital Forensics and Watermarking: a revolutionary quick self-restoration semi-fragile watermarking method that resists JPEG compression is used to authenticate the content of images. In: 0th International Workshop, IWDW 2011, October 23–26, Atlantic City, NY, October 21, 2011, pp. 72–85. Springer, Berlin, Heidelberg (2012)
12. Cheddad, A., Kevitt, P.M., Condell, J., Curran, K.: An enhanced, safe self-embedding algorithm to prevent digital document forgeries. In: Shiozaki, A.A., Ogihara, M., Iwata, T., Hori, M., Shiozaki, A.: Digital watermarking technique for JPEG picture tamper detection and recovery, Theory Its Applications (2010). p. 2324 pp. 309–314
13. Gonzalez, R.C.: Digital Image Processing. Pearson Education, India (2009)

14. Morello, A.: Mignone V.DVB-S2: the second generation standard for satellite broad-band services. Proc. IEEE **94**(1), 210–227 (2006)
15. Said, A., Pearlman, W.: A new, fast, and efficient image codec based on set partitioning in hierarchical trees. IEEE Trans. Circuits Syst. Video Technol. **6**(3), 243–250 (1996)
16. Pavan, A.C., Somashekara, M.T.: An overview on research trends, challenges, applications and future direction in digital image watermarking. Int. Res. J. Adv. Sci. Hub **5**(01), 8–14 (2023). https://doi.org/10.47392/irjash.2023.002
17. Cox, I., Miller, M., Bloom, J., Fridrich, J., Kalker, T.: Digital Watermarking and Steganography, Second Edition. Elsevier, Amsterdam (2008)
18. Costa, M.: Writing on dirty paper. IEEE Trans. Inf. Theory **29**, 439–441 (1983)
19. Pavan, A.C., Somashekara, M.T.: Watermarking for Tamper Detection, Copyright Protection, and Rightful Ownership of a Digital Image: A Literature Survey, 15 December 2022. SSRN: https://doi.org/10.2139/ssrn.4304022

Author Index

Printed in the United States
by Baker & Taylor Publisher Services